D1426489

A SHORT HISTORY OF IRELAND, 1500–2000

A SHORT HISTORY OF IRELAND, 1500-2000

JOHN GIBNEY

Yale

UNIVERSITY PRESS

New Haven and London

Published with assistance from the Mary Cady Tew Memorial Fund.

Yale University Press books may be purchased in quantity for
educational, business, or promotional use. For information, please
e-mail sales.press@yale.edu (U.S. office) or sales@yaleup.co.uk
(U.K. office).

Set in Janson type by Integrated Publishing Solutions,
Grand Rapids, Michigan
Printed in the United States of America.

ISBN 978-0-300-20851-1 (hardcover : alk. paper)
Library of Congress Control Number: 2017941374
A catalogue record for this book is available from the British Library.

This paper meets the requirements of ANSI/NISO Z39.48-1992
(Permanence of Paper).

10 9 8 7 6 5 4 3 2 1

Contents

Acknowledgments

THIS BOOK HAS A simple and straightforward purpose: to provide a relatively brief, accessible, and up-to-date account of modern Irish history for those who want, or need, to learn more about it. In researching and writing it I have incurred debts to a number of individuals and institutions, and would like to thank the following for offering sage advice on various sections of the text: Brian Hanley, Carole Holohan, Breandán Mac Suibhne, Ivar McGrath, Christopher Maginn, Eamon Ó Ciardha, Brian Ó Conchubair, Kate O'Malley, Micheál Ó Siochru, Gearóid Ó Tuathaigh, Jim Smyth, and Frank Rynne. Aspects of the research and writing were facilitated by visiting research fellowships at Marsh's Library, Dublin, and the Moore Institute at the National University of Ireland, Galway. I would also like to thank the staff of these institutions and of the National Library of Ireland, the Tyrone Guthrie Centre at Annaghmakerrig, County Monaghan, and Trinity College Dublin. At Yale University Press, Laura Davulis and Jaya Chatterjee have been patient and encouraging editors, and I would like to record my thanks to the anonymous referees for the press who commented on earlier drafts. Thanks are also due to Tomás Ó Brógáin for preparing the maps, and to Oireas Heritage Services for generously sponsoring them. I am responsible for any errors and omissions that remain. Finally, thanks to family and friends who made this possible in so many different ways, and above all to Liza Costello and Martha Costello Gibney.

A Note on Conventions

Before 1752, Britain and Ireland used the Old Style (Julian) calendar, which was ten days behind the New Style (Gregorian) calendar used elsewhere. All dates prior to 1752 have been given according to the Old Style calendar, but the year is taken to begin on 1 January rather than 25 March. Beginning in 1752, dates are given according to the New Style calendar.

The spelling used in quotations in the text has been standardized and modernized. Place names are given according to the current spelling used by the Irish Ordnance Survey, and are generally described in relation to the modern (post-1600) administrative division of Ireland into counties. Ireland is traditionally divided into four "provinces," each of which corresponds to the cardinal compass points: Ulster to the north (comprising counties Antrim, Armagh, Cavan, Donegal, Down, Fermanagh, Londonderry, Monaghan, and Tyrone), Leinster to the east (counties Carlow, Dublin, Kildare, Kilkenny, Laois, Longford, Louth, Meath, Offaly, Westmeath, Wexford, and Wicklow), Munster to the south (counties Clare, Cork, Kerry, Limerick, Tipperary, and Waterford), and Connacht to the west (counties Galway, Leitrim, Mayo, Roscommon, and Sligo). The provincial divisions have been used as shorthand for geographical designations.

With regard to personal names rendered in both Irish and English, I have generally opted for the commonly used English versions. I have made an exception for writers and literary figures whose primary language of expression was Irish. This is for convenience of usage, and should not be construed as a value judgement. The names have been standardized wherever possible according to the versions used in the Royal Irish Academy's *Dictionary of Irish Biography* (Cambridge, 2009). Unless otherwise indicated, all biographical details have been taken from the *Dictionary of Irish Biography* and the *Oxford Dictionary of National Biography* (Oxford, 2004). Throughout the text "Ireland" is taken to mean the entire island of Ireland prior to 1920, and unless otherwise indicated the independent state that existed after 1922 (including the Irish Free State). "Northern Ireland" is the official term for the six counties—Antrim, Armagh, Down, Fermanagh, Londonderry (or Derry), and Tyrone—that were given separate jurisdiction within the United Kingdom after 1920, and is used accordingly.

The island of Ireland, showing political boundaries and urban areas, with the main cities in italics. Technically, Ireland has only a handful of cities, arising from the status granted to certain urban areas from the Middle Ages onwards. The majority of urban areas are categorised as towns, regardless of size. (Map by Tomás Ó Brógáin)

Chronology of Key Events

1720	Declaratory Act permits British parliament to legislate for Ireland
1740–41	Famine
1760	Formation of Catholic Committee to lobby for Catholic rights
1778	First Catholic Relief Act begins to repeal "penal" legislation
1782	Legislative independence for Irish parliament
1791	Formation of Society of United Irishmen in Belfast and Dublin
1798	United Irishmen's rebellion
1801	Act of Union abolishes Irish parliament and brings Ireland into the United Kingdom
1823	Foundation of Catholic Association in Dublin
1829	Daniel O'Connell elected member of parliament for County Clare
1845–52	Potato famine
1867	Fenian rebellion
1869	Disestablishment of Church of Ireland
1870	First Land Act to reform Irish system of land ownership
1879–82	Land War
1912–14	Ulster Crisis, as passage of Home Rule bill through House of Commons leads to foundation of Ulster Volunteer Force and Irish Volunteers
1916	Easter Rising
1919–21	War of Independence and creation of Northern Ireland
1921	Anglo-Irish Treaty, leading to the creation of the Irish Free State
1922–23	Irish Civil War
1937	New constitution passed by referendum in Irish Free State
1939	Declaration of state of emergency on the outbreak of Second World War
1949	Official declaration of a republic in the twenty-six counties of the former Irish Free State

1969	Outbreak of conflict in Northern Ireland (the "Troubles")
1973	Ireland joins the European Economic Community (EEC)
1994	Paramilitary cease-fires in Northern Ireland
1998	Belfast Agreement ("Good Friday Agreement") establishes new power-sharing government in Northern Ireland
2010	Irish government enters the International Monetary Fund, European Central Bank, and European Union's bailout programme

Introduction

Ireland on the Edge

W HAT IS SO SPECIAL about 1500? Why choose that as a starting point? The date is often assumed to separate the medieval from the modern, and this assumption is justified by the cluster of significant events and phenomena that occurred in western Europe around that time: the capture of Constantinople and the fall of the Byzantine empire in 1453; the development of printing; the Renaissance; and, of course, the Reformation. In European history, 1500 is a convenient date. Yet the decades immediately after 1500 have profound implications for Irish history. This book really begins in the 1530s and 1540s, with a series of crucially important phenomena: a rebellion, the introduction of the Reformation, and the elevation of Ireland to the status of a kingdom to be governed by English, and later British, monarchs. Ireland at this time was on the brink of radical change. This introduction is intended to offer a brief overview of the country that was about to be changed.

Land

Ireland is an island on the western fringe of Atlantic Europe, and like much of this region, it is a creation of the last Ice Age. Despite its northerly location, trans-Atlantic currents—the Gulf Stream—

emerge from the Caribbean to warm the waters of Britain and Ireland, producing a mild but damp climate. Ireland is relatively small:
only 486 kilometres separate its northernmost and southernmost
points, and 274 kilometres separate the furthest points on the eastern and western coasts. Yet this relatively small land mass contains a
great deal of geographical and ecological diversity. Limestone un-
derpins most of the Irish landscape, with volcanic rocks such as
granite appearing on the eastern and western fringes and sandstones
comprising much of the northern coastline. The withdrawal of the
ice sheets twelve thousand years ago has left rich layers of glacial soil
(utilised as farmland) in much of the south and east, along with a
distinctive range of small glacial hills—the so-called "drumlin belt"
—stretching across the north and northwest. The interior is a mixture of lowland and upland, with central plains surrounded, for the
most part, by uplands and relatively low mountains, most of which
are found near the coast. Peat bogs are a significant feature of the
Irish landscape; these decayed remnants of ancient forests are most
evident along the Atlantic coast and in the more sheltered midlands.
Broadly speaking, two geographical zones can be discerned on the
island: the relatively rugged and wetter west and northwest, and the
drier, less challenging and more fertile east and south.[1]

People

Such is a thumbnail sketch of the physical environment; what of the
peoples who have lived on it and left their imprint? Ireland was first
populated from continental Europe in the millennia after the last
Ice Age, though much about the earliest settlers remains unknown
and unknowable. This changes as we move closer to the present.
Ireland was settled by waves of peoples in the pre-Christian era,
most famously the so-called Celts, and there is extensive evidence of
sophisticated pre-Christian settlement. The Céide fields in County
Mayo, on the west coast, offer the oldest evidence of land cultivation in western Europe, dating from circa 5000 B.C. The huge mega-
lithic tombs of the Boyne Valley in County Meath, near the east
coast, were built between 4000 and 3000 B.C., and they remain as
impressive monuments to another vanished civilization. New arrivals brought new cultures, new languages, and new beliefs. Beginning

in the fifth century A.D., missionaries from Britain and the continent brought Christianity to Ireland, most famously by the Briton Patricius: Patrick. But by the eighth century an indigenous Irish culture, woven from a variety of strands and usually termed "Gaelic," can be discerned. Gaelic society was militaristic, pastoral, and profoundly aristocratic, with its own language and dialects thereof, and a distinct intellectual and cultural life. A vernacular epic such as the *Táin* is one manifestation of this; the existence of distinctive traditions of law (details of which have been preserved in tracts dating back to the seventh century) is another.

Other cultural, intellectual, and religious traditions acquired a foothold in Ireland over time. Irish Christian monasteries, located on the fringe of Europe, became centres of learning after the fall of the Roman empire, and later served as missionary powerhouses that exported Christianity back to the continent in the early Middle Ages. The distinctive illustrations of the famous Book of Kells demonstrate the fusion between the new faith and the society it had become a part of. But links forged across the sea went both ways. From the end of the eighth century the Scandinavian raiders known as Vikings were attacking the Irish coast, and their establishment of bases from which to strike further inland laid the basis for the development of most of Ireland's coastal towns and ports. Dublin, on the east coast, was the largest Viking settlement and has been, for most of its history, the largest urban centre on the island. The influence of the Vikings brought Ireland into a trading empire that stretched from the Baltic to the Middle East. The sea did not isolate Ireland; rather, it offered innumerable pathways to a wider world.

Ireland did not, at this time, have a centralized political structure with a dominant power at a national level. Its political structure instead consisted of regional "kings" of varying degrees of status, wealth, and power; this was an aristocracy legitimated by tradition. These Gaelic lords presided over kinship groups—known as *derbfine* —in which succession was nominated or chosen from amongst aristocratic families. But such nominations and choices could be challenged, and often the most powerful prevailed, which proved to be a source of enduring instability. Due to a dynastic dispute in the southeast in the late twelfth century, Norman knights from England and Wales under the leadership of Richard Fitzgilbert de Clare, the earl of Pembroke, were persuaded to come to Ireland as mercenaries in the nominal service of Diarmait Mac Murchadha, the deposed king of the eastern kingdom (later province) of Leinster; this opened the door to conquest, colonisation, and settlement from England and Wales throughout the Middle Ages.

Ireland and Britain are geographical neighbours, and people have always moved between them. But from the twelfth century onwards migration from Britain assumed a new character, with deep and enduring consequences. The Anglo-Norman invasion of Ireland and the colonisation that followed spread rapidly: into the south, and extending northwards up the eastern coast, with small pockets of English settlement on the western seaboard around the cities of Galway and Limerick. These new conquerors and settlers viewed themselves as English, and both cities developed strong trading links to the continent. Yet the original conquest was never complete, and the very different culture and power structures of Gaelic Ireland remained intact across much of the island, most especially the northwest. Many Irish kings reached accommodations with the new regime based in Dublin, but equally, the original conquest ran out of steam in the thirteenth century. It is worth pausing at this point to consider both the conquerors, and those they sought to conquer.

Natives and Newcomers

The Gaelic Irish made up most of the inhabitants of Ireland prior to the arrival of the Normans.[2] Theirs was a pastoral society, with a marked emphasis on livestock, most especially cows, which were a crucial source of wealth and status. Dairy products played a major role in the Gaelic diet, and the most famous early Irish epic poem, the *Táin*, is about a cattle raid. Land units certainly existed—the traditional division of Ireland into four historic "provinces" is a surviving remnant of this—but were surprisingly fluid. The importance of livestock made this unavoidable. Equally, there was little in the way of internal infrastructure and, outside the major monastic centres and old Viking enclaves, larger permanent settlements were few and far between. Some later observers felt that Ireland seemed under-populated, but this assumption did not reflect the existence of a light and mobile population. Stone was used as a building material in the large settlements that did exist, but the normal building materials were wood, wattle, earth, and turf, though craftsmen working in metal were to be found in Gaelic Ireland. Agriculture was practised, with cereals being widely grown, as was flax for linen; wool was another important product. The bonds of hierarchy were enforced in the form of tributes or more concrete obligations, such as billeting the soldiers of a lord.

Gaelic warfare was light and mobile, and very different from the military practices of the Normans; it was suited to the internal conditions of Gaelic Ireland. Warfare was organised on a semi-feudal basis and took the form of guerrilla fighting by Irish soldiers (often described in the singular as *kern*, from the Irish term *ceithearn*, meaning a band of warriors). These were sometimes assisted by the Scottish mercenaries known as gallowglass (from the Irish *gallóglach*, a "foreign fighter"). In times of peace, Roman law, as mediated by the Christian church, was a major influence, and was enforced by the Gaelic lords, with arbitration by the hereditary lawyers known as *breithimh* (colloquially known as Brehons); punishments for crimes could range from payments and compensation to mutilation and death. The bonds of Gaelic society and culture and the mechanics of how it operated were sophisticated, and of long standing.

The political structure of Gaelic Ireland remains relatively easy to identify, as do its intellectual elites, such as the hereditary poetic caste of *filí*, who were generally retained by the lords. Everyday life is more obscure. Aside from the major rivers, there were virtually no inland routeways. The Christian church was a vitally important institution, though practices and customs differed according to region. It seems that there was a rich vernacular religion outside the institutional church, but again, it is hard to fully discern. The primary language was Irish (though there were, and are, a number of dialects). Norse would have been spoken in the old Scandinavian enclaves, and the new settlers would have spoken various dialects of English, with French being spoken by the colonial elite. Bilingualism would have been common amongst sectors of the ruling elites, and was almost certainly essential for merchants, but this was by no means universal.

The Normans were a warrior aristocracy. Unlike their Gaelic

counterparts, they were technically under the rule of a centralised authority, in the form of the English monarchy. Prince John was granted lordship of Ireland by his father, King Henry II, in order to rein in the knights who were ensconcing themselves on his western flank. The common law and English structure of local government were extended to the new English colony in Ireland, which was to be ruled by an appointed governor who would represent the king and his interests. Parliaments began to be called as consultative bodies in the thirteenth century. Yet the most obvious and profound changes that the new arrivals brought were physical and cultural. Large-scale immigration took place, primarily from England and Wales, and new forms of agriculture and crops began to be applied in the areas under Norman control. New languages and dialects were imported, as were new laws and territorial divisions; meanwhile, the fortified castles of the Norman elite took shape and became a new feature of the Irish landscape.

Lands that the Normans had seized were redistributed to the king, to the church, to feudal magnates, and even sometimes to the Irish. Road building took place to a limited degree within the new zones of English influence; trade links with cities such as Bristol and Chester were forged, built on the export of hides, tallow, butter, cloth, cereals, and fish, with luxury goods such as wine coming back the other way. English modes of tillage farming were to be seen in some areas (there was a much greater emphasis on pastoral farming in Gaelic Ireland). Ireland remained heavily wooded, and the administrative division of the island into counties had not yet happened. As time went on, interculturation took place; some Norman aristocrats became Gaelicized, while by the fifteenth century some Gaelic lords in the western province of Connacht and the southern province of Munster were adopting the types of military fortifications that the Normans had brought to Ireland.[3]

Yet there was perhaps more continuity than change within Gaelic Ireland; many Gaelic dynasties outlasted their newer Norman competitors. And the colony was weakened by internecine squabbles amongst its aristocratic leadership; weaknesses that came to fore in 1315 when Edward Bruce, earl of Carrick and brother of Robert Bruce, king of Scotland, arrived in the northeast at the head of an army. Styling himself as king of Ireland and intent on overthrowing the English colony at a time when Scotland and England were at war, Bruce found support amongst the Gaelic Irish of the northern province of Ulster, but also within the colonial community, and embarked on a devastating series of campaigns before being killed in battle in 1318. The arrival of bubonic plague in the middle of the fourteenth century—the "Black Death"—took a major toll on the population of English Ireland, and presumably of Gaelic Ireland too. Three of the four horsemen—war, famine, and plague—were regular visitors to Ireland in the later Middle Ages.

What also became evident in the later fourteenth century, as the colony weakened, was "degeneracy": a sense that the English in Ireland were, quite literally, adopting Gaelic ways and going native; the Statutes of Kilkenny in 1366, which forbade the adoption of Gaelic customs of all kinds, were a draconian attempt to solve an increasingly worrisome problem. If the English in Ireland became "more Irish than the Irish themselves," as the saying went, then the basis of the incomplete English conquest would be eroded. And the English colony was undoubtedly weakening and contracting in the later Middle Ages: the Gaelic Irish slowly but surely began to roll back the areas of English influence and authority. By the beginning of the sixteenth century, the rule of the English administration in Dublin was restricted to the "English Pale"—the modern counties of Dublin, Wicklow, Meath, and Louth—with the vast patrimonies of the leading aristocrats such as the Fitzgerald earls of Kildare or the Butler earls of Ormond remaining as outposts of English influence beyond this region, often within their own devolved jurisdictions or "liberties." There is an extraordinary contrast between the relative weakness of English rule in Ireland at the beginning of the sixteenth century and the successful conquest that had been completed a century later.

The Anglo-Norman conquest had reoriented Ireland's ports away from their traditional focus on Scandinavia. Dublin was the key town on the east coast and looked towards Britain, with which it had major trading links. North of it, Dundalk remained as a major trading centre, and inland there was a militarised network of new medieval towns such as Navan and Trim in County Meath. Urbanisation also brought a new religious phenomenon. The Normans, just like the Gaelic Irish, patronised religious orders, but they also supported the new orders of mendicant friars—Dominicans, Franciscans, Carmelites, and Augustinians—that began to arrive in their wake, and who began to minister within the newly established urban network.

But towns and cities had very definite limits; the Wicklow mountains, immediately south of Dublin, remained a Gaelic fastness, and the influence of Gaelic aristocrats could still be felt even in the earliest zones of English settlement. The rich southern lands of Munster fed into ports such as Waterford, Kinsale, and Cork, all of which had major trade links with Britain and the continent, though a Gaelic presence was still strong in the northern edge of Munster and in western Cork and Kerry. By the end of the Middle Ages towns and cities such as Limerick, Galway, and Sligo were increasingly isolated English outposts on the western fringes of Gaelic Ireland; otherwise, the northwest was under the sway of great Gaelic aristocrats such as the O'Donnells and the O'Neills. Moving east across Ulster, an English fringe could be found on the northeast coast in towns like Carrickfergus, but there was also an enduring Scottish presence: the Gaelic world extended to the Hebrides and western Scotland. Sometimes the dominion of Scottish aristocrats like the MacDonnells straddled the channel between Ulster and Scotland. The frontier zones that lay between these various regions were areas of interculturation as well as conflict.

Much had changed in Ireland since the Norman invasion and the creation of the colony. Ireland at the start of the sixteenth century could be divided into two distinct cultural and geographic blocs, divided in terms of law, custom, language, agriculture, styles of warfare, and much else besides, with a considerable grey area in between. But a brief overview such as this cannot hope to do justice to the complexity of Irish life on the eve of the profound changes of the sixteenth century; the beginning, one can say without exaggeration, of modern Ireland.[4]

PART I

The Sixteenth Century

CHAPTER ONE

New Faith, New Kingdom

The Kildare Ascendancy

The medieval lordship of Ireland had come into being in the 1170s, after the original Norman conquest. In 1177, King Henry II of England granted the title "lord of Ireland" to his eldest son, John, and the English crown thereby claimed jurisdiction over the entire island. Yet three centuries later, at the beginning of the sixteenth century, the reality that lay behind this claim was very different. English control was effectively restricted to the "English Pale"—the extended hinterland of Dublin to the north and west—along with the major towns and the territories of the English aristocracy. By the later fifteenth century, it was also obvious that English power in Ireland depended on the local power wielded by the leading noble families within the "Englishry." Preeminent amongst these were the Fitzgerald earls of Kildare, in their territories on the borders of the Pale.

By the beginning of the sixteenth century, the earls of Kildare were, in practical terms, the de facto rulers of Ireland. The disarray into which their great aristocratic rivals had fallen helped their rise. The remote earldom of Desmond, centred on Limerick and Kerry, became alienated from the crown after the seventh earl of Desmond was executed in 1468 on trumped-up charges of treason. The earldom of Ormond, centred on counties Kilkenny and Tipperary, was riven by chaos arising from a succession dispute that remained un-

11

resolved until 1515. Consequently, the earls of Kildare had the field to themselves.

Their power was secured by other factors. Their base was on the western border of the Pale, and as the zone of English influence contracted in the later Middle Ages, the Kildare territories had effectively become the frontier; the earls commanded considerable military power as a result. They had also cultivated an intricate network of alliances amongst both Gaelic and English families that no English government based in Dublin could hope to rival, and Kildare's forces were more than capable of enforcing the obligations such alliances entailed. Gearoid Mór, the eighth earl of Kildare, was appointed as lord deputy—the king's representative—on 5 August 1496, with a formal link to the royal family through marriage; the business of Kildare rule continued much as before up to and after 1513, when Gearoid Mór's son Gearoid Óg became the ninth earl after his father died from a wound received while campaigning in 1511.

Yet their power did not go unchallenged. In 1515 the ninth earl, while in London, was obliged to answer allegations that the integrity of the English colony had begun to degenerate over time due to Kildare's alignments with Gaelic Irish lords, and more disturbingly, that Kildare rule was ultimately intended to usurp the authority of the king. His adoption of the semi-feudal Gaelic practices known as "coign and livery"—the taking of free lodgings and sustenance, often by soldiers—were a particular bone of contention. The allegations were dismissed, but they highlighted perceived problems in Ireland that were assumed to have gotten worse under the rule of the earls of Kildare. In 1519, further complaints against the ninth earl prompted Henry VIII to confront the ambivalence with which English monarchs viewed their most important servant in Ireland, and Kildare was summoned to London to account for himself. The traditional English dependence upon Kildare may have been a pragmatic decision, but it also meant that this extraordinarily powerful subject had to be kept on-side. Equally, Kildare had to be scrutinised on occasion to ensure that the power he wielded remained firmly in the service of the crown; the eighth earl had, after all, lent his support to Lambert Simnel, a pretender to the English crown in the later fifteenth century.

Kildare was too powerful to fully disregard. In May 1520 he was replaced as lord deputy by Thomas Howard, earl of Surrey, who embarked upon military campaigns in Ulster, Leinster, and the midlands in order to bring Gaelic families such as the O'Neills to heel. But Surrey quickly realised that any comprehensive attempt to bring the Gaelic Irish to obedience was going to require a major and expensive investment of men and material. Henry VIII was unwilling to support this, and the English in Ireland proved unwilling to pay for it on the grounds that the king was obliged to provide for their security anyway. Instead, Henry enjoined Surrey to proceed by diplomacy, or, as he put it, "sober ways, politic drifts, and amiable persuasions, founded in law and reason."[1] But Kildare, disgruntled at being marginalised from a role that he and his family increasingly seemed to view as a birthright, mobilised his Gaelic allies to foment unrest; a further indication of how indispensible his power and influence was. Henry was distracted at this juncture by the possibility of a Scottish invasion of Ireland through northern England, not to mention the related prospect of war between France and the Holy Roman Empire, with which Henry was becoming aligned; Ireland slipped down the list of royal priorities.

Henry did become more involved in Irish affairs in the 1520s, as did his chief advisor, Cardinal Thomas Wolsey. Between 1522 and 1529 no lord deputy served for more than two years (there were nine in total). This reflected two things: the piecemeal nature of English policy making towards Ireland, and a desire to avoid depending on any one powerful noble to govern Ireland. But while Kildare could be stripped of formal office, it was another matter entirely to remove the real basis of his power: Kildare was essentially in a position to rule by default should he choose to do so. Henry had committed himself to not restoring him to the highest office in the land, and instead appointed Sir Piers Ruadh Butler, one of the rival claimants to the earldom of Ormond, to the position in March 1522. The subsequent revival of the old Kildare-Ormond rivalry saw both earls summoned to London to account for themselves in August 1526, and Kildare remained there until 1530. The power vacuum that resulted saw outbreaks of widespread unrest that seemed to confirm that Kildare was the only one qualified to govern Ireland. By July 1532 it was obvious that he would have to be relied upon again. His reappointment to the most powerful office in the land in 1532 suggested that, once again, little had changed. The assumption that this was indeed the case ultimately proved fatal.

In the 1530s Henry VIII, having unsuccessfully attempted to have his marriage to Catherine of Aragon annulled, broke with the papacy and repudiated the spiritual authority of the Vatican: the break with Rome heralded the introduction of the English Reformation. It also left England isolated as a Protestant power in predominantly Catholic western Europe, and thus left England vulnerable to attack by Catholic powers at the behest of the papacy or the Holy Roman Emperor Charles V, or both. Consequently, any internal threats to Henry's regime were likely to be taken far more seriously than had previously been the case. In 1534 Wolsey's successor Thomas Cromwell had drawn up proposals for reviving royal authority within the lordship of Ireland. While Cromwell's plan was not new, the eventual reaction to it was unprecedented.

Amongst Cromwell's prescriptions was a demand for a series of new appointments to key positions in the Dublin administration that Kildare had sought to block; he was well aware that these schemes were intended to clip his wings by placing patronage in the form of state offices out of his reach. He was officially reprimanded and was summoned to London to account for his activities. Kildare had shrugged off such efforts to restrict his authority in the past by exerting his power to remind the king that he could not realistically be sidelined; in this case he ensured that the royal armoury in Ireland was transferred to his own castles, most especially his seat at Maynooth in County Kildare. In February 1534 he departed for England, leaving his eldest son, Thomas, Lord Offaly, in his place. And in June 1534, Offaly took drastic action.

The Rebellion of Silken Thomas

Offaly—known to posterity as "Silken Thomas" due to the silk headpieces reputedly worn by the horsemen in his retinue—repudiated the king's authority on 11 June 1534. This was an attempt to remind Henry of his family's supposedly indispensible authority in Ireland; they had done this in the past. But the context in which Offaly embarked upon an open revolt was unprecedented: the break with Rome had prompted Henry's regime to consolidate and secure its authority in the north of England, Ireland, and Wales, against the backdrop of a potentially hostile international situation. Kildare himself was imprisoned in the Tower of London, where he died in September 1534. Offaly thus became the tenth earl of Kildare in the midst of the rebellion he was leading. While throughout the summer of 1534 Henry left avenues open for a diplomatic resolution, the prospect of full-scale rebellion in Ireland (now accompanied by Offaly's claim that he fought against a heretic king, which attracted the attention of the Holy Roman Emperor) could not be ignored. In October 1534 Henry VIII sent Sir William Skeffington to Ireland with 2,300 troops, along with artillery that was used to capture the Kildare stronghold of Maynooth Castle in March 1535; in a display of singular ruthlessness, 25 prisoners were decapitated outside the castle on 25 March. Kildare had been declared a traitor on Skeffington's arrival, and finally submitted in August 1535. After travelling to London, in October 1535 he was imprisoned in the Tower of London, in the same cell in which his father had been incarcerated.

Thomas, the tenth earl, had gambled and lost. He was executed along with five leading male members of his family on 3 February 1537, and the earldom itself was legally extinguished. In terms of ruling the lordship of Ireland, the English government were now in unfamiliar waters. Thanks to the vacuum left behind by exterminating the earldom of Kildare, Henry VIII had gained himself a sustained and unavoidable commitment to Irish affairs. In the immediate aftermath of the Kildare rebellion, the English authorities were uncertain of how best to proceed in this uncharted territory, but there were some straightforward reforms that could be introduced quickly. The government of Ireland was to be remodelled with an English-born governor, backed by a standing garrison and a good leavening of Englishmen in the new administration. If Ireland was to become a political extension of England, it would also have to become a religious extension: it was inevitable that the Henrician Reformation would be extended to the lordship of Ireland.

Reformations

The original status of Ireland as a lordship held by the kings of England originated in *Laudabiliter*, the papal bull in which Pope

Adrian IV had granted it to Henry II in the 1150s. Within this arrangement was a problem waiting to happen; if the pope was now irrelevant in English affairs, then the English title deeds to Ireland were faulty. Consequently, the early phases of the Henrician Reformation in Ireland were more concerned with authority than with doctrine. Its basic tenets were generally accepted by the colonial community. The parliament that sat in Ireland in 1536–37 (and which briefly followed the new lord deputy, Lord Leonard Grey, on campaign around the country) was responsible for passing the legislation that laid the bedrock for the Irish Reformation. The most important legal initiative was the recognition of the royal supremacy (the status of the monarch as head of the church). The legislation also made arrangements for its application, with the creation of a new (or, as it would claim, newly reformed) state church: the Church of Ireland. The relevant legislation was passed in Ireland, albeit with some limited opposition from low-ranking clergy, and the executions of Kildare and some senior members of his family were delayed until 1537 to facilitate their passage. By the end of the 1530s the lordship of Ireland had become, in principle if not in practice, a "Protestant" jurisdiction (though the term itself comes from a later era).

There was another question to be faced: was this political and religious change to be restricted to the Pale and the "Englishry," or was it to be extended to those beyond both? In 1536 the Irish parliament had decreed that the king's subjects in Ireland were to conform to English customs, most especially by speaking the English language (Irish would, over time, be seen as a symptom or source of rebellious and disloyal tendencies).[2] This had implications for the Gaelic Irish, as the inhabitants of the Gaelic lordships were not seen as "subjects." But the conquest of the lordships was not an option. It was not the case that the real power of the government was increased after the rebellion; instead, the dominant regional power that the crown had traditionally depended upon was removed. The new administration in Dublin was now faced with considerably greater responsibility in terms of ruling Ireland without any significant increase in the financial means with which they could do so, though the confiscation of Kildare lands and the lands of newly dissolved monastic orders offered some financial relief. The dissolution of

Irish monasteries was an inevitable outcome of the extension of the
Reformation to Ireland, though the redistribution of monastic
wealth amongst the laity seems to have contributed to a period of
modest economic growth and, according to its historian, "moderate
social improvement," as this newly released wealth was used to fund
the creation of almshouses, hospitals, and schools.[3] This may also
have softened the edges of the new and more interventionist policy
being undertaken by Ireland's English rulers.

While Kildare's allies had not risen against the government,
they still looked to the ghost of the family for potential guidance
and leadership. The government was loath to replace one over-
mighty subject with another; the earls of Ormond, for example,
were never going to be permitted to become as powerful as the earls
of Kildare had been. But that government was now forced to depend
on such allies in Ireland as could be found. By the late 1530s Grey
had embarked upon campaigns to deal with the "Geraldine league":
the former Gaelic allies of Kildare, spearheaded by magnates like
Manus O'Donnell and Conn O'Neill, who demanded the restoration of Kildare and would even go so far as to offer the crown of
Ireland to James V of Scotland. In August 1539, Grey decisively
defeated them at the battle of Bellahoe, on the Meath-Monaghan
border. But while successful, this was not a pattern that could realistically be continued.

Grey was replaced in July 1540 by a new lord deputy who was
supposed to take charge of this new situation: Sir Anthony St. Leger,
who possessed a number of vital attributes for his new position: a
good knowledge of Ireland, having served there previously; diplomatic experience; and secure backing at court. He was willing to use
force as he deemed necessary, as witnessed by his forays into Leinster to deal with families (or "septs") such as the O'Tooles and the
Kavanaghs. His key contribution to Irish affairs was, however, constitutional, in the form of the initiative he deemed necessary to secure the "reform" of Ireland: its elevation from a lordship into a
kingdom.

In 1541 the Irish parliament passed the Act for the Kingly Title.
Ireland was now formally transformed into a kingdom under Henry
VIII and his successors, as opposed to a lordship that was technically
held by the kings of England by a grant of the papacy. The principle

was simple. Under this new dispensation, the various factions and political groupings in Ireland could be brought under one single authority as loyal subjects of the crown to which they would now pledge their obedience. The symbolism of the act was exemplified by the earl of Ormond having its formal announcement at a service in St. Patrick's Cathedral in Dublin translated into Irish for the ben-efit of Gaelic chieftains who were present. The act could be seen as the culmination of calls for political and cultural "reform" that had been uttered at intervals since the start of the century. The subse-quent policy often termed "surrender and regrant" was to be its practical outworking.[4]

"Surrender and regrant" operated on a simple premise. Gaelic lords, who in legal terms were "non-subjects," would surrender their territories to the crown and submit to royal authority. They would then be "regranted" the same territories by the king, to be held by what were now lawful subjects. The policy entailed the cre-ation of an entirely new community of Irish peers, at every level of the peerage except the rank of duke. This was seen as a long-term process that would work itself out over generations, and that would implicitly facilitate the eventual conversion of the Irish from their allegedly barbarous ways. In the early to mid-1540s the policy seemed to have the potential to be a notable success. St. Leger did the rounds of various Gaelic chieftains, and Henry VIII's initial scepticism about the kingship act and its consequences was allevi-ated by a series of important aristocratic submissions in London. On the whole, in the 1540s this new departure seemed viable, and suc-cessful. It had arisen from the necessity for alternatives to an outright reconquest of Ireland, which had long been seen as impractical.

The Tudors were faced with the problem that there were alter-native political structures in Ireland that lay outside the jurisdiction of the English colony. These were based on alliances maintained on what had virtually been a national scale by figures such as the earls of Kildare, and to a lesser degree, their Ormond rivals. The creation of the kingdom of Ireland was intended to restore the stability of the old arrangement in the absence of a figure like Kildare; Ireland's diverse components were to be unified not under the rule of an over-mighty subject, but under the rule of the monarch to whom all would, in theory, give allegiance. Initially, this seemed to have worked. But many of the tentative arrangements created in this manner would ultimately be destroyed.

The New Order Versus the Old

In the decades after the Kildare rebellion, the priority of the Tudor regime was to secure its control over Ireland. A concrete indication of this was revealed by the growth of cartography, as the English administration sought to quantify their knowledge of the island that they wished to bring under firmer control. New and often beautifully detailed maps of Ireland were created throughout the sixteenth century by English cartographers such as John Goghe, Robert Lythe, and Richard Bartlett, amongst others. These were not just neutral, descriptive depictions of Ireland; they were also analytical and prescriptive. By rendering Ireland's physical, cultural, and political geographies intelligible to English observers, the maps were blueprints for the Tudor regime to consolidate its control over Ireland.[5] The creation of the kingdom of Ireland was a political initiative aimed at asserting this control, while the introduction of the reformation was a religious initiative harnessed to the same purpose. Yet there was a third, and more far-reaching strategy by which the Tudors sought to achieve their objectives in Ireland: social engineering, in the form of colonisation.

Henry VIII died in 1547 and was succeeded by his nine-year-old son Edward. His short reign was dominated by his aristocratic guardians, and in 1553 he was succeeded in turn by his half sister Mary, who unsuccessfully tried to roll back the Reformation. Yet it was during the brief reigns of these Tudor monarchs that the most significant English venture into early modern Ireland began. Colonisation had been suggested earlier in the century, but the first "plantations" in Ireland were established in the midland regions of Queen's and King's counties (modern Laois and Offaly) in the 1550s, areas that had traditionally been within the Kildare sphere of influence. The formal plantations had been preceded by the establishment of new garrisons in these regions (such as Fort Protector, which evolved into the modern town of Portlaoise). The purpose was straightforward: alongside these new defensive arrangements on the fringes of the Pale, the plantations would hopefully serve as examples of "civility" to the Gaelic Irish that would serve to extend English common law to them, and to persuade them of the virtues of a commercial economy based largely upon pastoral farming. The two settlements were not wholly successful, despite attempts being made to shore them up throughout the 1550s. But they were pioneering efforts at colonisation; and as such, they pointed the way towards its future use.

On the accession of Elizabeth I in November 1558 many of the traditional cultural and political boundaries between English and Gaelic areas remained largely intact. The west and north remained predominantly Gaelic, and "Gaeldom" stretched across the North Channel into Scotland. The Englishry still remained largely confined to Leinster, with Munster uneasily balanced between the two. Elizabeth, in the early years of her reign, was reluctant to embark on any radical new departure in Ireland unless circumstances demanded it; with the end of a war with France and Scotland, she did not want to become embroiled in another expensive military venture. But her apparent indecisiveness satisfied no one. Gaelic lords remained uncertain of how they were to be treated, while the "Palesmen" resented having to maintain an English army, along with an English-dominated government that was no longer as receptive to their overtures as it had been when they dominated it. On the other hand, the so-called "New English" settlers and administrators who had started to arrive in Ireland since the 1540s felt that these groups had been treated too leniently in the past. The English government in London remained baffled that Ireland had not been brought under control.

The most obvious and immediate feature of Elizabeth's reign was the renewed commitment to the English Reformation, after the attempts of her stepsister and predecessor Mary to reintroduce Catholicism in the course of her own brief reign. The Elizabethan religious settlement in England retained a great deal of residual ceremony reminiscent of the old religion, and she herself was given the status of supreme governor of the church, as opposed to her father who had been supreme head. These strictures were now applied to the Church of Ireland, but the propagation of the reformed religion was hamstrung by a lack of resources on the part of both the government and the church. A major reason for the failure of the Tudor reformation in Ireland was the simple fact that it was impossible to fully enforce it, and the deployment of extra resources (such as clergy) from England only reinforced the notion that the new faith was an alien imposition. More basic realities could also interfere with its mission: in 1562 the bishop of Kildare asked to be relieved of his position, on the grounds that most of those he sought to minister to spoke Irish rather than English.

The flaws in the new dispensation were made manifest in the 1560s, when Elizabeth's government in Ireland, now headed by Thomas Radclyffe, earl of Sussex, was obliged to grapple with the ambitions of Shane O'Neill. He was the youngest son of Conn Bacach ("the lame") O'Neill, earl of Tyrone, who had emerged as the appointed heir according to Gaelic law but not, alas, according to the new arrangements into which his father had entered; that status had been granted instead to his cousin Brian, second Baron Dungannon. Having seen off both his eldest brother (whom he had killed) and his father, Shane was installed as "the O'Neill" (the head of the sept or kin-group), and soon brought pressure to bear on traditional vassals of the O'Neills, such as the Maguires, MacMahons, and O'Reillys, to bring them back into the fold and to break the newly forged bonds of loyalty between these families and the government. At the same time he rekindled the traditional rivalry between the O'Neills and the O'Donnells, the other major Gaelic aristocratic family in Ulster. He also began to mount attacks in Connacht and upon the Pale. In essence, Shane O'Neill had begun to reassert the traditional preeminence of his dynasty.

He succeeded, though not in the way that might have been intended. Sussex took the view that the challenge presented by Shane's activities struck at the root of English authority in Ireland and would have to be stopped. Shane was declared a traitor, and Sussex went to war against him with a large and expensive army. It was obvious by 1561 that this had failed, but there was another possible solution to the problem. As early as 1559 Shane had been seeking the official title of earl of Tyrone, and in January 1562 he was presented before a bemused Elizabeth and her court in London. He sought the earldom, arguing that his rival Dungannon was illegitimate anyway, that he was willing to start negotiating with the English afresh, and that he was the natural candidate for the earldom because he was the appointed representative of his people, an argument that Elizabeth found compelling. Sussex argued against this, claiming that Shane was a usurper and that his status as the O'Neill was irrelevant in English law, which was technically correct. The negotiations that followed were intended to define what Shane understood by the powers of the earldom; in other words, they were intended to limit that power by ensuring that the traditional Gaelic authority of the O'Neill would not be carried on by the earl of Tyrone should Shane obtain that title. The awkward fact that the title was officially meant to pass to Dungannon was dealt with when Shane had the latter assassinated. Yet within these intrigues could be seen the clash of two very different political systems and legal codes. Shane O'Neill was potentially a problem on a national scale: hence Sussex's imprecation that "if Shane be overthrown, all is settled; if Shane settle, all is overthrown."[6]

The Treaty of Drumcree of September 1563 recognised Shane's position whilst promising him the earldom of Tyrone as soon as was legally possible. But by 1564, procrastination on this front was interpreted by Shane as evidence of bad faith. He decided to act by attacking the Scottish MacDonalds, who had a substantial presence in east Ulster, with subsequent attacks on the O'Donnell heartlands in west Ulster. He was undermined by his gamble; rather than view him as indispensible, the English government, now led by Sir Henry Sidney, concluded that he would never accept their authority, and resolved to defeat him. When O'Neill came to negotiate with the Scots with an eye to forging an alliance, the Scots were in the process of reaching their own accommodation with Sidney. In June 1567, their negotiations with O'Neill ended when they cut his throat. Soon afterwards, O'Neill's head was sent to Dublin to be impaled on a spike over Dublin Castle. The struggle between O'Neill and the English government encapsulated a clash between two very different and competing types of authority; a clash that would recur again before the end of the century, and on a much greater scale than ever before.

CHAPTER TWO

Elizabethan Ireland

Fault Lines

The English presence in Ireland was becoming notably more coercive in the second half of the sixteenth century. It was perhaps inevitable that the increasing use of force, and the inexorable growth of plantations (both private ventures and those sponsored by the state) would prompt reactions from the Irish and the older English community who felt that they were also being encroached upon; members of both embarked on rebellions towards the end of the century. In itself this was nothing new, but the contexts in which such revolts took place was now shaped (at least in part) by religion. Religion was not, however, the only distinction between these various groupings.

Gaelic Ireland possessed an old and rich culture; indeed, Irish aristocrats often deemed the English to be their inferiors. There existed a loose sense of national identity, based upon common characteristics across the island and the existence of ancient literary and cultural traditions. The existence of a Gaelic world extending into Scotland had traditionally helped to negate the development of a sense of distinctly Irish "Gaeldom," though this would begin to change in the latter half of the sixteenth century. Gaelic Ireland retained much of its territorial sovereignty and cultural hegemony; and crucially, it retained a loyalty to the older, Catholic, faith. These could all be interpreted as evidence of hostility to English rule. This was compounded by English views of the Irish as a primitive and savage people, which are often traced back to the writings of Giraldus Cambrensis in the twelfth century. The Irish, in some Tudor eyes, were not just primitive: they were barbarous, treasonous, and generally untrustworthy to boot. Indeed, political reforms were often couched in terms that implied a more fundamental cultural reform as well. From an English point of view, the reluctance of the Irish to adopt English ways and norms was a reflection not of problems with those English laws and customs, but with the Irish who were incapable of appreciating their benefits. Similar assumptions, namely that the Irish were incapable of receiving the word of God, would later be used to account for the failure of the Reformation.

As time went by, religious affiliation facilitated the definition of a third grouping in Irish society. The descendants of the original colonists—the "English in Ireland," as they had come to describe themselves—found their position under threat as the Tudor state reengaged with Ireland from the 1530s onwards. They had hoped that their existing status would also be incorporated into the new reformed Irish polity that was supposedly under construction. However, the arrival of a new cohort of English administrators, soldiers, and, as the century wore on, settlers, was a source of resentment, not least as the Old English were expected to pay for an increasingly expensive administration that was becoming increasingly oblivious to their interests; they were basically expected to cough up and shut up. One consequence was that the Old English became more inclined to exert an influence on the English-dominated government by withholding the financial subsidies that it depended on. Another was an increasing tendency to air their grievances in London rather than Dublin. The difficulty was that such tactics automatically brought their loyalty into question. And as the older English community also kept their allegiance to Catholicism, they began to be seen as suspect in other ways. The burgeoning tension between religious and political allegiance was becoming unsustainable over time.

Instabilities

The relative failure of the Reformation in Ireland should not obscure the fact that religion became an increasingly important distinction between these three key segments of Irish society. The Reformation had set newly Protestant England firmly at loggerheads with the great Catholic powers of Europe, most notably Spain and the papacy itself. In February 1570, Pope Pius V declared Elizabeth I to be a heretic, thereby excommunicating her. The implications of this were clear: Catholic subjects were now released from their allegiance to a heretic queen and could, at least according to canon law, lawfully resist her (though this remained a contentious issue for many Catholics). It further illustrated the necessity to extend the reformation across the Tudor dominions. In 1567 a Gaelic translation of the Book of Common Prayer had been published in Edinburgh using Irish orthography in the hope that it might be used in Ireland as well as Scotland, and the first book published in Ireland in the Irish language was published in 1571: an Irish-language primer, complete with prayers borrowed from the Book of Common Prayer. It was increasingly seen as a necessity to seek the conversion of the Irish from popery, and such efforts at proselytising would have to be conducted in Irish.[1]

This imperative to secure Ireland from the forces of international Catholicism was highlighted by a number of significant rebellions in the early decades of Elizabeth's reign. The first broke out in June 1569 when James Fitzmaurice Fitzgerald, a cousin of the earl of Desmond, began to attack English settlements in Cork in league with Donal MacCarthy, earl of Clancare, who abandoned his English title in favour of the Gaelic title of MacCarthy Mór (a parallel rebellion broke out in Clare, led by the earl of Thomond and prompted by more localised grievances). Along with numerous other Gaelic lords and the younger brothers of "Black Tom" Butler, the tenth earl of Ormond, who was also a cousin of the queen, these rebel forces mounted a campaign across Munster that extended up into the planted regions of the midlands. The rebellion adopted the rhetoric of Catholicism in an unsuccessful attempt to garner support from the continent, but it had been prompted by concerns about encroachments being made on Desmond lands by English soldiers and planters: a far more prosaic grievance. Ormond was tasked with dealing with it. He was upstaged as he did so by the lord deputy, Sir Henry Sidney, who resented his influence with the queen and embarked upon a furious campaign in Munster to suppress the rebellion. This was notable for the brutality of figures such as Sir Humphrey Gilbert, who in six weeks captured twenty-three castles and wiped out their inhabitants; he allegedly forced those submitting to his authority in the province to enter his tent via an avenue of severed heads. While most of the rebel leaders had submitted by December 1569, Fitzmaurice remained at large, having nothing to lose, and the future viceroy Sir John Perrot claimed to have executed eight hundred people (excluding those killed in battle) in a two-year campaign to suppress the revolt.

These events happened at a time when English colonial ventures were tentatively being embarked upon in North America, which provided a wider context against which to view the English experience in Ireland; contemporaries such as Gilbert and Sir Walter Raleigh spent parts of their careers on the other side of the Atlantic after cutting their teeth in Ireland, and others like Sir Thomas Smith, patron of a failed attempt at a plantation in Ulster, readily made such comparisons between the new world and the old. The key comparison, however, was that in Ireland, just as in North America, the English presence was obliged to coexist with a very different culture and socioeconomic order. The cultures of Gaelic Ireland and the native cultures of North America were themselves very different: Gaelic Ireland was Christian, and was linked to the broader culture of Europe in a way that native Americans were not. But the cultural differences perceived by English observers were sufficiently great that these indigenous peoples on either side of the Atlantic could both be seen as strange and barbarous.

By the 1570s it was evident that Gaelic Ireland remained culturally and politically largely intact. One conclusion to be drawn from this was that the Irish would have to be coerced into submission. Under Sidney in the later 1560s, new local administrations—provincial presidencies—were established in Connacht and Munster. These were primarily intended to extend English common law into outlying areas. They were to be equipped with an advisory council, a small military force, and two judges. Rather tellingly, the chief justice of Connacht, Sir Ralph Rokeby, noted that "it must be fire and sword and the rod of God's vengeance that must make these stubborn and cankered hearts yield for fear."[2] This new approach was to be paid for by taxes designed to replace the semi-feudal exactions practised by Gaelic and Old English lords, which had long been a source of complaint. A single regularised tax—"cess"—was to be paid by the various lordships to sustain what would be, in theory, a government that would administer justice impartially whilst upholding their interests, and which would, hopefully, spread law, order, and civility. But the new presidencies also had the added power of being entitled to investigate land titles, which had uncomfortable implications: to question the right to own land was to question the very basis of wealth and power in Ireland. The new institutions were exploited in this manner, notably the Connacht presidency under Sir Richard Bingham.[3]

Ireland offered scope for the unscrupulous to enrich themselves in ways that undermined any claim by the authorities to be acting as honest and impartial brokers. Official service in Ireland was especially attractive to the younger sons of English noble families, many of whom took the view that Ireland could be used as a springboard for their advancement, not to mention their enrichment: it was also closer to home than North America. The increasing proliferation of English rather than Anglo-Irish officials in both central and local administration was evidence of this enthusiasm. But this trend also seems to have contributed to a rise in the levels of violence employed by the Tudor state, with the increasing use of martial law from the 1550s onward. Between 1558 and 1578, 259 commissions of martial law were issued, providing its practitioners with summary powers of execution and the right to claim one-third of the goods and possessions of those executed: a profit motive that could encourage its use against a people increasingly viewed as barbarous and inferior.[4] And brutal actions took place. In July 1575 the earl of Essex, for example, while involved in a pioneering plantation venture in Ulster, had six hundred men, women, and children killed on Rathlin Island, the stronghold of the MacDonnells, under a commission of martial law. This was gradually extended across Ireland as the reign of Elizabeth wore on, and increasingly without distinction; summary execution became a widespread practice, and decapitated heads became a common feature of conflict, whether as trophies of victory or grisly receipts for rewards.[5]

There were, however, other justifications for the use of such extreme violence in wartime: thousands of survivors of the Spanish

Armada were executed in 1588 by Bingham on the coasts of Galway, Mayo, and Sligo. This treatment could also be extended to those Irish who were seen as inclined to align themselves with such hostile Catholic powers. By the 1580s it was becoming increasingly evident that the widespread use of repression (as directed against the Irish), often exploited for the purposes of personal profit, was provocative, and was serving to undermine any lingering English hopes of the political and cultural reform of the kingdom of Ireland. Force had long been advocated as a central plank of English policy, and English commanders like Humphrey Gilbert readily resorted to it. Yet it was not necessarily the preferred option, not least because of how much it might cost. The deployment of campaign armies, organised as required, was the most common large-scale recourse to force by Elizabethan governors. But they were not automatically suited to Irish conditions: bogs and woodlands made for difficult terrain, and the preferred Gaelic practise of guerrilla warfare made them vulnerable to hit-and-run attacks. English armies were also going to be faced with a welter of private armies in the control of the Gaelic and English lordships. The ad hoc nature of these English armies meant that real power and authority was usually retained by the lower-ranking officers, the often unaccountable "captains" responsible for recruiting, equipping, and leading the various units of the army. As the Irish came to be seen as reformable only by force, it was used more frequently. This state-sponsored repression was dictated by the need to secure control of Catholic Ireland as Protestant England became increasingly alienated from the great continental Catholic powers. But there was always the possibility that such heavy-handedness might provoke rebellions in their own right; a dangerous prospect against the backdrop of war with Spain, a fact that Elizabeth herself was acutely aware of.

Elizabeth's reign was punctuated by Irish uprisings. If the first Desmond rebellion was provoked by what was, to all intents and purposes, English land grabbing, the second Desmond rebellion began with the return to Ireland of James Fitzmaurice Fitzgerald (who had escaped to France in 1575) in July 1579. He arrived at Smerwick in Kerry with a number of Catholic priests and a small military force. The government, paranoid as they were about the possibility of continental intervention in Ireland, reacted swiftly and

severely: the expeditionary force of six hundred was killed after sur-
rendering, and Fitzmaurice himself was executed in August. Here
the matter might have rested, had the government not also out-
lawed Gerald Fitzgerald, the fourteenth earl of Desmond, thus leaving him little option but to embark upon a rebellion himself after
being proclaimed a traitor in November 1579. The conflict thus
expanded enormously.

The Desmond rebellion was the single biggest challenge to
English rule in Ireland between the 1530s and the 1590s. It was
characterised by low-level warfare, with at least 170 military engagements taking place. Campaigns led by Ormond were followed
by a scorched-earth policy by the lord deputy Arthur, Lord Grey de
Wilton. Desmond tried to adopt the mantle of Catholicism to garner support, but was also willing to negotiate with a government
that was receptive to such overtures, up to a point; the precise point
is hard to determine, because the rebellion ended when he was captured and decapitated six miles outside Tralee in November 1583.
The subsequent confiscation of his vast territories paved the way for the
greatest Elizabethan initiative in Ireland: the Munster Plantation.

The Munster Plantation

Plantation had originally been attempted in the midlands in the
1550s, and there were sporadic (if short-lived) attempts at further
plantations in east Ulster in the 1570s after grants of land were given
to Sir Thomas Smith and Walter Devereux, earl of Essex, after the
death of Shane O'Neill. These were envisioned as almost a form of
private security, and were intended mainly to act as a bulwark against
the Scottish presence in the northeast. Plantations were also created
in Munster in the 1580s, but these new ventures were on an unprecedented scale. The suppression of the Desmond rebellion had been
brutal and exceptionally destructive, as much of the province had
been laid waste by English forces. In attempts to destroy the heartland of the rebellion, massive seizures of crops and livestock had
been accompanied by widespread scorched-earth policies that destroyed the Munster economy; the destruction of its society soon
followed. Perhaps 7,000 were killed in fighting, but the subsequent
famines may have pushed the total death toll from the rebellion to

in excess of 48,000: almost 10 percent of the projected population of Ireland at this time.[6] The most notable commentary on the devastation was provided by Edmund Spenser, an English official in the Munster presidency who was one of many to obtain lands in the province in the aftermath. His account was that of an eyewitness who had followed the brutal proceedings of Lord Grey de Wilton, who by his own admission executed 1,485 members of the gentry, not to mention "those of meaner sort . . . the account of which is besides number."[7] Spenser observed the devastation, and wrote an account of the aftermath:

> The proof whereof I saw sufficiently ensampled in Munster, for notwithstanding that the same was a most rich and plentiful country, full of corne and cattle, that you would have thought they would have been able to stand long, yet ere one year and a half they were brought to such wretchedness, as that any stony heart would have rued the same. Out of every corner of the woods and glens they came creeping forth upon their hands, for their legs could not bear them. They looked anatomies of death, they spake as ghosts crying out of their graves, they did eat the dead carrions, happy where they could find them, yea and one another soon after in so much as the very carcasses they spared not to scrape out of their graves, and if they could find a plot of watercresses or shamrocks, there they flocked as to a feast for the time, yet not able long to continue therewithal, that in short space there were none almost left and a most populous and plentifull country suddenly left void of man and beast.[8]

After 1586, that void was to be filled by the plantation. Munster had been surveyed as land was confiscated in the aftermath of the rebellion, in a rough arc stretching from Cork to Limerick. It was to be granted to "undertakers," who would hopefully take up to 12,000 acres at a time: 298,653 acres were granted to thirty-five undertakers: soldiers, officials, merchants, and investors (including Walter Raleigh, who received over 40,000 acres). They were to bring in exclusively English tenants, and the remaining Irish were to be removed. That said, many of the original inhabitants were pardoned, and some regained their lands through successful litigation. The plantation in Munster was different from its predecessors. The problem with military settlements was that by their nature, they did not necessarily guarantee that Irish society might be remoulded in the long run. What was attempted in Munster was more radical: it was essentially a form of social engineering intended to replicate the society of southeast England in Munster from scratch. Undertakers were also obliged to build English-style villages on specified outlines and subject to strict conditions, and to settle tenants there according to English law and tenurial customs. They were also to ensure that the plantation would be strong enough to withstand Irish attack. It was intended to create a society with a strict hierarchy, to ensure that over-mighty subjects would not emerge, and it was to employ English forms of agriculture to replace the pastoral farming of the Gaelic Irish. The plan was formulated by senior members of Elizabeth's government—such as William Cecil and Francis Walsingham—and the creation of this new world would hopefully serve as an example to be emulated by the Irish.

This was the theory. In practice the plantation failed to meet its objectives—settler numbers were lower than expected, sufficient villages were not built, the climate of Munster did not always suit the chosen forms of agriculture, and many of the undertakers lacked the capital necessary to fully deliver on their obligations; indeed, some were perfectly happy to retain Irish tenants and collect rent from them, contrary to the conditions under which they had participated. Alongside this gap between the theory of the plantation and its practice, the original Desmond rebellion that facilitated the Munster plantation had, in the meantime, spawned another rebellion that involved an explicit combination of Old English and Gaelic Irish, albeit for somewhat different reasons.

The Revolt of the Palesmen

The old colonial community of the Pale had become increasingly estranged from the government in Dublin through the middle decades of the sixteenth century.[9] Even aside from the mistrust that built up towards them as they either refused to pay for the government or simply bypassed the lord deputies to appeal directly to the queen, the Palesmen were also marked out by their "recusancy": their refusal to publicly commit themselves to the Church of Ireland, which was shorthand for retaining their traditional allegiance to Catholicism. They themselves were of the view that their political grievances and their religious beliefs would not necessarily interfere with their fundamental loyalty to the crown, but these were precisely the grounds upon which they were viewed with mounting suspicion.

It was probably inevitable that someone within the Pale would eventually state their opposition to the Tudor regime on religious grounds. The figure in question was James Eustace, Viscount Baltinglass, who had spent time at the court of Pope Gregory XIII, and who in July 1580 came out in arms against Elizabeth, denouncing her as an oppressor and a heretic. Baltinglass had secured support from figures within the Pale for his revolt but also from Gaelic septs such as the O'Tooles and O'Byrnes in Wicklow, especially under the leadership of Feagh McHugh O'Byrne. But the Gaelic septs of Wicklow did not join Baltinglass out of zeal for the true faith. The O'Byrnes and O'Tooles had good reason to be concerned that any new expansion of English rule into Wicklow would come at their expense and were intent on opposing this; by the 1580s both septs were concerned at the increasingly aggressive activities of Sir Henry Harrington, the seneschal of Wicklow. They had reasons to rebel, and made common cause with Baltinglass (who only decided to open hostilities once he was assured of their support). O'Byrne, Baltinglass, and their respective followers found themselves facing the same enemy for different reasons.

The most notable engagement of the Baltinglass rebellion was the defeat of an English army in the isolated Wicklow valley of Glenmalure in August 1580. The conflict then moved back to a pattern of guerrilla warfare, and was slowly strangled by the deployment of English forces in and around Wicklow from late 1580 onwards. The Desmond rebellion guaranteed that there were enough troops in Ireland to do this; the fact that this was the first rebellion from within the Pale since the Geraldine revolt of 1534 ensured that Lord Grey de Wilton took it seriously. Last but not least, its Catholic tinge ensured that a zealous Protestant such as Grey de Wilton would, and did, devote considerable attention to it.[10]

The O'Byrnes and O'Tooles had provided the bulk of the rebel forces, though they eventually came to terms with the government by the end of 1581. Baltinglass, on the other hand, had mainly been important as a figurehead, and escaped to the continent with some of his close confederates in November 1581. In the aftermath, however, Grey de Wilton shifted his attention to the Catholic community of the Pale, whom he suspected of complicity in the rebellion. He conducted widespread interrogations, often with brutal torture, within the Pale and executed around twenty leading figures before his departure from Ireland in August 1582. Elizabeth did not approve of his excesses.

Grey de Wilton did not feel that the Palesmen were entitled to any special treatment on account of their origins. They had proven themselves to be unreliable in the distant past, and rebels in the recent past, and the close-knit nature of the Pale community could be taken to mean that most of it was suspect. Last but not least, while they might have been rebels, they were also Catholic rebels, disloyal by definition. Hence the indiscriminate nature of the crackdown, which illustrated to many in the Pale that figures such as Baltinglass had been correct to rise up in the first place. The Catholic community of the Pale was sustained not just by tradition, but by strong links to continental Europe, many of which were of an increasingly religious nature, and were themselves strengthened by the course of events in an increasingly Protestant kingdom. The Elizabethan acts of supremacy (recognising the monarch as head of the Church of Ireland) and uniformity (demanding adherence to that church) had accelerated the outflow of Irish clerical emigrants in the 1560s, and the network of Irish missionary colleges in places such as Salamanca, Lisbon, Douai, and Louvain that would prove so crucial to the growth of the early modern Catholic Irish diaspora was evident by the 1590s.

Members of the Old English community were prominent in this movement. The dissolution of the monastic orders in the 1530s had inadvertently cleared the way for a new Catholic missionary drive in the latter decades of the sixteenth century. As the Counter Reformation took shape, its ideals were being taken on board by Irish clerics abroad and were being imported back to Ireland. Clerics such as Peter Lombard, who came from an Old English background in Waterford and later became professor of theology at the University of Louvain and archbishop of Armagh, assiduously tried to foster an Irish Catholic "community of faith." The Irish were also being incorporated into the martyrology of the Counter Reformation. Richard Verstegan's *Theatrum crudelitatum haereticorum nostri temporis* [The Theater of Cruelty of the Heretics of Our Time], for example, published in Antwerp in 1587, depicted the cruelties Protestants exercised on Catholic martyrs such as the archbishop of Cashel, Dermot O'Hurley, who was tortured and executed in 1584 as part of an ongoing investigation into Catholic dissent in the Pale that stemmed directly from the Baltinglass rebellion.[11]

Religion was thus added to the cultural and political divisions between Gaelic Ireland and the Tudor state. As the bulk of the Gaelic Irish remained Catholic, they were now also faced with an enemy that was primarily foreign, perhaps incidentally English (the Spanish might have garnered a similar response, given the brutality of their colonial ventures in South America) but undoubtedly Protestant. It was a stance that was increasingly shared by the Old English. There were plenty of practical secular grievances that could and did prove provocative, but the later decades of the sixteenth century saw the emergence of a heightened sense of an Irish identity—prompted by the perceived and actual threat posed by the Tudor state, which was now intertwined with Catholicism in the face of the Protestant nature of that state. The ensuing overlap of ethnicity and religion would, and has, survived for centuries.

CHAPTER THREE

Tyrone's Rebellion

The Nine Years War

The Great O'Neill

Hugh O'Neill (earl of Tyrone or the "Great O'Neill," depending on one's perspective) was born circa 1550 in County Tyrone, the second son of Matthew O'Neill, baron Dungannon, who had been the appointed heir to the earldom of Tyrone under a surrender and regrant arrangement of 1542, and who had subsequently been killed on the orders of Shane O'Neill. Hugh O'Neill was brought up in the household of an English settler in County Dublin, Giles Hovendon. In the early part of his career, his appointed role was little more than that of a puppet for the government to ease the implementation of their plans for Ulster; or, as Elizabeth herself put it, "a creature of our own."[1]

The Elizabethan government was obsessed with avoiding expensive ventures wherever possible, so the "reform" of Ulster had instead been farmed out to private interests, such as the earl of Essex or Sir Thomas Smith. Hugh O'Neill served in Essex's brutal campaigns in Ulster, was involved in the suppression of the Desmond rebellion (where he was commended for his often lethal enthusiasm), and throughout the 1580s and early 1590s was increasingly called upon for military service by the government. O'Neill benefited from this. He was able to unofficially extend the lands under his control, forged strong links with the new English settler elite, became acquainted with modern forms of warfare, and above all, his perceived loyalty opened the door to his eventually being granted the title of earl of Tyrone.

At this stage in his life and career O'Neill's status was essentially no different from that of an English captain; but he was also an O'Neill, and was interested in securing the ancient title to the lordship. To this end he successfully built up alliances amongst the Gaelic families of west Ulster. This was tolerated as it suited the government, and O'Neill was recognised as earl of Tyrone in the 1585–86 parliament. But at the same time, plans were being drawn up by the then lord deputy, Sir John Perrot (a veteran of the 1569 Desmond revolt) to divide the lordship again and create another provincial presidency in Ulster that would naturally threaten O'Neill's ambitions. In 1587 O'Neill visited court, arguing that he was entitled to the entire earldom by pointing to his loyal record of service to the crown. With the backing of the earl of Ormond, O'Neill was granted the full lordship of Tyrone; essentially what his grandfather Conn Bacach had received from Henry VIII in 1542. Thus, O'Neill was implicitly recognised as the leading magnate in Ulster, regardless of whether any English provincial government was subsequently created. He affirmed his loyalty as was required, overseeing the massacre of survivors of the Spanish Armada in west Ulster in 1588.

But his rise to power was resented, most especially by Sir Henry Bagenal, the marshal of the Irish army, who coveted the prospect of being appointed to any new position of authority in Ulster. To further this ambition he embarked upon a whispering campaign aimed at undermining O'Neill via accusations of disloyalty and treason in London and Dublin. O'Neill sought to get around this by marrying Bagenal's sister Mabel in 1591, a decision that backfired, as Bagenal took it as a personal insult. By the early 1590s, O'Neill's actions were being scrutinised, his power was being challenged on the ground, and his loyal reputation was being questioned. He had sought to assert his family's traditional dominance in Ulster, but was canny enough to realise that this could be done successfully only by convincing the English government that it was in their best interests to accept this. His attempt to straddle this middle ground became increasingly untenable as time went on, and came to a head in 1594.

The Nine Years War

The "Nine Years War" was precipitated when O'Neill's allies Hugh Roe O'Donnell and Hugh Maguire besieged the town of Enniskillen in modern County Fermanagh in June 1594 and subsequently attacked an English supply convoy nearby, leaving fifty-six English soldiers dead at the so-called "ford of the biscuits." O'Neill immediately appeared in Dublin to affirm his loyalty and offer his support to the government; indeed, he made numerous attempts to reach an accommodation with the Elizabethan authorities. Elizabeth was unwilling to countenance this, and ordered that her existing garrisons in Ulster be strengthened. O'Donnell and his allies then besieged the garrisons in question, and at this point Tyrone declared his hand, defeating 1,750 troops under Bagenal in Monaghan in June 1595. O'Neill was proclaimed a traitor later that month. In September, however, in a gesture of immense symbolism, the same Hugh O'Neill became "the O'Neill"—a title with no standing in English eyes—after the death of Turlough Luineach O'Neill, the previous incumbent. Tyrone does seem to have wanted to work with the English government, and had sought to restrain many of his followers and associates. But he had concluded that he had no choice but to join the rebellion that had broken out. The only realistic alternative was to turn against his own people, in the service of a crown whom he had concluded could not be fully trusted. He had seen this coming, and had built up his forces accordingly by training them and arming them in the light of his own military experience in the English service; O'Neill's army was more formidable than any previous Irish army. But the pattern of the war they waged was the familiar one of guerrilla warfare, the only practical option for O'Neill in the long term, unless more support was forthcoming from elsewhere.

This was not, however, a vague and forlorn hope. O'Donnell and others had, as early as 1593, made overtures to Philip II of Spain. After 1595 O'Neill had unofficially endorsed these efforts, and increasingly began to do so on religious grounds. He was not particularly enthusiastic about this alignment with Spain, as he wanted to keep his options open with the crown and was aware that the Spanish bogey was of great concern to Elizabeth. But he strengthened his military position anyway, and 1595—98 was characterized by guerrilla warfare that inexorably extended beyond Ulster, punctuated by halting attempts at negotiation. The battle of the Yellow Ford (in modern county Armagh) in August 1598, when Tyrone defeated 4,300 troops under Bagenal, who was killed in the engagement, changed matters. This defeat illustrated the potential weakness of the English government in Ireland, while such a striking victory increased the possibility of active Spanish involvement in Ireland: O'Neill's rebellion now looked like a safe bet. After the battle the war began to be extended across the island. The Munster plantation was attacked, and collapsed, as many of the settlers fled. The rebel position was being strengthened as appeals to Spain were renewed.

The prospect of a Spanish intervention in Ireland could not be disregarded by the Tudor authorities in the midst of a war with Spain. In April 1599, Robert Devereux, second earl of Essex and the queen's favourite, left for Ireland with 17,300 troops: the largest English expeditionary force sent anywhere in the reign of Elizabeth I. Tyrone continued to seek negotiations, but Essex was soon discredited for contemplating his offers. Having returned to England, he was replaced by the more belligerent Charles Blount, Lord Mountjoy, in February 1600. The war then took a different form, and O'Neill concluded that the time for negotiating was past. Prior to the war, O'Neill had recognisably been an adherent of Catholicism, but this had posed no difficulties in terms of his dealing with the state. In January 1596, however, he had demanded liberty of conscience from the government, and via proclamations, circular letters, and the preaching of the Catholic clergy, he increasingly began to depict himself as a defender of the faith in an attempt to reach out to the Old English. In 1599 O'Neill produced a manifesto consisting of twenty-two articles (dismissed as "ewtopia" [*sic*] by Elizabeth's secretary of state Robert Cecil), amongst which were demands for the full restoration of the Catholic Church and the removal of all English officials (bar the viceroy) from their positions, and their replacement with Irish appointees.

Within these demands was a subtle fusion of religion and a burgeoning sense of national identity; "faith and fatherland," as it has been labelled.[2] The faith aspect was self-explanatory; the concept of fatherland ("patria") was more of a pragmatic attachment to one's land than an ethnic or nationalist concept, and had its origins in classical concepts revived in the Renaissance. It had been deployed by the Palesmen earlier in the century, but became intertwined with the ideals of the Counter Reformation due to the presence of increasing numbers of Irish Catholic clerics on the continent in the later sixteenth century. Its employment by O'Neill was a significant milestone, one bolstered by his inauguration as the O'Neill. But he also wanted to secure papal support and legitimacy for his actions. The defence of O'Neill's stance provided by figures like Peter Lombard offered a coherent exposition of this new ideology, in terms of a war being waged against a heretic queen. This expansion of the conflict in ideological terms was mirrored by its expansion in physical terms.

Successful lobbying for Spanish assistance finally paid off on 21 September 1601, when twenty-eight Spanish vessels, with 3,300 men under Don Juan del Aguila, arrived at Kinsale in County Cork. But from O'Neill's point of view, this was the worst possible location for a Spanish landing: it was too far from his northern heartland. O'Neill had previously suggested that if the invasion force was greater than 6,000 men, it should land in Munster, where it would provoke a rebellion (this, in the event, did not happen). He had also suggested that any smaller force should land in Connacht, where either he or O'Donnell could reach them, but bad weather had forced the Spanish to land in Kinsale, thus leaving O'Neill and his cohorts with the worst of both worlds.

Mountjoy had already subdued the rebellion in Munster using scorched-earth tactics. O'Neill was reluctant to leave Ulster unprotected by going south. But the Old English did not rally to O'Neill's standard: their lingering suspicions of him guaranteed their loyalty to Elizabeth, which deprived O'Neill of potential allies outside Ulster and left him no choice but to meet Aguila in Munster. It is worth noting that Pope Clement VIII was unwilling to give his full backing to the Spanish expedition, as the recognition of a Spanish foothold in Ireland was bound to alienate the French from the papacy. But for the English government, the fact that the old fear of a

Spanish landing had actually come to pass was enough of a problem
for them. Mountjoy blockaded Kinsale while waiting for the rest of
his army to join him. Ironically, by doing so he had pulled most of
his forces from Ulster and the borders of the Pale. Unfortunately
for O'Neill, Aguila was too weak to break out from Kinsale to capi-
talise on this, and was unable to get reinforcements.

For O'Neill and O'Donnell this was a quandary: if they went
south to assist the Spanish they would leave their own territory open
to attack. James VI of Scotland had already offered military support
to Elizabeth; he was, after all, in line to succeed her. The Irish leaders went south despite this, with a formidable force that could probably have bested Mountjoy, who was supported by another force
under the earl of Thomond (one of the success stories of the old
policy of surrender and regrant). On 24 December 1601, O'Neill
and O'Donnell attacked both of the government camps. In military
terms the Irish were a match for the English forces, being trained
and equipped to a similar standard, but they attacked in an uncoor-
dinated manner that was successfully held off by the English defences and, crucially, by cavalry. The Irish had attacked in this manner
to allow the Spanish to use their own cavalry, but Aguila suspected a
trap and declined to do so. The battle lasted two hours; Mountjoy
had been lucky. Some Spanish reinforcements finally attempted to
land, but were successfully fought off by English warships.

One of the great questions in Irish history is: what if the English
had been defeated at Kinsale? It would surely have emboldened the
Spanish to invade en masse, and Ireland (and England) might well
have become part of a Spanish empire, with enormous implications
for Irish, British, and indeed European history. Its actual and immediate consequence was the long retreat of O'Neill and O'Donnell to
Ulster. Despite the disaster of Kinsale, the war would drag on for
another two years. In that time, Mountjoy hunted down his enemies, issued pardons to those deemed worthy of it, and pursued his
prey into Ulster, where garrisons were rebuilt and the countryside
was laid waste. This had been done before by figures such as Sir
Arthur Chichester who had approvingly reported that he had wiped
out every living thing around Lough Neagh in May 1601. However,
in June 1602 Mountjoy embarked on a scorched-earth campaign
whose systematic nature and sheer scale marked it out as distinctive

even in European terms: livestock, crops, buildings, and people were simply eradicated across the north of the island. Sir Henry Dowcra attacked O'Neill's heartland from the northwest, Mountjoy from the south, and Chichester from the northeast. This was accompanied by slaughter and destruction on a huge and unprecedented scale; indeed, the destruction was thorough enough to make it difficult to maintain the English armies, which often had to be supplied from England. The basic thrust of the campaign was to induce a man-made famine by the winter, thus to destroy O'Neill's power base.[3]

The English conduct of the war from this point onward was quite indiscriminate. But the consequences of the scorched-earth policy shocked even those English forces who carried it out. Mountjoy's secretary Fynes Moryson (whose writings often displayed a notable contempt for the Irish), for example, recorded a horrific encounter near Newry (presumably mediated through a translator) with three small children,

> (whereof the eldest was not above ten years old), all eating and gnawing with their teeth the entrails of their mother, upon whose flesh they had fed 20 days past, and having eaten all from the feet upward to the bare bones, roasting it continually by a slow fire, were now come to the eating of her said entrails in like sort roasted, yet not yet divided from the body, being as yet raw. The governor went to the place to see it, and demanded of them why they did so: they answered they could not get any other meat. It was demanded where their cows were, and they said the Englishmen had taken them away.[4]

The soldiers gave the children some food before departing. Even if the account is exaggerated, coming as it does from a source that was unsympathetic to the Irish, it points towards enormous hardship in the aftermath of Kinsale. Such ruin in Ulster may have had the same unplanned consequences as the destruction of the Desmond rebellion in Munster twenty years earlier, in that it eased the way for the plantation that ultimately followed.

The impact of the defeat at Kinsale was to destroy O'Neill's chances of negotiating with the crown from a position of strength.

He held out in Ulster where he was hemmed in on all sides, but there were some things in his favour: the English state was hovering on the verge of bankruptcy due to its war in Ireland, and there was a possibility that the imminent succession of James VI of Scotland to the English throne might result in a pardon. In these circumstances, Tyrone was quite willing to revert to his original prewar demands for recognition of his rule in Ulster. It was no coincidence that when Mountjoy was authorized to come to terms with him, he made sure to do so before Tyrone learned of the death of Elizabeth in March 1603. The Treaty of Mellifont ended the Nine Years War three days after her death. The key terms were generous: Hugh O'Neill was to retain the title of earl of Tyrone, abandon any links with Spain, and relinquish his Gaelic title of O'Neill: in an immensely symbolic show of strength, Mountjoy had previously destroyed the ancient inauguration stone of the O'Neills at Tullahogue in Tyrone. In political terms, the clock was being turned back to the 1580s.

The Flight of the Earls

The war against O'Neill had nearly bankrupted the Elizabethan state. His name was lauded across Catholic Europe, and echoes even seem to have survived in English folklore.[5] The accession of James I to the throne of England, Ireland, and Scotland had been lauded by Irish poets, in the expectation that he would surely favour Catholicism despite being a Protestant himself (James's mother, after all, had been a Catholic).[6] But any aggressive attempts to impose a new law and a new faith on Ireland had to be balanced against the need to maintain an even newer postwar equilibrium. The settlement agreed to by Mountjoy had left questions pertaining to religion unresolved, and offered little punishment to those who had supported O'Neill, or whose loyalty had wavered during wartime. Yet even as early as 1603, O'Neill perceived that his position was by no means secure. In the aftermath of a failed Catholic conspiracy to assassinate King James I by blowing up the houses of parliament in London in 1605 (the "Gunpowder Plot"), more vigorously anti-Catholic policies were adopted across the three kingdoms of England, Ireland, and Scotland. In Ireland the government affirmed that all in the realm were the subjects of the king, not of any lord or chief. The implications of this were obvious, and tensions between O'Neill and the state intensified in subsequent years. The Dublin authorities were intent on dealing with him in some manner, but on 14 September 1607, O'Neill, along with some key allies and retainers, left Donegal on a French ship bound for Spain, never to return.

Questions remain about the precise circumstances of "the flight of the earls." Certainly, O'Neill and other Gaelic aristocrats were facing legal encroachments from the established church and the state, and the fact that O'Neill had been summoned to London for adjudication in one of these cases seems to have precipitated his departure. There were suspicions that he had continued to plot with the Spanish; perhaps he had, which would explain his departure as an act driven by fear. O'Neill died in Rome in 1616, having unsuccessfully sought assistance from Catholic powers in Europe to win back what was—to him at least—rightfully his. Yet events in Ireland after the Flight of the Earls hinted at what might have lain in store for him had he stayed. Sir Cahir O'Doherty of Inishowen in County Donegal, who had taken sides with the English against Tyrone, had helped the English war effort in the northeast, and was the foreman of the jury that indicted O'Neill for treason after his flight, rebelled in April 1608 by seizing recently established English garrisons at Derry and Culmore. The rebellion lasted eleven weeks, and resonated across Ulster until O'Doherty was killed in battle. He had risen in response to what he deemed to be contemptuous treatment by the governor of Derry; a hint, perhaps, that the Irish were to be relegated to second place in the emergent colonial order. In the case of O'Doherty and O'Neill, their status was a moot point. They were gone, and their absence opened the door to British colonisation on a scale that surpassed what had previously been attempted in Munster, in the form of the plantation of Ulster.

Where Historians Disagree

THE SIXTEENTH CENTURY in Ireland is notable for two major developments: the introduction of the Protestant Reformation, and the extension of English power over the entire island by the end of the century. Each of these issues raises a question.

The first is: why did the Reformation not succeed? Its "failure" has long vexed historians. Brendan Bradshaw argued that the reformation had failed in Ireland by 1558; Nicholas Canny, on the other hand, argued that if such was the case, it happened much later, and that in some ways Bradshaw missed a crucial point: "that the majority of the native population remained outside the structure of the rival churches and clung tenaciously to pre-Tridentine religious practice."[1] In this reading, Bradshaw was too preoccupied by the institutional basis of the reformation, and overlooked a "native-born Protestant group who were critical of the official approach to launching the reformation" and "Catholic survivalism."[2] It is a debate that, by its nature, operates from inference and deduction. As Karl Bottigheimer observed, "the fact that we cannot assign a precise date for the event does not prove that it did not happen."[3] It should be noted that the boundary between vernacular religious practises can be extremely loose; religious institutions did not automatically reflect the reality of religious cultures as they existed. Could the ultimate failure of the Reformation in Ireland be characterised as successful resistance to the imposition of an alien religion

44

by a foreign power, or a stubborn refusal to abandon the older faith? Ireland remained the only part of the Tudor dominions to retain a predominantly Catholic population. The Reformation succeeded in Wales despite linguistic and cultural differences with England. A different form of Protestant faith took root in Gaelic Scotland, which possessed a very similar culture to that of Gaelic Ireland. On the other hand, examples abound on the continent of successful attempts to resist and reject any attempt at religious reformation. Thus, Ireland was not necessarily distinctive in ultimately rejecting the English Reformation. There were attempts to proselytise on the part of the authorities; equally, Old English and Gaelic links to the continent opened the door to the Counter Reformation, as the Catholic Church fought a rearguard action against its new rival in Ireland.[4] But was the failure of the reformation down to a more mundane reality? James Murray, in a recent major study of the Dublin diocese, concluded that "the principal cause of this failure was the English Irish community's attachment to a survivalist form of Catholicism. And that this attachment itself had been actively and effectively defended during the Marian period and the opening decade of Elizabeth's reign."[5] In other words, the resources simply were not available to fully impose the new Episcopalian state church on a diverse population that remained strongly attached to Catholicism; an attachment that would, over time, become intertwined with their respective senses of who they were.

The extension of English power over Ireland in this era raises another question: was there a "Tudor conquest"? Ireland was undoubtedly conquered in political and military terms, but had this been an unyielding process that remained constant throughout the century? The question is tied up with questions of motive. Steven Ellis has argued that the extension of English control across Britain and Ireland from the fifteenth century onwards was simply the extension of the frontiers of both Ireland and northern England: a process of state formation rather than conscious imperialism, and one that was not unique to Ireland.[6] Yet did ideology shape English policies in Ireland? If so, was it the imperatives of Protestantism, as suggested by Brendan Bradshaw, who has argued the case for a "constitutional revolution" in Ireland? In this argument, from the end of the fifteenth century the Tudors were increasingly inclined to reform the government of Ireland and bring it under closer control. This accelerated due to the Reformation and the break with Rome, and culminated in the Act for the Kingly Title in 1541 and the practical working out of its implications.[7]

A contrasting perspective, put forth by Nicholas Canny, was that the ideological impulse that underpinned English policy in Ireland was one of imperialism, based on the notion that the native Irish were an inferior people who needed to be civilized or conquered.[8] If either of these assumptions were true, did notions of "civility" arising from the intellectual ferment of the Renaissance have a role to play; in other words, did the English embark upon what they might have deemed to be a civilising mission in Tudor Ireland? The argument for conscious imperialism might be challenged on the grounds that a sizeable proportion of the Irish population were not Gaelic. Instead, Ciaran Brady has argued that insofar as there was an English ideology of conquest, it arose from the notion that Ireland was in desperate need of political and cultural reform according to English norms; that the policy of English governments was formulated in a piecemeal, almost haphazard style, rather than being part of a detailed programme for conquest; and ultimately, that an incremental clash of cultures lay at the heart of the conflicts of the sixteenth century.[9]

But is this too subtle, and does it minimise or overlook some of the grislier elements of the history of sixteenth-century Ireland? More recently it has been pointed out that, regardless of the ideologies behind it (if any), the reality of Tudor rule was brutal and violent, and this violence escalated as the century wore on. The Kildare rebellion was suppressed with unprecedented ferocity, and by the 1540s the policy was to expand the Pale and to curb Gaelic power. The new divisions that the Reformation had opened up in Europe made this an imperative, and greatly increased levels of violence, including ruthless attacks on civilians, were deployed in pursuit of this objective. The Tudor era was therefore much bloodier than is often assumed.[10] In other words, Ireland was conquered violently. This emphasis on the religious and political history arises in part from the fact that much of the social and economic history of the period remains difficult to reconstruct, but there are some valuable studies that reveal much about at least some of the realities of life on the ground in both Gaelic and colonial Ireland.[11]

PART II

The Seventeenth Century

CHAPTER FOUR

Plantation

Ireland in 1603

The Nine Years War had highlighted the unwelcome prospect that Ireland was potentially within easy reach of the Spanish in time of war. In the aftermath, the unprecedented expenditure required to defeat Tyrone was to be offset by the confiscation of lands, but the relatively lenient settlement that followed the war was unpopular, most especially with those who had expected to receive some largesse. The Act of Oblivion in 1603 pardoned many of those involved in the war, and the Commission for Defective Titles of 1606, which was intended to examine land ownership, had seemed to forestall the prospect of new plantations in many areas. But the Flight of the Earls changed this situation drastically. The government was now in a position to lay claim to the vast O'Donnell and O'Neill territories in central and western Ulster. Alongside the resettlement of the Munster plantations, which had been overthrown during the war, huge tracts of southern and northern Ireland were now open to British settlement and colonization on an unprecedented scale.

What kind of country was Ireland at this juncture? It had long been an early venue for English imperialism, and this continued apace—indeed, intensified—in the early decades of the seventeenth century. Ireland had been conquered in devastating fashion by 1603, though the island remained, in large part, culturally quite diverse.

The Irish, English, and Scottish made up the major ethnic groups, but even within these broad categories there were differences, most especially with regards to religion. The Catholicism of the descendants of the medieval English colonists, for instance, now qualified them for a label to set themselves apart from the newer Protestant settlers: "Old English." Distinctions of this kind would become increasingly important with the passage of time.

Despite the horrific devastation produced by the scorched-earth policies that characterised the latter stages of the war, much of Ireland remained extensively wooded. In the seventeenth century these woodlands would be stripped away for fuel, raw material for woodworking—shipbuilding and cooperage—and ironworking. Much of the arable landscape was still devoted to tillage and pastoral farming; the latter explained both the relative absence of buildings and the continuing importance of dairy products to the Irish diet. Inland communications networks remained poor and underdeveloped: rivers were very significant as routeways. Such urbanisation as existed was still mainly confined to the coasts of Leinster and Munster, though there were newer garrison towns further inland, and more towns would be developed as plantation took hold once again. Many of the existing towns and cities—Dublin, Cork, Galway, Limerick, Wexford—retained their defensive walls, a testament to the ongoing upheavals of the Tudor era. The coastal ports were also key points of contact with the wider world. Dublin had major links to England, Waterford with Spain and Bristol, while Galway and Cork remained focussed upon Spain and France.

A tangible illustration of the manner in which the English had asserted a greater degree of control and influence over Ireland prior to 1603 is that trade with England had increased while trade with the continent declined. Exports of livestock, rough textiles, and staves were already well established. Goods were imported as well; indeed, by the 1590s perhaps as many as four hundred different types of consumer items were passing from Bristol to Ireland, from French glassware and spectacles to utensils, furniture, tobacco, laxatives, cider, spice, and much more besides. Consumer demand had increased from the 1540s onwards (though the overall value of trade had actually declined). The trade with Bristol was largely (though not exclusively) concentrated on the southeast, and these goods were consumed in colonial areas, most especially by the elite. Western merchants from Limerick and Galway also imported via southeastern ports such as Waterford. A range of commentators in the late sixteenth and early seventeenth centuries observed that such consumer goods were by no means unknown in Gaelic society.[1] In administrative terms, the shiring of the country into distinct counties was completed by 1606 with the creation of Wicklow, ending a process that had begun with the Normans. Yet hints of stability in the aftermath of war had other implications; Ireland offered great potential to those willing to take chances, and the aftermath of the Flight of the Earls offered opportunities to take them.

The Ulster Plantation

The Ulster plantation was foreshadowed by private settlements established on lands owned by the lord deputy Sir Arthur Chichester, who had settled former soldiers in Antrim; his experience would influence the much bigger project that he soon oversaw. By 1608 the counties of Armagh, Cavan, Coleraine (later Londonderry), Donegal, Fermanagh, and Tyrone were in the hands of the government, and these were to be used for a new plantation. As early as January 1609, a plan for the plantation of Ulster was drafted. Between July and September 1609 the land available to the crown west of the River Bann after the departure of O'Neill and O'Donnell was being surveyed with an eye to its future usage, and by April 1610 the conditions of the plantation were announced (these probably owed more to the attorney-general, Sir John Davies, than Chichester). A key stipulation of the scheme that emerged was that that new British settlers should outnumber Irish natives. The lands in question were assigned to a number of corporate bodies: Scottish and English undertakers, "servitors" (military veterans), Trinity College Dublin, the city of London, along with a number of individuals. The so-called "deserving Irish" received lesser amounts. While the servitors were permitted to have Irish tenants, the English and Scottish undertakers were not.

Lessons had been learnt from the earlier plantations of the sixteenth century. Small plantations proliferated in early modern Ireland: counties Wexford, Longford, Leitrim, Offaly (King's County),

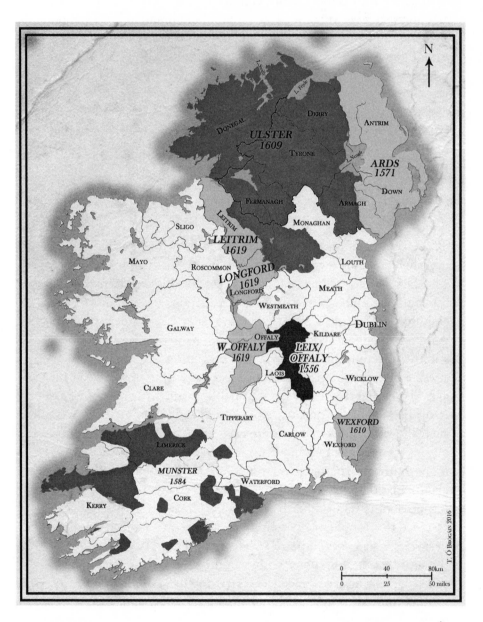

British plantations in early modern Ireland prior to 1641. (Map by Tomás Ó Brógáin)

Laois (Queen's County), and Westmeath had all seen plantations of some kind at one time or another. Chichester's original ideas for the plantation of Ulster seem to have echoed the principles behind these earlier settlements. But the new northern colony was to be more concentrated than its southern predecessors, with designated areas for the Irish natives, who could thereby be kept under surveillance (perhaps ironically, it was grafted on to existing Gaelic patterns of landholding, which survived surreptitiously). The servitors did not do as well as they had hoped, receiving perhaps 13 percent of the total acreage. Forty percent was reserved for "undertakers": private investors who would receive between one thousand and two thousand acres (with a small number of three-thousand-acre holdings), subject to very specific guidelines relating to rentals, types of building, defensive arrangements, and the forms of agriculture to be used. The amounts of land were deliberately kept low as a security measure; the crown wanted to keep an eye on things, and to ensure that the newly settled regions west of the River Bann would not be dominated in the future by a new generation of regional magnates.

The entire county of Coleraine went to the corporation of the city of London, to facilitate private investment from London companies; a tangible outcome was the establishment of the new northwestern city of Londonderry (the second part of the name derived from the Irish *doire*, meaning an oak forest). Another 14 percent of land in Ulster went to "native freeholders"; 18 percent went to the Church of Ireland to support its missionary endeavours; and 1 percent went to support schools for planters and for natives who were open to "civility." The desire to inculcate English cultural values amongst the natives gave an ideological dimension to the plantation, which was far more systematic than its sixteenth-century predecessors. The Ulster plantation was social engineering on a massive scale. Economic, religious, and legal life were to be reshaped in a manner intended to promote English norms. To English eyes—those of soldiers, settlers, officials, traders, and travellers—Irish cultural and social life was deemed to be so radically different from what they were used to that it was judged as inferior, though a basic lack of understanding of what such observers were actually seeing compounded what were, all too often, profoundly negative judgements. Not only was the plantation project to generate wealth for those who participated in it, the cultural, economic, and social changes that it involved might yet serve as models to be emulated by those—the Irish themselves—who were, in theory at least, to be left on the outside looking in.

Civility was, as ever, intertwined with the desire to evangelize the native Catholic population. To this end, the sons of Catholic gentry were encouraged to attend Trinity College rather than continental universities with a Catholic ethos, the better to foster a religious example from the top down. The same could be said of the expanding Irish peerage, who might also set an example to those below them. At the start of the seventeenth century there were twenty-seven members of the Irish peerage, about four-fifths of whom were Old English. Thanks to the sale of noble titles in the reign of James I, Ireland's peerage had ballooned to ninety-two by 1641, only sixty-eight of whom were actually resident in Ireland. A third of those resident peers were "New English," part of a newer cohort of settlers: a concrete reflection of the increasing colonisation of Ireland in the seventeenth century. By 1641, 49 percent of the peerage were still Old English (the largest group of landowners), 33 percent were New English, 10 percent were Gaelic Irish, 7 percent were Scottish, and the remaining 1 percent were Welsh; these proportions were still roughly valid as late as 1685. Alongside this shift in the origins of the peerage was a shift in their religious affiliation: there were three Protestant peers in 1603, but this had increased to thirty-nine by 1670.[2]

The desire for cultural assimilation and political reform that could be seen in the early sixteenth century had been overridden by the necessity for political and military conquest. Now political, economic, religious, and cultural change was to be imported and imposed; hopefully the natives could assimilate these changes, but this was not an absolute necessity. The ruthless use of martial law in early Stuart Ireland pointed to the fact that the plantation ultimately rested upon force. But the plantation would also have to pay for itself, and consequently, economic development was essential to colonisation. The Gaelic economy had traditionally not operated as a cash economy, but the aftermath of the war against O'Neill saw the extension of English common law and the accelerated development of a new cash economy, partly due to indebtedness incurred in the war. But a genuine economic recovery was discernable after 1603, and sectors of the economy such as textile production and livestock continued to expand up to 1641. The shift to pasture was significant: sixteen Irish cows had been landed in Chester in 1607; by 1639 the number was just under sixteen thousand.[3] That said, the pace of change took less productive forms: timber shortages were being noted by the 1630s, as the massive and rapid export of wood for cooperage and shipbuilding took a toll on Irish woodlands. Short-term opportunism was by no means unknown in plantation Ireland.

The New Ireland and the Old

In addition to these socioeconomic changes, the imposition of a new culture had its own implications for the society that already existed in Ireland. Gaelic Ireland had, since the later sixteenth century, become increasingly integrated into the European world of the Counter Reformation. Networks of Irish colleges had been established across Europe by Irish Catholic clerics, primarily in the Low Countries (the Franciscans of Leuvan were especially interested in the Irish language and Irish history), but also in Spain, Italy, and the Austrian Habsburg lands, as far east as Vienna. The Counter Reformation was crucial in offering an intellectual and ideological bond to Gaelic Ireland's fragmented network of aristocratic lordships, in which Irish, English, Latin, and Spanish would have been spoken, to varying degrees.

The advent of the new order did not automatically imply the cultural eclipse of the old one: quite the opposite. Irish literature and genres of expression diversified in what was a period of remarkable intellectual innovation in the Irish language. But the anomaly of a Protestant state and church attempting to rule a Catholic population seemed to prompt an intellectual shift and a redefinition of Irish identity in more consciously sectarian terms. Catholicism was increasingly seen as synonymous with the Irish, though many of the Irish aristocracy did seek to reach an accommodation with the state. Equally, the policy of the Irish Catholic hierarchy, as approved by provincial synods in 1614, 1618, and 1624, was for obedience to the monarch in temporal, if not spiritual matters. Royalism and loyalty to the new Stuart dynasty was reflected in new terms imported into the Irish language, such as *teideal* (title) and *an choróin* (the crown).[4]

Alongside this a more distinct sense of Irish identity—*Eireannach*—was emerging slowly but surely in the face of the increasingly assertive Protestant regime in Ireland (and possibly Jacobean assumptions of cultural superiority towards the Irish). The anonymous satire *Parliament Chloinne Thomáis* [The Parliament of Clan Thomas], seemingly written between 1605 and 1615, hinted at an awareness of such encroachments, and the changes brought in its wake, not least in terms of the threat they posed to the traditional Gaelic aristocracy.

One culture was coming under pressure from another. The encroachment of the new order and the erosion of Gaelic aristocratic power had implications for the bardic elite who traditionally depended upon their patronage. After the death of Domhnall O'Sullivan Beare, a former ally of Hugh O'Neill, in Madrid in 1618, the poet Domhnall Ó Dálaigh composed an elegy that could also be taken as a lament for the passing of the old order in the face of the relentless colonisation:

> Re Gallaibh go nuaidhe a-niogh
> Aoinfhear do ghasruidh Ghaoidhiol,
> A gcoai imreasuin ní fhuil
> Fá fhinnleasuibh Chraoi Cobhthuigh
>
> [In all the fair dwellings of Ireland there is
> Today no man of the Gaelic company capable
> Of resuming the struggle against the foreigners][5]

Yet all was not lost: the early seventeenth century also witnessed a renaissance in Irish prose writing. This was fostered and influenced by European intellectual trends, as mediated though the Irish colleges on the continent, most obviously and significantly in the form of histories written by both Catholic clergymen (both Gaelic and Old English), such as *Annála Ríoghachta Éireann* [Annals of the Kingdom of Ireland] and Seathrún Céitinn's *Foras Feasa ar Éireann* [The Foundation of Knowledge of Ireland].[6] The latter was of a piece with humanist national histories being composed across Europe in this era. Educated in France, Céitinn (also known as Geoffrey Keating) was of Old English stock, and wrote his work to refute the hostile commentaries of English authors such as Edmund Spenser and

Fynes Moryson, while at the same time constructing a version of Irish history that could accommodate a distinct Catholic identity that would be oblivious to the ethnic distinction between Gaelic and Old English. Composed in the 1630s, his work was assimilated into the Irish scribal tradition by the 1650s, and survived there for centuries.

But there is a more complex story than just a clash of cultures. English ideological antagonism to the Irish must be contrasted with the pragmatic reality that the settlers were obliged to engage with Gaelic culture on the ground, and vice versa. Bilingualism in Irish and English was common; even the Church of Ireland recognized the need for the use of Irish to spread the gospel. Print culture in Irish, on the other hand, was essentially confined to the continent. And the Irish diaspora in early modern Europe was not composed of just clerics and students; after 1603 a military diaspora migrated to the Spanish service. By the 1630s, Austria and France also became established as crucial destinations for Irish soldiers, and Irish merchants had also become a permanent presence in key Atlantic ports such as Nantes and La Rochelle.

Yet Catholic emigration needs to be contrasted with Protestant immigration, which had a far more profound impact. Perhaps as many as one hundred thousand British settlers, mostly (though not always) Protestant, settled in Ireland in the first four decades of the seventeenth century. The resulting population increase was weighted towards the northeast of the island, and Protestants of one type or another may have made up 18–20 percent of the total Irish population by 1641. If Ulster had traditionally been seen as a Gaelic stronghold prior to 1603, then in the first decades of the seventeenth century the plantation ensured that the northern province underwent a profound and permanent transformation.

That said, the number of migrants populating the Ulster plantation was lower than expected, which ensured that many Irish were permitted to remain on their lands. By 1622, when the progress of the plantation was surveyed by a royal commission, it was seen to have fallen short of some of its initial objectives. Nonetheless, a new population had arrived in the north of Ireland, and the land holdings of the native Irish there had been sharply eroded. Within this new settler population was a very substantial Scottish presence, who left an enduring mark. Above all, the landscape and culture of the region was radically remoulded in the first four decades of the seventeenth century; alongside a new population came new infrastructure and a new urban network. These changes may have fallen short of the ambitions of those who had designed the plantation, but they proved to be enduring and radical changes nonetheless. The new British presence in Ireland was firmly ensconced by the 1630s, yet an uneasy peace prevailed. The original stipulation that planters were to build defensive housing had been made for a reason, for the plantation ultimately rested upon dispossession on an enormous scale. The resentments bred by that stark reality would continue to fester.

The Government of Wentworth

Despite the hopes of the Irish Catholic intelligentsia, the early years of the reign of James I witnessed a fiercely anti-Catholic government based in Dublin embark on increasingly vigorous campaigns to suppress Catholicism. This culminated in the execution of Conor O'Devany, the bishop of Down and Connor, in Dublin in 1612. Catholic political power was to be further eroded by the expedient of creating new parliamentary boroughs and thereby packing the Irish parliament with Protestant members. For the Old English in particular, the outbreak of war with Spain in the 1620s was seen as an opportunity to prove their loyalty to the monarch, by arguing that any allegiance they owed to the papacy was a purely private, spiritual matter; once again, the necessity for parliament to approve the finances due to the government gave the Old English their leverage. The government's financial requirements saw the drafting of the "Graces," a set of demands set forth by the Old English that placed a marked emphasis on the toleration of Catholicism. If the Old English were to pay for the raising of an army to defend Ireland against Spanish attack, they were going to expect something in return. It was practically difficult for the government to pursue an anti-Catholic agenda—there were, quite simply, too many Catholics in Ireland—and tentative negotiations took place with Old English representatives. But the end of the war with Spain 1629 ended any need to indulge these, and the anticipated Irish parliament never met. More overtly anti-Catholic policies had been reintroduced by the early 1630s, a stance that dovetailed neatly with the authoritarian rule of the viceroy Thomas Wentworth.

Wentworth came from a minor gentry background in Yorkshire. Having been elected to the English parliament, he was initially viewed warily by Charles I (who had succeeded his father James as king in 1625). But Wentworth was gradually brought into the royal fold, being created Viscount Wentworth in 1628, and appointed to a number of offices where he proved himself an efficient and loyal, if high-handed, servant of the king. In January 1632 he was officially appointed lord deputy of Ireland. He was unenthusiastic about his new post (as were many of those who held it over the centuries), but Wentworth was shrewd enough to recognise that his blunt manner was best deployed away from court.

Wentworth's tenure in Ireland needs to be seen as part of a concerted effort by Charles I to strengthen his authority across all three of his kingdoms, in both political and religious terms. In the 1630s Charles had sought to get around the English parliament by ensuring it did not meet, and by raising the monies he needed for his government from additional taxes in England. The first priority for Wentworth was to make Ireland profitable to the crown as well, and his Ireland would have no room for "over-mighty" subjects. Wentworth was prepared to maintain cordial links with Catholics for practical reasons, even hinting that the "Graces" of the 1620s would finally be put into law. Yet this was more of a tactic than a strategy; the long-term objective of Wentworth's government was to bolster the scanty resources available to both the crown and the Church of Ireland, thus strengthening the position of the former while better enabling the latter to carry out its mission to convert the natives. In part, this was a response to the presence of rival Protestant faiths that had arrived in the northeast of Ireland with Scottish settlers. Presbyterianism would not be formally established in Ireland until the 1640s, but an embryonic puritanism with a Calvinist bent was present from the early seventeenth century, and Wentworth had little regard for it. He also attempted to impose reforms on the Church of Ireland along the lines of those being applied to the Church of England in the 1630s by Archbishop William Laud, though he met with stiff resistance as he did so.

It is virtually impossible to disentangle the political history of Ireland in the 1630s from Wentworth's career. In parliament he played Catholic and Protestant against one another to secure the subsidies he required, but Catholics were increasingly unhappy at his stated unwillingness to confirm one of the key elements of the "Graces": the confirmation of land titles more than sixty years old (a stance that provoked great hostility from both Protestant and Catholic members of parliament). The prospect of new plantations in Connacht was to be used to bring the Catholic gentry there into line, though Wentworth mollified Protestant opinion with a promise to confirm land titles under the plantation of Ulster. He eventually managed to wrest control of financial subsidies from the Irish parliament, which, true to his autocratic instincts, he viewed as useful rather than necessary. But Wentworth ultimately alienated every significant interest group in Irish life; instead of mastering them, he made enemies of them, though with the backing of the king he continued to govern Ireland in an aggressive and autocratic manner. His inquiries into land titles resulted in extortionate increases in rental incomes that were available to the crown, which naturally had the full support of Charles I.

Wentworth governed in an almost monarchical manner (a point not lost on some of his enemies); his house in Jigginstown in Kildare would have been the largest private residence in the Stuart kingdoms had it been completed. While it was intended to be sufficiently grandiose to accommodate the king should he ever visit Ireland, the heightened ceremony of the viceregal court in Dublin increasingly resembled that of a monarch. Public discontent was easily quashed by the army, thirty-four hundred strong, which Wentworth readily deployed. But his unpopularity placed him in a precarious position. In January 1640 he was appointed lord lieutenant and was ennobled as earl of Strafford. It appears that Wentworth's style of heavy-handed government was to have been applied in England as well as Ireland, but a promising future as the king's right-hand man was brought to an abrupt end when he was impeached for treason and tried in March 1641 by the English parliament. Over half of the charges against him related to Ireland, having been assembled by an unlikely coalition of Catholic and Protestant representatives. Before the trial could continue, Wentworth was executed by order of the English parliament on 12 May. Yet his actions in Ireland led to an unexpected outcome.

The 1641 Rebellion

In 1637 a rebellion against Charles I had broken out in Scotland after an attempt to impose the English Book of Common Prayer on the Presbyterian Scots. Charles had been unable to defeat the rising, and Wentworth was instructed to raise an army in Ireland to help him do so. Before these troops could be brought into the field the Scots invaded England as far as Newcastle, and stated that they would return home only if any settlement with the king was also approved by the English parliament. After a decade of watching the king rule without any recourse to the English parliament, when it finally met it became a forum for the widespread discontent built up throughout the 1630s; this ultimately sealed Wentworth's fate. Yet the overwhelmingly Catholic army he had raised in Ireland remained in existence, and as it had never been used against the Scots, there were genuine fears in England that it might be used to impose the king's will on the English parliament and his English subjects instead.

As this crisis dragged on, it presented both a danger and an opportunity to the Old English and the Gaelic Irish, who were increasingly wary of anti-Catholic utterances emanating from Scotland and England, and who were also aware that the issues of most concern to them—the free exercise of their religion and the security of their lands—remained dangerously unresolved. But if the Scots had successfully won terms from the crown, might the Irish be able to do something similar to get the assurances that they wanted? By the summer of 1641 at least some leading Old English, along with members of the Gaelic aristocracy, felt that this was precisely what they should do. The Catholic gentry of Ulster hatched a plot to stage a limited rebellion to give themselves a bargaining position with the king (they were later at pains to stress that they acted not as rebels, but as loyal, if disgruntled, subjects). And so, on 22 October 1641, Sir Phelim O'Neill, MP for Dungannon, led the seizure of Charlemont Fort in Armagh. His personal history hints at his possible motivation: O'Neill was a Gaelic aristocrat who had accommodated himself to the new colonial order. His grandfather was killed in crown service in 1608, and he was forced to wait for his inheritance. Having been educated at Lincoln's Inns in London, he later served as an official in Ireland and even planted his estates with Protestant tenants. Yet by the summer of 1641 he was heavily indebted and willing to get involved in the conspiracy to give him and others a degree of leverage for negotiating with the king. O'Neill gained entry to the Charlemont Fort on the pretext of coming for dinner—which speaks volumes about his relationship with the authorities—and his violent actions were mirrored across Armagh and Tyrone over the next few days.

But the limited uprising planned by O'Neill and his associates gave way to a popular revolt carried out by Irish who had been dispossessed under the plantation of Ulster. What made this uprising distinctive as it spread out across the island was its undeniable sectarian character. English Protestants were explicitly targeted for attack, although Scots were apparently left unmolested in the early stages. Many were robbed and killed, and many others reported acts of desecration, as in the case of an anonymous Irish rebel in Armagh who, one account claimed, "opening the sacred Bible pissed on the same saying I would do worse with it if I could."[7] But it was the killing of Protestants that garnered the greatest attention, as allegations of horrific cruelties began to emerge. And as the authorities put it:

> Certainly this kingdom and the lives of us all here, and all the Protestants in the kingdom, were never in so great danger to be lost as at this instant, no age having produced in this kingdom an example of so much mischief done in so short a time as now we find acted here in less than a fortnight's space, by killing and destroying so many English and Protestants in several parts, by robbing and spoiling of them and many thousands more of his Majesty's good subjects, by seizing so many castles, houses and places of strength in several parts of the kingdom, by threatening the English to depart or otherwise they will destroy them utterly, and all their wickedness acted against the English and Protestants with so much inhumanity and cruelty as cannot be imagined from Christians even towards infidels.[8]

As such allegations made their way to both Dublin and London, rebellion morphed into war.

CHAPTER FIVE

The Wars of the Three Kingdoms

The Official Response

The imminent outbreak of the rebellion was revealed to the authorities in Dublin on 22 October 1641, thereby foiling an attempt to capture Dublin Castle and its arsenal. One Owen Connolly, a confidante of the rebels, revealed details of a plot to rise up against the English who had conquered them in order that the Irish "should soon be delivered from bondage and slavery under which we groaned." He was told by one of those involved that "our design was to take the castle of Dublin, which we can easily do, and destroy the warders, they being silly old men, and that this night betwixt 8 and 9 of the clock all the English towns in the whole kingdom will be surprised by our party, who we have desired in each county to their several places and so all the English on a sudden shall be cut off, which done, and we are possessed of the castle of Dublin, the kingdom is then our own . . . there was besides great artillery powder and ammunition was then in the castle to furnish out completely 30,000 men." He heard this in a tavern, and having left to go to the lodgings of one of the conspirators, he detached himself from the group to "make water" and slipped away to alert William Parsons, one of the lord justices (the officials who headed the government in the absence of the viceroy) at his home.[1]

The subsequent response of the authorities to the uprising was ferocious as the brutality of the Catholic rebels was repaid in kind. Government forces carried out bloody retaliations in Leinster and Munster and unofficial retaliations by settlers took place across Ulster. Yet the attacks on Catholics in and around Dublin were crucially important, for the targets there were the Old English who were unconnected with the rebellion that had broken out in the north. Figures such as Parsons and the notorious Charles Coote seemed intent on waging indiscriminate sectarian war upon all Catholics in Ireland. Consequently, the Old English elite sought strength in numbers and reached out to the Gaelic Irish. In late 1641, at a meeting in Meath, Gaelic and Old English leaders came together to defend their common interests. Their enemies in the Dublin administration naturally viewed this alliance as further proof of a Catholic conspiracy, an interpretation which some Catholics felt was simply a justification for further land confiscations. Irish Catholics of all stripes, however, were at pains to point out that they remained loyal subjects who were now forced into fighting against an unjust and oppressive government in Dublin.

Confederates

This alliance between Gaelic and Old English led to the formation of the Confederate Association, whose motto clearly stated the thinking of its members: *Hiberni unanimes pro deo rege et patria* (Irishmen united for God, king, and country). Their official seal had both Catholic and royalist insignia. Based in Kilkenny in the southeast, where the confederate assembly met for the first time in October 1642, the confederates acted as a government, establishing local administrations, collecting taxes, and of course, raising armies. They sought a degree of common cause between the Catholic and Protestant segments of the Irish political elite, and did not insist upon ethnic or religious qualifications for membership or influence. They were at pains to emphasise their loyalty to the crown; while the confederate elected general assembly was modelled on the Irish parliament, there was no assertion of its sovereignty. The confederates operated in a much more fluid manner than might have been expected, with a considerable degree of common ground between their

various constituent parts. But they never entirely rid themselves of
the tensions that existed between the Old English and native Irish.
Given that the aim of the Confederate Association was to defend
and represent Irish Catholics (clerics remained prominent in it
throughout its existence), it sought to draw the sting from this issue
by promoting an interpretation of Irishness based on birth, rather than
on ethnic origins: an embryonic form of Irish nationalism.

Yet the immediate purpose of the confederates, in the circumstances of the 1640s, was to fight a war; and in this they were not
alone. There were perhaps 45,000 troops in arms in Ireland in the
1640s, including troops sent from England and Scotland, though
the conflict was more a war of attrition, with scorched-earth campaigns and sieges being more representative of its conduct than set-
piece battles. There were at least five armies in the field at various
points in the 1640s: royalist, confederate, parliamentarian, Scottish,
and the Laggan Army, composed of Scottish settlers in Ulster. The
relative lack of a cash economy in the Gaelicized northwest hamstrung the resources of the confederate army in Ulster; supplies
were more difficult to obtain. The war that the confederates fought
was conducted against the backdrop of the civil war in England, and
Protestant Ireland had similarly split into royalist and parliamentarian
factions; among the latter were the Scots of Ulster. The outbreak of
the rebellion seems to have forced them to align themselves more
firmly with events in Scotland; hence the arrival of a 10,000-strong
Scottish army in the north of Ireland in April 1642, which facilitated
the formal establishment of Presbyterianism in Ulster, as Scottish
ministers embarked on preaching missions there.

Amidst a plethora of smaller engagements, there were perhaps
only a handful of major battles in the 1640s: at Kilrush (April 1642),
Liscarroll (August 1642), Benburb (June 1646), Dungan's Hill (August 1647), Knockanuss (November 1647), and Rathmines (August
1649). By 1646–47 the confederates may have had as many as 20,000
men enlisted in their "regular" armies. Their forces had been bolstered by the return to Ireland of military veterans such as Garret
Barry, Owen Roe O'Neill, and Thomas Preston, who had all learned
their trade as soldiers on the continent during the Thirty Years' War
and now attempted to apply their experiences to the newly formed
forces at their disposal; the early modern "military revolution" was

thus brought to Ireland. The confederates also sought external assistance for their struggle, and a variety of emissaries from Catholic powers such as Spain and France reached out to them. Alongside the internal war, the confederates commissioned privateers to act as a de facto navy operating out of southeastern ports such as Wexford and Waterford. Perhaps 450 vessels were seized by confederate privateers between 1641 and 1653 (in 1649 it was noted that "the cellars and storehouses of Waterford are full of Englishmens goods");[2] although this was vitally important in logistical terms, it attracted the attention of the English parliament as time wore on.

The brutal fighting that took place throughout the decade was punctuated by cease fires that led to negotiations, as the confederates sought the satisfaction of their demands and Charles I attempted to secure their forces for his prosecution of the war against the English parliament. Even these tentative approaches had problematic offshoots: the 1643 negotiations, for example, forced Scottish settlers in Ulster to gravitate towards the English parliament. The cease fire or "cessation" of 1643 ended one phase of the war, and the distraction of the civil war in England, which prevented further reinforcements reaching Ireland, gave the confederates room to grow and breathe. A critical issue that rendered the internal politics of the confederates especially fractious was the question of what might be acceptable terms for a settlement with the king. This ongoing problem was further complicated by the stance taken by a papal nuncio, Gianbattista Rinuccini, the archbishop of Fermo, who, having arrived in Ireland in 1645, effectively split the confederates by opposing any settlement with Charles I that was deemed to offer too little to Catholics. Those Catholics who adhered to peace terms agreed with the king in 1646, for example, were excommunicated. What made such internal division more significant was the fact that as the decade wore on the military position of the confederates was weakened. O'Neill's Ulster army (which Rinuccini favoured) defeated the Scots at Benburb in Tyrone in 1646. But the king's Irish Protestant viceroy, James Butler, earl of Ormond, was so reluctant to come to terms with Catholics that he went so far as to surrender Dublin to his erstwhile parliamentarian opponents in June 1647, thus giving them a strategic foothold in Ireland. A parliamentarian army subsequently wiped out the confederate army of Leinster at

Dungan's Hill in Meath in August 1647, and the Munster army was destroyed at Knockanuss in Cork in November 1647.

Despite these setbacks, by January 1649 royalists and confederates had finally come to terms with one another. By 1649 there were perhaps eighteen to twenty-eight thousand Catholic troops in Ireland, opposed by twenty-five to thirty-eight thousand Protestant troops. Yet the confederates proved fatally indecisive in political terms, and this undermined any prospect of a successful military struggle. The eventual success of their protracted but intermittent negotiations with royalists in 1649 proved illusory, as events were overtaken by the invasion of Ireland at the behest of the English parliament.

The Cromwellian Conquest of Ireland

Charles I was executed by the English parliament in January 1649, and the parliamentarian reconquest of Ireland began within months. Parliament was unwilling to tolerate the prospect of Irish reinforcements assisting the royalist war efforts in Britain. The lurid atrocity propaganda that had been generated by the 1641 rebellion, which regaled readers (and listeners) with horrific accounts of Catholic cruelties inflicted on Protestant settlers in Ireland in 1641, fostered a sense that the perceived sufferings of Irish Protestants needed to be avenged. Finally, and most significantly, lurking behind these was the fact that in March 1642 the English parliament had passed the so-called "adventurers" act, which raised money to pay the army that was to suppress the original Irish uprising in 1641 using land nominally confiscated from Catholic "rebels" as collateral. This had been channelled into the parliamentarian war effort during the English Civil War, but there was still a debt to be collected.

Oliver Cromwell, who had risen rapidly through the ranks of the parliamentarian forces, headed an army twelve thousand strong that arrived in Dublin in August 1649. The New Model Army under his command embarked on a swift and ruthless campaign over the next nine months. Parliamentarian control of the Irish Sea kept their forces amply supplied, unlike their Irish opponents. The bloody captures of Drogheda and Wexford were the most notorious incidents in a war that saw Cromwell's forces traverse much of Leinster and Munster, which became key theatres of war. A notable defeat was inflicted on them at Clonmel in Tipperary, but the parliamentarians strengthened themselves even further by forging alliances with the Scottish forces in Ulster, and won the allegiance of the Protestant population across the island.

By the summer of 1650 the confederate war effort was broken in the field and Cromwell himself departed from Ireland, leaving his son-in-law, Henry Ireton, in command. Guerrilla conflict, rather then set-piece engagements, became the norm as the structures of the confederate armies began to fracture; as one commentator had quipped in 1642, the "best fort" of the Irish soldiers was "a bog."[3] The brutal conflict saw guerrilla warfare waged across substantial regions and being met with extraordinary severity: the counties of Carlow, Cork, Kilkenny, Laois, Offaly, Tipperary, and much of Waterford and Wicklow were deemed, quite literally, to be outside the law. Scorched-earth tactics were used in these areas, which experienced systematic destruction and extermination. The suffering caused by the prosecution of the war was exacerbated by the arrival of bubonic plague in Galway in July 1649, seemingly from Spain. Outbreaks of plague were recorded across Munster and Leinster (including Dublin) between 1650 and 1653. Thanks to the intertwined ravages of war, famine, and disease, the overall mortality rate in Ireland from 1649 to 1652 may have been as high as 15–20 percent.[4] The war ended with the final defeat of the confederates in 1653. Perhaps thirty-five to forty thousand confederate soldiers emigrated in the aftermath, while some fifteen to twenty-five thousand civilians were transplanted to English plantations in the Caribbean as indentured servants. The human cost of war, as always, extended far beyond those who had done the fighting.

CHAPTER SIX

The Cromwellian Conquest and
the Restoration

The Cromwellian Settlement of Ireland

With the ending of the war came a strategy for defining the nature of the peace. The "Act for the Settling of Ireland" of August 1652 was drafted even before the end of the war, and its prescriptions for the settlement of Ireland began by separating the enemies of parliament from its friends. It set out a number of categories that were to be completely exempted from any postwar pardon, including all those who had been in arms before 10 November 1642 (the date of the first sitting of the confederate assembly); Catholic clerics (who were collectively assumed to have encouraged and abetted the "murders or massacres, robberies or violences committed against the Protestants and English"); and a wide range of other categories that were assumed to define degrees of guilt or innocence. The price for guilt was to be the confiscation of lands and, in many cases, execution.[1]

The broad contours of the settlement were laid out by Cromwell's son-in-law, Henry Ireton, who died in 1651. His successor, Charles Fleetwood, was, like Ireton, hostile to the Catholic Irish. While the settlement had envisaged the confiscation of lands belonging to Protestant royalists, many landowners who fell within the specified categories successfully lobbied Cromwell for an outcome that would be favourable to them. Consequently, the brunt of the confiscation fell upon the Catholics, though Cromwell was by no means unsympathetic to the claims of some Irish Catholics in the 1650s.[2]

While the Cromwellian settlement seemed neat and organised in theory, its implementation was inevitably contentious. The final version of the settlement emerged after much negotiating between different interest groups, most especially the original "adventurers" of 1642 who had invested in the parliamentarian war effort and the Cromwellian soldiers who had actually done the fighting and now expected their reward. Ten counties (Armagh, Down, Antrim, Meath, Westmeath, Laois, Offaly, Tipperary, Limerick, and Waterford) were reserved to satisfy the demands of these two groups. Their claims were assigned by lottery, but there was a difference between the land allocated and what was actually available: hence the necessity for the pioneering Down Survey conducted in the late 1650s under the supervision of William Petty, which mapped Ireland in minute and unprecedented detail.[3] Matters were complicated by the fact that many of those soldiers who had been paid with parcels of land simply sold it on and returned home. Given that army units were expected to settle together, a thriving market in land developed as enterprising parliamentarian officers acquired larger estates than had been expected at a good price. Equally, many of the older Protestant settler population had adhered to the parliamentarian regime, and they also profited from the settlement. The lingering problems caused by uncertain and conflicting claims to Irish land remained unresolved for decades.

The settlement envisaged the removal of Catholic landowners from three of the four Irish provinces: by April 1653 it had been decided that Connacht and County Clare were to be transformed into a Catholic reservation hemmed in by the natural barrier of the River Shannon, with an additional buffer zone around the coast. Catholics who did not qualify for complete dispossession were to be relocated and compensated with smaller holdings in the west of Ireland. The fact that the geography and landscape of the Atlantic counties was made up of poorer, rockier soil was not lost on some observers such as the Cromwellian officer Edmund Ludlow, who observed of the bleak limestone landscape of the Burren in Clare that it had "not water enough to drown a man, wood enough to hang one, nor earth enough to bury him."[4] Although the actual enforcement of the transplantation remained incomplete, the disruption it entailed was significant. Moreover, the more general economic downturn of the 1650s had a major and detrimental effect on Irish towns such as Galway. This was accentuated by attempts to purge Irish towns and cities of Catholics, though hints of urban recovery could be seen before the end of the 1650s.

The implementation of the land settlement after 1655 was impressive in principle but less successful in practice. Yet after the Ulster plantation, it is perhaps the single most important attempt at social engineering in modern Irish history; and its impact would be felt long after the restoration of the monarchy to the thrones of England, Ireland, and Scotland in 1660.

The Restoration

In December 1659, Dublin Castle was seized by a coalition of Cromwellian officers and older Protestant settlers. They anticipated that the commonwealth established by Oliver Cromwell could not survive his death, in 1658, and they viewed its likely collapse as a potential threat to their newfound (or newly enriched) status in Ireland. In May 1660 the monarchy was restored to power in England, Ireland, and Scotland with the return of Charles II, son of the executed king, who had spent the intervening years in exile on the continent. The Church of Ireland, which had been suppressed under the commonwealth, was also restored. The various laws and statutes passed by the commonwealth since the death of Charles I in 1649 were assumed to have been passed illegally by a usurping regime, and were now repealed. One notable exception, however, was the Irish land settlement of the 1650s.

Irish Catholics had consistently proclaimed their loyalty to the monarch in the 1640s and had signed a peace treaty with his representative in 1649; it was not unreasonable that they would expect the reign of the new king would see the reversal of their dispossession and the restoration of their lands. The Protestants who now owned that land, however, stood in the way. The crisis of the previous two decades had welded the members of Ireland's diverse Prot-

estant community together in defence of their shared interests. By
1660 they had become the masters of much of the country thanks to
the Cromwellian settlement, and were unwilling to see this undone.
Protestant leaders such as Sir Audley Mervyn stated this very vocally
in the Irish parliament that sat from 1661 to 1666; it was clear that
the price of accepting the return of the monarchy was the confirmation of the Cromwellian confiscations. At the same time, it was impossible to fully disregard the claims of Catholics. In the 1660s a
court of claims reversed some of the confiscations, and a handful of
Catholics had land returned to them. The competing claims of
those who had estates to gain or lose caused Ormond (who had been
reappointed as viceroy) to quip that they would need a second Ireland to keep everyone happy. But the price of Protestant allegiance
to the restored monarchy was to be the maintenance of Protestant
power, as established in the 1650s. The settlement in Ireland rested
upon this fact, and it was maintained by an army that was to defend
Ireland against internal and external threats, along with local militias organised by members of the Protestant aristocracy. In 1641
Catholics owned 42.2 percent of Irish land, predominantly outside
Ulster; by 1670 this percentage had been reduced to 16.6 percent.[5]
Despite some limited redress (and even then it was the Old English
rather than the Gaelic Irish who benefited the most), the bulk of
the lands confiscated from Catholics during the 1650s remained
in Protestant hands, and the Protestant "interest" was thereby secured.[6] Catholic discontent was hardly surprising.

Table 1. The seventeenth-century revolution in land ownership, revealing the
extent of land confiscated and transferred from Catholic to Protestant
ownership following the Cromwellian and Restoration land settlements.

	1641	1670
Land owned by Catholics	42.2%	16.6%
Land owned by Protestants	42.1%	69.8%
Common/unprofitable land	3.8%	1.6%
Other	12%	12%

Source: *The Down Survey of Ireland: Mapping a Century of Change* (http://down
survey.tcd.ie)

A far-reaching consequence of the 1640s and 1650s in Ireland was that sectarian identities—Catholic, Protestant, non-conformist (those Protestants, such as Presbyterians, who were not members of the Episcopal state church)—came to take precedence over ethnic identities. It was perhaps inevitable that representatives of both Catholic communities came to articulate a common rhetoric of dispossession. The Irish poet Seán Ó Connaill wrote *Tuireamh na hÉireann* [Ireland's Dirge] in Munster in the latter half of the 1650s. Its commentary on the devastation wreaked in the course of the Cromwellian conquest had an enduring relevance beyond 1660.

'S iad do chríochnaig *conquest* Éireann,
do ghabh a ndaingin 's a mbailte le chéile
ó Inis Bó Finne go Binn Éadair
's ó Chloich an Stacáin go Baoi Béarra.
. . . .

Cá ngeabham anois nó créad do dhéanfam?
Ní díon dúinn cnoc ná coill ná caolta.
Níl ár leigheas as liaig í n-Éirinn
Acht Dia do ghuí 's na naoimh i n-aonacht

[It was they who completed the *conquest* of Ireland,
and seized its fortresses and towns together,
from Inishbofin [west] to Howth [east]
and from the White Lady [north] to Dursey [south]
. . . .

Where will we go now or what will we do?
We have no shelter from hill, wood or marshes.
The physicians of Ireland cannot heal us
we can only pray to God and the saints in unison.][7]

The poem was copied scribally and disseminated for generations. After all, the return of the monarchy had done relatively little to change the circumstances that had originally given rise to Ó Connaill's lament. Nicholas French, the Old English bishop of Ferns, had been active in the Confederate Association in the 1640s and blamed leading Protestant grandees in Ireland for forcing the king to maintain the Cromwellian confiscations. This was all the more unjust, argued French, because of the steadfast loyalty that Irish Catholics had shown to the monarchy.

Interpretations of recent history had a role to play here. The case against Irish Catholics after the restoration rested on the assumption that, having rebelled in 1641, they had collectively attempted to exterminate British Protestant settlers. The continued dispossession of Catholics was justified in the 1660s as a necessary measure to prevent any repeat of 1641 in the future.[8] On the other hand, Catholics looked to the peace treaty agreed between Ormond and the confederates in 1649, which had offered significant concessions in terms of both religious toleration and security of land tenure. The Catholic community had been the losers of the 1640s and 1650s, and wanted this reversed. There were other consequences to this defeat. Banditry by "Tories" became endemic in some regions (the name derived from *tóraidhe*, an Irish term for a raider that was later applied to royalist factions in the British parliament). Irish Tories such as Redmond O'Hanlon became folk heroes, and Europe once again became a key destination for Irish Catholics prepared to serve in the armies of a foreign power, most especially the France of Louis XIV.

The Peoples of Ireland in the Reign of Charles II

Europe was not just a theatre of war for Irish soldiers. Just as they had earlier in the century, the Irish colleges of the continent facilitated a flowering of Irish intellectual life. The Catholic cleric John Lynch, for example, was born in Galway, educated in Galway and France, and wrote in Latin for an audience far beyond Irish shores. It is no exaggeration to view him as an archetypal renaissance humanist. Likewise, Irish-language texts continued to be written and printed on the continent during the seventeenth century, and many of these were part of the "religious propaganda" of the Counter Reformation. Such works were intended to disseminate beliefs opposed to the increasing dominance of Protestant colonial society in Ireland.[9] The government accepted that Irish Catholics were by no means reconciled to the dashed expectations of the 1660s and 1670s; biblical motifs of bondage were applied to the plight of Irish Catholics in the work of contemporary poets such as Dáibhí Ó Bruadair.

An inadvertent commentary on sectarian tension was provided by a verse allegedly written on the gates of Bandon Bridge in Cork circa 1670 by Roger Boyle, the zealously Protestant earl of Orrery:

Jew, infidel, or atheist
May enter here, but not a papist

To which a quick-witted "papist" supposedly added:

Who wrote these words composed them well,
The same are written on the gates of hell.[10]

Yet Ireland's Protestants were not homogeneous, in terms of either social status or religion. The established Church of Ireland had been restored after 1660, but alongside this Anglican community existed those Protestant "dissenters" who had arrived in Ireland as Scottish settlers in the 1630s or as Cromwellian soldiers in the 1650s. Throughout the reign of Charles II dissenters were discriminated against and viewed with great distrust by the Anglican establishment; Scots Presbyterians, strongest in Ulster, were a particular cause for concern. By the 1670s, however, many dissenters had sought to come to an accommodation with the crown, which was, for practical reasons, in no position to take too stern a line with them; the *regium donum*, a state grant given to Presbyterian ministers from 1672 onwards, was proof that they were here to stay, and could not be ignored. Senior figures like Ormond (viceroy again in 1662–69 and 1677–84) still felt that dissenters were more dangerous than Catholics, but for others the Catholic threat allowed for a degree of solidarity between denominations at times. Presbyterians may not have been the right kind of Protestants, but they were better than nothing.

By the 1670s Ireland had acquired a Protestant population that, according to Sir William Petty, consisted of 200,000 English (predominantly Anglicans) and 100,000 Scots (predominantly Presbyterian). Within this was a new, overwhelming Anglican ruling class, a land-owning elite that had benefitted enormously from the upheavals of the seventeenth century. The extent of aristocratic landholding could vary enormously, from the vast patrimonies of the earls of

Antrim, Clanricarde—both of whom were Catholic—and Ormond, to name but three of the wealthiest, to the scattering of more modest (but still substantial) holdings that were characteristic of the peerage as a whole. Some had made huge gains thanks to the confiscations of the 1650s: the Annesley family, ennobled as earls of Anglesey after the restoration of the monarchy in 1660, went from owning just 15,000 acres in 1641 to 145,000 in 1670.[11] But such enormous wealth at the top table should not distract from the society that existed below the aristocracy.

In economic terms, Ireland had by the 1680s recovered remarkably from the devastation of the 1640s and 1650s. This was probably to be expected, given the official emphasis on colonisation: settlers began to arrive in Ireland once more, though nowhere near the levels that the authorities hoped for. One striking phenomenon was the attempt to lure continental Protestants to Ireland as settlers, and after the revocation of the Edict of Nantes in 1685 that had guaranteed religious toleration in France, substantial numbers of French Protestants—Huguenots—began to arrive in Ireland. Many of these were skilled workers, and settled in the towns and cities. Ireland was now a more urbanised society, although the Catholic Irish were often officially excluded from towns. The growth of Dublin was perhaps the most spectacular example of urban expansion; the laying out of the Phoenix Park in the 1670s and the building of the Royal Hospital in the early 1680s were the most impressive and durable manifestations of this.

As for the Irish economy, livestock remained a crucial product. The English Cattle Acts of the 1660s banned the export of live Irish cattle to England; consequently, exports of meat (beef) and dairy (butter) took over. North America and the West Indies were major destinations for meat, with vast quantities of tobacco making the return trip; France and the Low Countries were key markets for dairy products. Cork also began to eclipse Galway as a major port, largely due to this new emphasis on the provisions trade to the Atlantic world. The increased export of hides was another consequence of the reduced export of livestock, while ongoing demands for wood to be used in tanning, or as staves, or timber for ships, or fuel for ironworking, took a continuing toll on Irish woodlands. There were attempts at economic diversification, with linen production finding a foothold in the northeast, and mercantile emigration picked up for the first time since the 1650s; then the push factor had been the Cromwellian regime, but within a generation the pull factor was the opportunity to profit in the expanding Atlantic world.

This growth should not, however, be taken to imply that Ireland in the reign of Charles II was a country at peace with itself. Irish Protestants, of whatever status or denomination, lived alongside a Catholic population that, according to Petty, numbered in the region of 800,000, vastly outnumbering them.[12] In the 1670s and 1680s, Catholics still wanted the implications of their defeat to be undone. The early 1670s had seemed to offer some hope, as Charles II moved towards an alliance with Catholic France; there were even hints that the land settlement might yet be reviewed in their favour, along with greater, albeit unofficial, toleration of the Catholic Church. But hostility to such initiatives in England soon brought them to a halt, and the Catholic intelligentsia continued to bemoan the reality of Catholic dispossession. The potentially precarious situation of the "Protestant interest" in Ireland was highlighted during the period of the so-called Popish Plot (1678–81), which arose from allegations of a Catholic plot to assassinate Charles II in England and to extirpate Protestants there. In Ireland, grandees such as Roger Boyle, earl of Orrery, went to great lengths to foster allegations of Catholic plotting to this end, complete with fears of a French invasion. While this forced the viceroy, Ormond, to pass some anti-Catholic measures, Ireland remained stable and at peace throughout the crisis (though the Catholic archbishop of Armagh, Oliver Plunkett, was implicated on trumped-up charges of organizing a Catholic rebellion and was executed in London in 1681). Yet the apparent quiescence of Irish Catholics did not mean that they had become reconciled to the dashed expectations of the restoration: the 1680s would offer them another chance of redress.

CHAPTER SEVEN

Two Kings

The Road to Revolution

On 6 February 1685, Charles II died, and his brother James, duke of York, succeeded him as James II. Since James had been publicly acknowledged as a Catholic since 1673, his accession was met with apprehension by Protestants across the Stuart kingdoms, a sentiment compounded in Ireland by the elevation to power of Colonel Richard Talbot, newly ennobled as earl of Tyrconnell, a scion of a prominent Old English family and an old associate of the new king. Tyrconnell came to prominence and notoriety as a spokesman for the Irish Catholic interest after the restoration. His ambitions to better their lot in the early 1670s were thwarted; by the later 1680s this wheel had turned full circle. As head of the Irish army, and subsequently as viceroy from February 1687, Tyrconnell presided over a de facto Catholic "counter-revolution."[1] In the army, Catholic officers and men replaced Protestants on a massive scale, and the machinery of government (the judiciary, borough corporations, county sheriffs) was rapidly transferred to Catholic hands in what were, essentially, purges. Alongside these developments, the Catholic Church began to emerge from the shadows.

Some of this could be seen as a form of redress for grievances that had been outstanding since the 1660s; James's reign offered a window of opportunity for Irish Catholics that might not recur again.

But the most contentious question of all soon became evident, as Tyrconnell contemplated a substantial revision of the restoration land settlement. Admittedly, he did not envisage its reversal, but his ambitions to tinker with it went further than those of his master. James took the view that in simple political terms, the settlement was best maintained. His government in Ireland was by no means intent on the destruction of Irish Protestants, but its policies were bound to erode their privileged position in Ireland.

Yet prior to 1688 this was not set in stone. James, while unpopular, could be tolerated due to his age; his reign was likely to be relatively short, and while he had numerous children, he had no legitimate son. His heir was his eldest surviving daughter, Mary, who was married to the Dutch prince William of Orange. The sense that normal service might be resumed with a Protestant succession after a Catholic interlude sweetened a bitter pill. But this changed dramatically in 1688, when James finally produced a legitimate son. The prospect of a Catholic royal dynasty precipitated the so-called "glorious" revolution, whereby James rapidly lost the support of his English subjects, who made clear their preference for Mary and William. Under James there was a distinct possibility of an Anglo-French alliance that would be unfavourable to the Dutch; William decided to intervene in British affairs in order to avert this, and to ensure he would not be abandoned in Europe in the face of the threat posed by Louis XIV's France. Consequently, on 5 November he arrived in England with a massive army, claiming to have been invited to settle a range of grievances aroused by the authoritarian, pro-Catholic regime of James. James was prepared to fight, but lost his nerve as his support in England collapsed; he fled to France in a fishing boat piloted by an Irish naval commander. William effectively forced the English parliament to offer him the crown, and the "convention parliament" invited Mary and William to rule as joint sovereigns. The Glorious Revolution derives its glory from the assumption that it was a peaceful transition. But in reality there was a war fought over the succession to the thrones of the three kingdoms, and this war was primarily fought in Ireland.

For Irish Protestants, William and Mary's accession seemed to offer salvation from almost certain destruction, and many (though not all) backed the revolution quite openly at a time of increasing sectarian tension under Tyrconnell's regime. Against this backdrop, violence was increasingly directed at Protestants in Ireland, some of whom began to flee amidst concerns that a massacre along the lines of 1641 might yet be on the cards. The situation in Ireland was compounded not just by the intersection of a British dynastic dispute with domestic sectarian tensions, but also, after November 1688, by the outbreak of European conflict as France declared war on the Dutch Republic. The French saw an opportunity to open a second front in Ireland, and James was pressured to return to a kingdom of which he was still legally king and to rally forces to win back his other two thrones. He arrived at Kinsale on 12 March 1689.

James's Catholic subjects welcomed him in Ireland rapturously; the arrival of this Catholic king offered hope that the newly enriched Protestant elite would be stripped of their lands, which could then be returned to what were perceived as their rightful owners. After travelling to Dublin, James reluctantly presided over an overwhelmingly Catholic parliament summoned in May 1689. It declared that the English parliament had no right to legislate for Ireland but did not elevate the Catholic Church to the status of the established Church of Ireland. It did, however, resolve to repeal both the restoration land settlement and the plantation of Ulster. And this proved to be the point of no return. Any lingering Protestant loyalty to James evaporated. The fate of the city of Derry acquired a particular resonance; having become effectively a Protestant refugee camp in the northeast, it was famously besieged by Jacobite forces until July 1689, when a blockade on the River Foyle was successfully breached by the English navy. The successful defence of the city, and the assumption that this had saved its Protestant population from certain doom, could stand as a metaphor for what was seen to be at stake in this war.

The War of the Two Kings

The prospect of French backing for James guaranteed that William would respond: the first of his forces to arrive in Ireland landed near Belfast on 13 August 1689. The Antrim town of Carrickfergus was successfully recaptured before the Williamite forces (19,000 troops by the end of September) established winter quarters near Dundalk, fifty miles north of Dublin, but they lost perhaps half their strength to disease. The initiative passed to the Jacobites. Winter saw some limited action, such as the capture of Sligo by the future Jacobite hero Patrick Sarsfield in October 1689, but on the whole they did little to capitalize on their advantage. Ultimately William took matters into his own hands, despite his unhappiness at this distraction from the European war. A second Williamite invasion force was assembled in April and May 1690, and on 14 June William himself landed in Ireland with a substantial army and the desire, as he allegedly put it, not to let the grass grow under his feet. By this time French troops had landed in Cork. William went south, and rejecting French advice to go west, James went north to meet him. The two kings, at the head of their armies, finally faced each other in the Boyne valley in County Meath on 30 June 1690: 36,000 Dutch, German, Danish, English, and Protestant Irish troops led by William faced 25,000 Irish and French troops led by James. Monday was traditionally considered unlucky, so while there was no actual engagement on 30 June, a bombardment prompted rumours of William's demise. But on 1 July he disproved this in resounding fashion with a decisive victory. James, acting on the advice of Tyrconnell and the French commander, Antonin de Caumont, comte de Lauzan, fled south with alacrity. He departed for France from Kinsale on 4 July, subsequently being castigated for doing so by at least one Irish poet who dubbed him *Séamus an chaca*: James the shit.[2]

The loss at the battle of the Boyne was surprisingly small, despite the size of the two armies involved, with only a thousand Jacobite and five hundred Williamite casualties. But while not decisive in military terms, the presence of the two kings gave it a potent symbolic resonance. Depending on one's perspective, a Catholic king (or pretender) had faced the Protestant king (or pretender). And the Protestant king had won a victory that would be celebrated for centuries.

In the absence of James, Tyrconnell favoured negotiations after the Boyne, a stance which prompted the emergence of a group under Patrick Sarsfield who advocated the continuation of the war; tensions between the Irish and Old English elements of the Irish Catholic coalition began to surface as a result. The Jacobites regrouped at the western city of Limerick, which was besieged in August 1690. But the siege was lifted by the end of the month; artillery that might have assisted the Williamites in their attempt to capture the city was delayed after a famous nocturnal raid led by Sarsfield, and winter was also drawing in. The abortive siege suggested that William had underestimated the strength of the remaining Jacobite resistance, and its failure opened the door to a negotiated settlement by confirming that an overwhelming victory would probably come at too high a price.

William subsequently departed for England, and Tyrconnell for France, as did most of the French force; a sign that both sides in the European war were detaching themselves from the Irish theatre. Raids by Jacobites continued throughout the winter, and their hopes were sustained by the lingering promise of more French aid. James ordered Tyrconnell to renew the war effort on the earl's return from France in January 1691, and ennobled Sarsfield as earl of Lucan in an attempt to ease growing tensions between the two Jacobite leaders. In May 1691, Charles Chalmont, marquis de St. Ruth, arrived from France with extra weapons, but, critically and revealingly, no additional French troops. The opportunistic nature of the French involvement in Ireland was evident; given their own desire to secure Irish troops for the war on the continent, the French would hardly risk their own in what was increasingly seen as a distraction (indeed, the prospect of obtaining an intact Jacobite army from Ireland at the end of the war was the essential reason for the continuing French involvement in Ireland). Aside from the major engagements, the war was increasingly characterized by partisan warfare conducted by the irregular forces known as "rapparees" (derived from the Irish *ropaire:* "rapier"). This resulted from the mobilization of the peasantry in the Jacobite cause; mopping-up operations to deal with these continued into the 1690s, but by then the war itself had reached its conclusion.

St. Ruth dedicated himself to strengthening the resolve of the Jacobite forces in Ireland by reorganizing them, as well as by rearming them. In June 1691 the Williamites attacked the Jacobite stronghold of Athlone on the River Shannon and crossed into Connacht. On 12 July the two armies met at Aughrim, near Galway, with St. Ruth choosing the ground. While the Jacobites were initially successful, the death of their French commander (decapitated by a cannonball) turned it into a rout as they retreated in disarray. The ensuing pursuit by Williamite cavalry resulted in carnage. Aughrim, at which perhaps seven thousand were killed, remains the bloodiest of Irish battles: twenty years later, the battlefield was still littered with skulls.

After this, a Jacobite surrender was simply a matter of time. A second siege of Limerick in September 1691 became their last stand, and ended with a reluctant surrender by Sarsfield, who had succeeded Tyrconnell as head of the Jacobite forces after the latter's death in August. The subsequent negotiations were cordial, and on 3 October the Treaty of Limerick officially brought the war to an end. The settlement had two distinct elements: military and civil. The military side was straightforward: the export of the Jacobite army to France. The civil articles proved more problematic, holding out as they did the promise of religious toleration and a general amnesty, along with guarantees of property and civil rights for Catholics.

William's purpose in coming to Ireland was primarily to prevent the French acquiring a foothold there. Having effectively defeated the Jacobites, he and his advisors were in favour of a speedy settlement to end the war in Ireland. Yet this broader purpose did not tally with more local concerns. From the point of view of Irish Protestants, and especially the Protestant elite, the Williamite victory of 1691 saved them from destruction at the hands of a hostile Catholic community that outnumbered them. The settlement William presided over was far too lenient for their liking, and did nothing to alter a sectarian arithmetic that could hardly be said to favour Protestant Ireland. The status and security of the broad Protestant community that had emerged victorious from the upheavals of the seventeenth century would have to be maintained at the expense of those Catholics who had hoped to supplant them.

The Williamite victory confirmed what had already been happening for generations: the domination of Irish society by a wealthy Protestant landed class, whose power would last for centuries. It also confirmed the final destruction of the political and military power of the old Gaelic and Catholic order and marked the final point at which the distinctions between Irish and Old English would actually matter. Both were to be united in defeat and in exile. In short, the Williamite conquest shaped Ireland for centuries. Its significance to the Protestant minority was to be revealed in the tradition that sought to celebrate the victory of a Protestant monarch on behalf of his Protestant subjects. But the significance of the last conquest of the seventeenth century to the Catholic majority was neatly encapsulated by the term used to describe it by the poet Dáibhi Ó Bruadair: "An longbhriseadh," or the shipwreck.

Where Historians Disagree

O NE OF THE MOST important areas of disagreement among historians of this period is whether or not early modern Ireland—from the sixteenth to the eighteenth century—is best viewed as a kingdom or a colony.[1] Some critiques of colonialism as an interpretive framework view it as completely inappropriate in the context of nineteenth- and twentieth-century Ireland, but concede its applicability to the early modern period.[2] The suggestion that Ireland—or at least substantial parts of it—became a British colony in this period has been vigorously reasserted in recent years in major works by the historical geographer William J. Smyth and the historians David Dickson and Nicholas Canny.[3] A kingdom in theory could also be a colony in practice, and many among the Protestant interest in Ireland viewed themselves as a colonial community during the Restoration period.[4] The representatives of the dominant external power sometimes had revealing views on the matter; Arthur Capel, earl of Essex, viceroy in the 1670s, described Ireland as a plantation, "for in reality it is little other."[5] So was early modern Ireland (broadly defined) a kingdom, a colony, or a mixture of both? It may be that "no neat imperial or civilizing model can be easily applied to early modern Ireland."[6]

The "kingdom or colony" dichotomy is broadly applicable to early modern Ireland, but with regards to the seventeenth century, one influential trend in historical writing relates to what was often called the "new British history," in which the various interactions of

England, Ireland, Scotland, and Wales were examined as a fluid and interlinked process, sometimes against the wider backdrop of European and Atlantic history.[7] This was a departure from purely national histories, though it came in for some criticism. "New British history" tended to focus on moments of crisis and upheaval like the 1640s, and for some, there was nothing particularly new about it: the "new British history" was basically the old Irish, Scottish, and Welsh history from a different angle.[8] Historians of these countries, after all, had been examining the past in the light of relations with English power for a long time.

One single event looms large in seventeenth-century Ireland: 1641. The precise events of the rebellion were disputed from the outset, as Protestants and Catholics created versions of 1641 that emphasised their victimhood, and which have been used as justifications for political beliefs and identities up to the present day.[9] Many of these polemics drew upon the testimonies taken from mainly Protestant refugees in the aftermath of the rebellion, including the infamous "depositions" held in Trinity College Dublin, which were digitized and published online in 2010.[10] While a small fraction of them contain lurid allegations of atrocities visited upon Protestants by Catholics, along with eyewitness accounts, scholars in recent decades have begun to examine them as sources for the social and cultural world in which British Protestant settlers lived.[11] For example, accounts of raids by Catholic insurgents relate what was said by them to their captors in Irish, which shows that some colonists lived in a bilingual world where the boundaries between settler and native were more fluid than might be assumed. That said, reexamining 1641 poses all sorts of questions. Was the rising a bolt from the blue? Or did it arise from long-standing tensions caused by colonisation and dispossession, as suggested by David Edwards?[12] In other words, what sort of society existed in Ireland in the decades prior to 1641? Was it at peace, or was a rebellion bound to come? Given the manner in which 1641 precipitated the "wars of the three kingdoms" and the subsequent Cromwellian conquest, and was used as a pretext for the later land settlements, questions like this are of fundamental importance.[13]

PART III

The Eighteenth Century

CHAPTER EIGHT

Ascendancy

Protestant Interests

The Treaty of Limerick was signed on 3 October 1691 by delegations led, respectively, by Sarsfield and the Williamite commander, Godard van Reede van Ginkel. From the Williamites' point of view, it was a reasonable (if not perfect) agreement that would enable them to return their attention to the war in Europe. Ironically, a key provision of the treaty was that the Irish Jacobites' army would be removed to the continent, and many ended up in the French service: the so-called "Wild Geese." Those Catholics who remained were to be confirmed in their estates and permitted to practice their professions (and even to bear arms, depending on their social status). They were also to be granted an ambiguous form of religious toleration, and would be insulated against any retrospective legal retribution for their actions in wartime. Yet the perceived leniency of these terms outraged Irish Protestants, who were unhappy that they would not be compensated for losses they had endured in the war and that Catholic Ireland remained, in their eyes, undefeated and dangerous. There was no attempt to ratify the treaty in the first postwar Irish parliament, called in 1692, and another attempt in 1695 was abandoned. The Irish parliament did not ratify the treaty until 1697, and even then it was only in a greatly diluted form that omitted the clauses relating to civil and religious toleration.

One side effect of England's Glorious Revolution was the emergence of an all-Protestant parliament in Ireland, which first sat in 1692. From the outset, it was dominated by constitutional questions that were ultimately about who was actually in charge. Was it the government, usually headed by an English aristocrat, with English appointees in key offices, or was it to be the representatives (such as they were) of Ireland assembled in the parliament? It was obvious that British and English interests did not automatically correspond to Irish interests in general, and to those of Irish Protestants in particular. It had suited the Williamite government, after all, to strike a deal with the Jacobites. But the signing of the Treaty of Limerick, complete with clauses that the Irish Protestant interest found highly objectionable, seemed to suggest that they and their concerns would ultimately be consigned to second place. And this could not be tolerated. Money was also an issue for the Irish parliament, as the question of parliament's "sole right" to initiate financial legislation to fund the government and administration of Ireland emerged, and MPs recognized that control of the purse strings could be used once again to exert a wider control over Irish affairs in the face of English oversight. On the other hand, from the 1690s the government began to utilise "managers" who would massage the parliament to pass legislation by deploying patronage on a large scale. Both styles of governance continued to evolve in the decades that followed.

The "sole right" claim was initially made by the Irish parliament in 1692, and the deadlock that ensued eventually forced the government into a compromise in 1695, which ultimately resulted in the advent of regular parliamentary sessions in Ireland. Thereafter, along with the passing of a modified version of the Treaty of Limerick, the lingering fears of Protestant Ireland began to be addressed by the gradual passing of the popery, or penal, laws. Catholics had been barred from the Irish parliament as early as 1691, after members were required to swear the oaths of supremacy and allegiance, and to take a declaration against transubstantiation, measures that Catholics would find repugnant. The first of two penal laws passed in 1695 officially limited Catholic ownership of weapons and horses over five pounds in value, lest these prove useful to either a future invader or a Catholic rebellion from within. The second penal law of 1695 effectively sought to curtail the numbers of students attending Irish colleges on the continent, and thereby the links between Irish Catholics and their European co-religionists. Given that the Wild Geese added a new military dimension to Catholic Ireland's already extensive intellectual and mercantile networks on the continent, these can plausibly be described as security measures in time of war.[1] Further restrictions followed.

Collectively, the laws passed from 1695 to 1709 were intended to hobble the intellectual, religious, and political leaders of Catholic Ireland. The ecclesiastical hierarchy and regular clergy were to be banished. A limited number of secular clergy were permitted to stay but were required to register with the authorities, and by 1709 these were also obliged to repudiate the Stuarts, who had been welcomed into exile in France and who were widely perceived as being intent on taking back the thrones of the three kingdoms. Given that landed wealth was essentially the basis of political and military power, many of the "penal laws" were aimed at restricting Catholic land ownership. Catholics were barred from purchasing land in 1704 and could not lease land for more than thirty-one years. The manner in which they inherited land was also restricted in 1704: instead of inheritance by primogeniture, whereby an eldest heir might inherit a land holding in its entirety, Catholics could only inherit land by gavelkind, in which case the land in question was to be divided amongst the family, thereby reducing the size and profitability of the land holding.

Security concerns were also reflected in some of the other penal laws. In 1728 Catholics were deprived of the franchise, and by the 1730s Catholics were barred from local government offices, attending Trinity College Dublin (then the only university in Ireland), and practising at the bar.[2] These restrictions on political and economic rights (especially in relation to land) and on involvement in the state, the professions, and the armed forces were essentially aimed at securing Anglican Ireland from what was seen, for much of the eighteenth century, as a Catholic and Jacobite threat that, while based overseas, retained a potent following in Ireland. With regard to the restrictive nature of the penal laws, at least some members of the Protestant community debated whether or not they were simply instruments of repression, or could be an inducement for Catholics to convert to the established church: after all, would conversion not

be a long-term solution to the problem? There were occasional attempts to promote conversion, especially through education, but
this was the work of a minority. Some Catholics did convert, and
some Protestants helped Catholic neighbours and relations to side-
step the provisions of the penal laws. They were devised in a piecemeal fashion, and were not always fully enforced. But collectively,
the penal laws facilitated the creation of an officially Anglican state
in eighteenth-century Ireland. Dissenters were also victimised, most
obviously by the sacramental test of 1704 that made adherence to
the Church of Ireland a prerequisite for state office, a condition that
dissenters found repugnant. Those Protestants who did not conform to the state church also forfeited their right to participate in
the state itself.

The passage of the first penal laws had paved the way for the
ratification of the Treaty of Limerick. In line with its provisions,
land confiscations followed in the 1690s, but the settlements that
ended the war—the articles of Galway and the Treaty of Limerick—
offered legal protection to most of those who were vulnerable to
punishment. Pardons were offered in some cases, and in others families were permitted to claim back at least some of what was confiscated: usually land taken from those who had been killed, or who
had departed for France. The Williamite confiscations were not on
the scale of their Cromwellian predecessor, but they eroded the
share of Catholic-owned land in Ireland even further. By the middle
of the eighteenth century Catholics may have owned as little as 5–10
percent of Irish land—an extraordinary transformation.

It is worth pausing to reflect on who now owned this land. By
1700 Ireland had acquired a Protestant population of various denominations and social classes that made up perhaps 20 percent of
the whole, split between the established church and nonconformists
(the latter grouping had been topped up in the 1690s by a renewed
surge of Presbyterian immigration). They were usually of British
descent, but also had continental elements thanks to immigration by
groups such as Huguenots in the later seventeenth century. And
some of these had done very well indeed. But the ruling elite was
Anglican. Protestantism was the key, and the bond provided by
Protestantism was bolstered by the punctual commemoration of key
dates in what could be described as a Protestant calendar: William's

birthday on 4 November; the execution of Charles I on 31 January; the restoration of the monarchy on 29 May; the outbreak of the 1641 rebellion on 23 October; and the discovery of the Gunpowder Plot on 5 November. These dates were marked by official and unofficial ceremonies—bells, bonfires, drinking, often elaborate fireworks, parades, and church ceremonies—that appealed across social classes, so long as those classes were Protestant. The discovery and outbreak of the 1641 rebellion was marked by the Church of Ireland in a way that reminded Irish Protestants of their deliverance from destruction at the hands of Irish Catholics (and could also be used to inculcate a moral message). As time went by another anniversary was added to the list: the battle of the Boyne on 1 July (old style).

These reminders of the past also served to keep an awareness of the lurking Catholic threat alive, and such fears remained a crucial component of Protestant identity in the early eighteenth century. From the point of view of Protestants of all kinds, the Catholic danger had not receded in the years after 1691; it had simply been exported. The "Wild Geese" constituted a strong and vigorous Irish military tradition on the continent throughout the eighteenth century, with the exploits of the "Irish Brigade" in the French army at the battle of Fontenoy in 1745 attracting particular renown. There were genuine fears in Britain and Ireland of a Jacobite resurgence in the generations after the Glorious Revolution. The repercussions of the Jacobite rebellions of 1715 and 1745 were weaker in Ireland than in England or Scotland, but they had certainly heightened tensions, and until the middle of the eighteenth century Protestant Ireland retained the lurking fear that a Catholic danger lay across the seas and would eventually attempt to strike at them.

If such fears posed the question of what Protestant Ireland should do to protect itself, then the answer lay in security. In the 1690s Ireland's defences were seen to be in a poor condition, and from 1698 a new network of residential barracks was built throughout the island (the Royal Barracks in Dublin, which was the largest barracks in Europe when it opened in 1710, was the most spectacular example of these). The new military installations were also intended to deal with the lingering threat posed by rapparees in certain areas, but having persisted in the aftermath of the war this threat receded in the 1720s. Fears of Jacobitism survived, however, and

Jacobite scares often prompted the seizure of Catholic weapons and horses, the detention of suspects, and bans on public assembly. From 1699 to 1769 the Irish army was nominally 12,000 strong in peacetime, increasing to 15,500 thereafter, although the real numbers enlisted were always lower. From 1701, Catholics and Irish Protestants were officially barred from the army, though these strictures were often relaxed in time of war, and both Catholics and Protestants could always be found amongst the rank and file. The ban on Irish Protestants was designed to maintain the integrity of the Protestant community by ensuring that it was not weakened by having substantial numbers of Protestants on overseas service; recruits instead came from Britain. Anglicans seem to have been accepted within the ranks from the 1740s onwards, though dissenters were still barred. But during the Seven Years' War of 1756–63 the demand for manpower saw the recruitment of Irish Catholics.

The Irish army in the eighteenth century was usually perceived as an external imposition due to both its composition and its quartering in barracks that were separated from the community at large. This also became a way of maintaining a standing army for service across the burgeoning British empire that would have been unpopular to maintain in Britain itself: instead, the army would be kept out of sight, out of mind, and ready for use in the new barracks in Ireland.[3]

The Exercise of Power

How did Protestant Ireland govern? The viceroy stood at the head of the government, but was usually English and non-resident unless parliament was in session; senior officials usually ran things on a day-to-day basis. Beneath this came various levels of administration and bureaucracy, of office holders and sinecures. These other layers of the apparatus of state were populated by Irish Protestants. Naturally, the same was true of the Church of Ireland, despite a widespread assumption that it was overwhelmingly populated by English clerics. The established church was essentially an arm of the state in its own right, and was perennially concerned with the condition of the Protestant community while being preoccupied with educational and proselytising schemes to expand the base of that community.

The law was administered by the judiciary, which was based in

Dublin but travelled around the country on the intermittent assize circuit. Then there was a plethora of local officials: magistrates, sheriffs, and justices of the peace. These positions were dominated by the gentry and were responsible for local judicial activity, along with the maintenance and development of infrastructure and public works. Essentially, the county grand juries lay at one end of the administrative spectrum, with parliament at the other end, and an increasingly elaborate bureaucracy in between.[4] The parliament itself was based on its English counterpart, with the two chambers meeting on an increasingly regular basis from the 1690s onwards, which was very different from the infrequent meetings of previous centuries. The upper house (lords) was populated by the Irish peers and the twenty-two bishops and archbishops of the established church. The lower house (commons) consisted of three hundred members sitting in two-seat constituencies, many of which were dominated by the gentry, and as such were little more than sinecures. The rural electorate consisted of Protestant landowners, though a wider franchise could be found in the urban boroughs where members of corporations and freemen could vote. Whig and Tory alignments were replicated in the Irish parliament during the reign of Queen Anne, though these distinctions faded away by the 1720s and did not re-emerge until the latter decades of the century.

But there were ultimately limitations to the parliament's power. The Declaratory Act of 1720 affirmed, amongst other things, the right of the British parliament to legislate for Ireland. In 1722 the decision to award a patent (sold on by the king's mistress) to mint copper coin to William Wood of Wolverhampton prompted a furious backlash. The idea was intended to replenish Ireland's depleted currency in circulation. This prompted ferocious hostility on the grounds that Ireland would be flooded with worthless coin, and it was successfully resisted. But the affair was seen to have had symbolic overtones as a clash between Irish and British interests, most famously articulated from outside the parliament by Jonathan Swift's *Drapier's Letters* (1724–25), the fourth of which addressed his concerns to the "whole people of Ireland." In the aftermath, the government resolved that in future all senior offices would remain in English hands, and that parliament would be rendered malleable by "undertakers."

The key to the undertakers lay in their name: in the absence of the lord lieutenant, they "undertook" to manage the meetings of parliament, being consulted about legislation and being granted access to the considerable patronage at the disposal of the government, the better to smooth the passage of bills through the parliament. The concept of "managing" parliamentary factions had existed earlier in the century, but became more firmly entrenched from the 1720s on. The task was usually given to figures of considerable wealth and prestige, who usually occupied senior positions, most notably William Connolly up to 1728 and Henry Boyle after 1732. Essentially, they sought to cajole and bribe on behalf of the government, and continued to do so until the 1760s.

Wealth

In 1731 the opening of a new Parliament House in Dublin gave impressive expression to the power of Ireland's Protestant ruling class: the so-called "Protestant ascendancy" (the term itself apparently dates from the 1780s but was—is—applied retrospectively).[5] After 1715 parliament was meeting on a biennial basis; in the eighteenth century Dublin, as the seat of parliament, became a magnet for the Protestant ruling elite, as the city expanded enormously against the backdrop of a lengthy economic boom. The Irish economy recovered slowly after the devastation of the Jacobite-Williamite war, though the 1720s were a period of particular hardship, with a succession of poor harvests causing famine conditions in some regions. Harvest failures and epidemics were by no means uncommon, as was seen to horrific effect during the nationwide famine caused by the Arctic winter of 1740–41.

But the long-term trajectory of the eighteenth-century Irish economy was upwards; from the 1660s to the 1770s there was a fivefold increase in Irish exports. Different ports had a different focus. Drogheda and Belfast dealt in linen; Dublin, Limerick, Cork, and Waterford exported livestock and food. There was no direct trade with the British colonies from 1696 to 1731: Irish exports, along with imports of sugar and tobacco, rum, timber, and flaxseed all went via Britain, as the larger ports squeezed out the smaller ones. Internal economic expansion was also facilitated by changes in the man-made environment. Landed estates and urban networks had been expanding since the seventeenth century, but the development of infrastructure such as roads, towns, and market fairs accelerated in the eighteenth century; the first turnpike roads had been established by 1729, and there were three thousand fairs established by the 1770s.

At the start of the eighteenth century there were perhaps two thousand estate farms in Ireland, the majority of which were smaller than four thousand acres, with some major estates as the exceptions.[6] Larger grazing farms for cattle emerged in Munster, Leinster, and east Connacht, putting pressure on smaller holdings. They also had another long-term impact: by using up the lowland pastures the prevalence of big farms accelerated the shift to widespread cultivation of the potato, which was easily grown in poorer upland soil. The large-scale shift to dairy farming had been prompted by the Atlantic provisions trade to the colonies, though Britain had become the primary market by the end of the century; it was the destination for 79 percent of Irish exports in 1800, having been the recipient of 45 percent in 1700. Salt beef and dairy products were the mainstay of the colonial trade, which shifted from the West Indies to North America over the course of the century.[7] Wealth and commercial expansion also left a mark in the Irish ports from which goods were imported and exported.

Catholic and dissenter mercantile interests remained unaffected by the penal laws, which were principally directed at landed wealth. Textiles such as linen remained major exports, and the linen heartlands of the northeast would become the wealthiest region in Ireland by the end of the century. The massive expansion of the linen trade in Ulster was encouraged by landlords, in part due to poor land yielding low rents; landlords also facilitated markets at which to sell the new produce, and the Armagh–Dungannon–Lisburn "linen triangle" of east Ulster became one of the great centres of economic growth in the second half of the eighteenth century. The linen industry eventually reached west to the Atlantic seaboard (for kelp) and south to Dublin (to the Linen Hall), which kept its preeminence as the centre of banking and capital flows. The street names around the location of the old linen hall in Dublin—such as Lisburn Street, named after the eponymous Armagh town—still bear testament to the link to Ulster via the linen trade, just as the elongated houses of eighteenth century weavers remain a feature of the vernacular architecture of the northern regions of Ireland; the extra length was needed to accommodate their looms. Another physical expression of wealth and security that could be seen across the island was the change in the nature of gentry residences and demesnes from the 1730s onwards, as they evolved away from the semi-fortified dwellings of the past. "Georgian" Ireland left a rich architectural legacy, and the aristocratic residences of the eighteenth century are perhaps the most important component of that. Yet tensions remained beneath the surface of the society ruled by the "Protestant ascendancy," for the new "big houses" remained embedded in the countryside of what was still an overwhelmingly Catholic country. It is to this reality that attention must now be turned.

CHAPTER NINE

Hidden Irelands

Catholics and Jacobites

In July 1711, Richard Thomas, the zealous vicar and rector of Headford in County Galway, wrote to John Vesey, the bishop of Tuam, to inform him that he was optimistic of converting two leading members of the O'Flaherty family, "which would strike a great stroke in making that a Protestant country, that is, if we do not meet with an extraordinary opposition from the moles the priests and friars that work underground."[1] There are two things that can be taken from this: that the Church of Ireland (or at least individual members of it) felt compelled to attempt the conversion of leading Catholics to exploit their influence within the Catholic community; and that they faced major obstacles from their Catholic opponents as they tried to do so (there was a long-running contemporary debate over whether or not the purpose of the penal laws was to prompt the conversion of Catholics). If Ireland was, in legal terms, a country in which only members of the Church of Ireland could participate fully in public life, then that excluded most of the population on purely sectarian grounds. This letter is a subtle reminder of that stark fact. The existence of a "hidden" Ireland, or Irelands, as used here refers to those segments of the Irish population that were excluded from formal political public life. Ironically, that means that the vast majority of the Irish population in the eighteenth century could be described as hidden.

Catholics made up most of the population but were excluded from participation in the state. That is not to say, however, that the life of Catholic Ireland was of no account; its political affiliation was of great concern to Protestant Ireland. Jacobitism—allegiance to the deposed Stuart monarchy—remained strong in Catholic Ireland throughout the eighteenth century, with support from some influential Protestants. Jacobite loyalties were reflected in Gaelic poetry and song, which still constituted a vibrant oral and scribal tradition. Despite the seventeenth-century renaissance, the pressure brought to bear on the Gaelic order since the sixteenth century had taken a toll on its intellectual life and its learned classes (which had long been viewed with hostility by the English authorities). But secular schools for poets, genealogists, lawyers, and doctors had survived well into the seventeenth century and beyond. The social cachet of the poetic class may have declined, but its members continued to respond to the world in which they now found themselves. Poetic genres such as the *aisling* (depicting a vision that often conveyed an allegorical message) survived and were adapted to new purposes, becoming far more demotic as they did so. There was a line of descent from the poetic elite of the seventeenth century to the Catholic schoolmaster of the eighteenth and early nineteenth centuries.

A good example is found in the career of Aodh Buí Mac Cruitín. Born in County Clare around 1680 into a family with a tradition of serving as hereditary historians to the O'Briens of Thomond, he wrote poems eulogising members of the local gentry before progressing to more explicitly Jacobite verse. He moved to Dublin and translated numerous works before publishing a book in English that drew on the work of Seathrún Céitinn to challenge the writings of Protestant historians of Ireland such as Richard Cox. Moving to Louvain, he edited and published a manuscript on Irish grammar before joining the French army in 1728. In 1731, in Paris, he assisted in the publication of an English-language dictionary before returning to his native Clare and establishing a school. As a poet, Jacobite, scholar, soldier, and teacher at home and abroad, Mac Cruitín encapsulates many elements of the Irish Catholic world of the early eighteenth century.

Catholic allegiance to the Stuarts was long-standing, and survived long after they had lost the thrones of England, Ireland, and Scotland. This was not mere nostalgia: Jacobitism held out the prospect that the new Protestant dispensation in Ireland could be reversed to the benefit of Irish Catholics. If the Stuarts regained the thrones they had lost, surely they would reward the Catholic subjects who had remained loyal to them, it was believed. A residual Catholic gentry had survived the confiscations of the early eighteenth century, but as land holders, tenants, and tenant farmers rather than land owners. Perhaps as much as 20 percent of Irish land effectively remained in unchanged hands, and although those hands belonged to "middlemen," these remnants of the older aristocracy —the "underground gentry," as they have been termed—retained this status within their community.[2]

Jacobitism was often associated with other forms of unrest, such as the threat posed by rapparees prior to the 1720s. It also had the sanction of the Catholic Church: 124 of 129 Catholic bishops appointed to Ireland from 1687 to 1765 were officially approved by the exiled Stuarts. But Jacobitism was sustained and made all the more threatening by continued links to the continent, as hinted at by the testimony of an informant aboard a ship moored in County Kerry in 1727. On hearing the ship's master toast "Jemmy," he asked who this was, to be told "damn his blood if he valued a halfpenny who heard him and that he meant King James the Third and accordingly drank his health in the aforesaid terms and then struck at a gentleman in company when he and I drank King Georges health."[3] Celebrations of the pretender's birthday, seditious toasts, and recruitment for foreign military service all served as reminders to Protestants that the return of the Stuarts might yet be a possibility, and many leading Catholics (and some Protestants) would have favoured such an outcome.

Yet the prospect of a Stuart restoration depended on the disposition of powers such as Spain, France, and to a lesser extent Sweden and Russia. After the Jacobite rebellion of 1715, for instance, the French, who were the most obvious ally of the Jacobite cause, had come to an accommodation with the British against the Spanish that lasted into the 1730s. Lingering hopes that continental powers might be induced to land in Ireland ebbed and flowed throughout the eigh-

teenth century, but the Jacobite rebellions of 1715 and 1745 garnered
virtually no support in Ireland. The Jacobite cause in Britain and Ireland never recovered from the failure of the Jacobite rebellion in
1745; the death of James II's son and heir James Francis Edward (the
"Old Pretender") in 1766 marked the end of the Stuart cause.

Irish Jacobitism could not be detached from Catholic Ireland's
links to Catholic Europe. In many ways, the centre of gravity of
Catholic Ireland had been dispersed into émigré communities.
Alongside the existing network of Irish colleges and Irish military
emigration, Irish Catholic merchants had established themselves in
such cities as Nantes and Bordeaux; some certainly dabbled in the
slave trade from these ports, but the trade in wine and wool with
their former patrimony remained the primary occupation to most.
The Catholic mercantile elite who had emerged in Ireland's towns
and cities in the second half of the eighteenth century reached out
to their counterparts (and often their relations) on the continent.
Some Irish Catholics did reasonably well at home and abroad.

This is not to say that the socioeconomic issues that affected the
majority should be overlooked. Between 1740 and 1815 the dairy
industry expanded from west to east. A number of distinct regions
could be identified: dairy in the south and cattle fattening in west
Leinster and east Connacht, with tillage in Leinster. The latter facilitated food processing such as brewing and milling. But tillage
needed labour: hence the growth of an "underclass" of landless labourers. The less profitable western seaboard, on the other hand,
came to be dominated by small farms. Communal farming practices
such as *rundale* (in which a landholding was shared by a number of
individuals or families, with individual plots being allocated by lots
on a rotating basis) helped regulate the pressure of a growing population, by maximising the use of scarce resources on poor land.

This world was not hidden, and was not unsophisticated; but it
was often viewed with incomprehension by observers who dismissed
it as primitive. The expanding economy also stoked tensions between landlord and tenants. The relationships between these was
often policed by a range of secretive peasant societies, most famously
the Houghers and "Whiteboys" of Munster (the latter so called
after the rough disguises they wore). Agrarian unrest was often con-
flated with allegations of Catholic disaffection and Jacobite plotting

—white, after all, was a colour associated with the Jacobites—though sometimes such claims were little more than a pretext for harsh repression on the part of the magistrates drawn from the landed elite. Yet as the century wore on, change was in the air. In 1758 restrictions on full Catholic membership of guilds was successfully challenged. In 1760, during the Seven Years' War, a small French force briefly seized the Ulster town of Carrickfergus, which prompted a flurry of protestations of loyalty from a range of Catholic voices and led in turn to the creation of the "Catholic committee," an organisation composed of largely urban middle-class Catholics arguing for the repeal of the penal laws. The "Catholic question"—the readmission of Catholics to political and economic rights—would become one of the defining political issues of the second half of the eighteenth century.

Dissenters and Their Diaspora

Catholics were not the only victims of punitive legislation: Protestant dissenters were also targeted by the Anglican state. Ireland's Anglican elite were traditionally suspicious of nonconformists, but the Williamite war had seen Presbyterians fight alongside Episcopalians. This fortuitous coalition led some members of the Church of Ireland to conclude that ultimately Presbyterians and Anglicans would come together if faced by a common Catholic danger. Therefore, the necessity to ease restrictions on dissenters was not an imperative. Presbyterians naturally viewed the sacramental test of 1704 that restricted their participation in public life with great hostility, though by the 1720s a degree of de facto toleration was evident once again. Yet the penal laws continued to victimise Presbyterians and other nonconformists, albeit to a lesser degree than Catholics. Presbyterians, for example, could vote, but thanks to the 1704 act they were barred from holding public office. In addition, their marriages were not recognised by the law—an issue with very serious implications for the manner in which they might inherit land. On the whole though, their exclusion was less thorough than that of Catholics. A concrete sign of this was that Presbyterian clerics tended to be far more vocal commentators on public affairs than their Catholic counterparts.

The migration that had brought Presbyterians to Ulster in the first place had mainly come from lowland Scotland, which brought with it distinct cultural traits, such as local dialects, educational practises, vernacular architecture, and the oat diet. Links to Scotland remained strong; indeed, given that that they were effectively barred from attending Trinity College Dublin, Presbyterians who could afford a university education traditionally looked to the Scottish universities of Edinburgh and Glasgow. The last major influx of Scottish immigrants had come in the 1690s, but this was soon overshadowed by another migration, as many of the Scots in Ulster began to emigrate to North America. Unfavourable economic conditions —increases in rents and downturns in the textile trade—were crucial drivers of this migration, though the appeal of more land and fewer petty restrictions on the other side of the Atlantic should not be underestimated. Perhaps 150,000 Presbyterians left Ireland for North America between the 1680s and the 1830s (along with very substantial numbers of Catholics). The Delaware region became a key destination for Ulster emigrants, and the frontier regions of the Carolinas, Georgia, and Virginia saw major settlement from Ulster. Extensive transatlantic links were thereby forged in the eighteenth century: flaxseed imported from America subsidised people going the other way. Both Catholics and Presbyterians were deeply divided from one other in the Ireland of the ascendancy. Yet to a far greater extent than their Anglican rulers, both Catholics and Presbyterians lived in worlds whose mental and geographical maps extended far beyond Irish shores.

Women and Ethnic Groups

It may seen bizarre to consider women as part of a "hidden" Ireland; yet if membership of this hidden Ireland is defined by exclusion from public and political life, then Irish women were most definitely a part of it. Political life was, in purely institutional terms, a male preserve. Yet politics extended far beyond the membership of institutions such as parliament, and involved a much wider sphere of cultural politics that did include women. Even within the ruling elites of medieval and early modern Ireland, aristocratic women had played an influential role in political life; the right of women to inherit land and property gave them a degree of political, economic and social influence. Yet this only applied to the elite; further down the social scale, women could find a role for themselves as domestic servants. By the eighteenth century women were still excluded from formal political power, but the opportunities available to them expanded quite considerably. Women could carve out their own spheres of influence by setting up their own businesses, often in clothing and crafts, though some women in urban areas were forced into prostitution.

Marriage remained the most obvious gateway to women's formal status in society. But the institution of marriage was also linked to the "vicious and reprehensible" crime of abduction, which was often accompanied by violence and rape, ending in a forced marriage. As a crime, abduction was primarily economic in motivation and was very much a crime of the "middling" classes in origin, but violence against women was casual and common. Yet the fact that abduction was a capital crime hints at a more complex reality than just the existence of a patriarchal society.[4] A woman like Letitia Bushe, for instance, the daughter of a relatively minor landowner from Kilkenny who had intermittently held some public offices, could carve out a fulfilling and relatively independent life amidst "polite society" in Dublin and Meath in the mid-eighteenth century, while maintaining her own views on issues such as politics and war that were, in official terms, assumed to be purely male preserves; the very real constraints imposed upon Irish women in this period and others cannot tell the whole story of their experience.[5] Likewise, the intermittent presence in Hanoverian Ireland of black men and women from Africa or the East Indies—often domestic servants or slaves—points towards other dimensions of human experience that can be overlooked by historians.[6] There were many "hidden Irelands" in eighteenth-century Ireland.

CHAPTER TEN

Patriots

IN THE SECOND HALF of the eighteenth century a new, if loose, ideology, became fundamental to the self-image of many amongst Ireland's Protestant ruling class: "patriotism." The Protestant elite were British in ancestry, but as time went by, subsequent generations were Irish by birth, and became increasingly conscious of a distinct, and collective, Irish identity that was separate to that of Britain and was sharpened by resentment at Ireland's political subordination to Britain: surely Irish Protestants were the equal of their British counterparts, and should therefore enjoy the same rights without infringement? The legal basis of Irish Protestant "patriotism" lay in the implications of the Act for the Kingly Title in 1541 that had made Ireland a separate and distinct kingdom with a status commensurate to its English counterpart. This aspiration to equivalence had to be tempered by the blunt reality that Protestant security in Ireland—and Irish "patriotism" was a Protestant phenomenon —ultimately depended on the English (and later British) parliament; the power relationship between the two was profoundly unequal. But there was sufficient grounds for tension between the theory and the practice of the Anglo-Irish relationship to survive anyway. This could be seen in controversies over such issues as the "sole right," the disputed right of the Irish parliament to initiate financial legislation, which came to have a symbolic value as an issue on which the Irish parliament could assert its rights in the face of English influence in government.

One of the earliest and most famous statements in defence of the Irish parliament's right to govern without outside interference had come in 1698, after a collapse in English wool exports due to the exigencies of war prompted an attempt to ban Irish woollen exports to maintain a competitive edge. While this was achieved in 1699, it also prompted the publication of William Molyneux's tract *The Case of Ireland . . . Stated* (1698), which denied the right of what was then the English parliament to exercise its authority over its Irish counterpart (England and Scotland were united as a single kingdom with a single parliament in 1707). The controversy over William Wood's patent to mint coins for Ireland, as it played out in the 1720s, highlighted the key political issue that animated Irish patriots: English interference in what they increasingly perceived to be Irish affairs. Patriotism was not an unbroken tradition; but it was certainly a recurring theme, and it became more pertinent in public life from the 1740s onwards.

In 1741 an apothecary from Clare, Charles Lucas, was nominated to sit on Dublin's Common Council, the governing body made up of representatives of the guilds and other appointees, along with the lord mayor and twenty-four aldermen. The rights of the council were based on various medieval charters granted by the crown, but Lucas began to agitate for reforms of the council, contending that it was not governing in the interests of the citizens and was actively breaching the rights enshrined in the older charters. In 1749 he stood for election to parliament, and established his own campaigning newspaper, *The Censor*, to give full vent to his argument that the Protestant citizens and freemen of Dublin had rights that could be traced back to the middle ages, and that these had been eroded by the misconduct of the powers that be and centuries of British dominance. Lucas eventually had to flee Ireland after the House of Commons ordered his arrest. He went to Paris, Leiden, London, and Rheims before returning to Dublin in 1760. But he had let a genie out of a bottle. If, as he argued, the Protestants of Ireland were entitled to the same rights and privileges as their British counterparts, then the British parliament, and British administrators, had no right whatsoever to govern Ireland. This was the single biggest issue that Ireland's Protestant rulers would grapple with between the 1760s and the 1790s.

The manner in which they did so took new forms; the "Lucas affair" pointed towards the growth of polemical print culture and newspapers that could foster and reflect public opinion. This was not entirely new: Swift's *Drapier's Letters* had been a very public campaign against Wood's halfpence in the 1720s. But print culture was becoming increasingly important to Irish political and economic life. Literacy in English was increasing in the eighteenth century, fostered by various official and unofficial educational systems (such as the "hedge schools" that offered a basic education to many of the Catholic peasantry). Dublin was the world's second largest centre for printing in English, and the absence of any meaningful regime of censorship or copyright restrictions prior to 1800 allowed the print trade to flourish (often thanks to reprints and translations of British and continental publications). Political polemics may well have been restricted to Protestants who could officially take part in politics, but not all politics was institutional; the emergence of the Catholic question also prompted ventures into print from outside the formal boundaries of political life, as Catholic clerics and intellectuals like Cornelius Nary, Charles O'Conor, and John Curry tried to make sense of the circumstances in which their community found itself.[1]

Sectarian issues influenced intellectual life in surprising ways. Both Curry and O'Conor readily engaged in the pamphleteering which arose in part from a heightened antiquarian interest in the Irish past that developed in the course of the eighteenth century. This may have held out the possibility of revealing a history before the English conquest that Catholics and Protestants could engage with. But this posed awkward questions about the superiority (or otherwise) of the cultures that arrived after it; there could be a sectarian edge to antiquarian debates carried out by Catholic and Protestants over the nature and origins of the ancient Irish.

Perhaps inevitably, Quakers and Catholics were prominent in publishing in Dublin. Provincial publishing really only took off in the nineteenth century. Prior to that, the printers of Dublin had a long reach: there were well-oiled distribution networks for books, bolstered by the informal activities of small traders; there were perhaps eighteen hundred licenced pedlars in Ireland in 1750.[2] Printing in eighteenth-century Ireland took place overwhelmingly, but not exclusively, in English, though it would be wrong to assume that literacy was automatically confined to English and vice versa. It is true that the shift by which English replaced Irish as the vernacular language of most of Ireland's population was under way in the eighteenth century, but this language shift did not automatically require literacy. Scribal culture in Irish may have compensated for the dominance of English in print, and this remained vigorous well into the nineteenth century. It would also be wrong to say that the cultural and intellectual worlds of Irish and English operated in mutual isolation; quite the opposite.[3]

The scope for public debate was widened by political changes both at home and abroad. By the 1760s a sense had emerged that the "undertakers" who traditionally managed legislation through parliament had grown too powerful. This came to a head during the tenure of George Townshend, Viscount Townshend, who served as lord lieutenant in 1767–72. Having lost patience with the old system of parliamentary "management" as practiced by figures like John Ponsonby, Townshend sought to reassert the primacy of the government over an occasionally obstreperous parliament by cultivating new alliances in parliament, regaining control of the patronage that had previously been conceded to the undertakers, and also by establishing a visible presence in Dublin by residing in it more or less continuously, as he became the first eighteenth-century viceroy to do so. This new style of British government was naturally opposed by the burgeoning patriot constituency in parliament, but this group remained a fragmented and ineffectual coalition of diverse interests. What eventually welded them together into a more formidable and effective lobby was the crisis that erupted on the other side of the Atlantic in the 1770s.

Revolution in America

Ireland's links to the Atlantic world were strong and well developed by the 1770s, but the outbreak of war in the thirteen colonies in 1775 had a huge impact in Ireland, and for very distinct reasons. Given that the Irish parliament was technically subordinated to the British one, and that considerable trade restrictions had been imposed on Ireland since the end of the seventeenth century, the issues that animated colonists in North America—political authority, representation, sovereignty, the right to trade—undoubtedly had a resonance in Ireland. The rhetoric of Irish patriotism echoed similar concerns from across the Atlantic; as Benjamin Franklin had remarked, there were "many points in similarity" between the British dominions on either side of the ocean.[4] Even aside from the implications of the outbreak of the Revolutionary War for the Irish patriots, at least some Catholic poets (writing in Irish) rejoiced in the fact that the British were under pressure in North America, though this did not equate to overt sympathy with colonists who could be viewed, somewhat ambiguously, as akin to Ireland's Protestant elite.[5] In the decades after the failed Jacobite rebellion of 1745, the ideological focus of the Gaelic intellectual world began to transform from an explicitly Jacobite stance to one that could be categorised as Jacobitism without the Stuarts; it became increasingly attuned to Catholic identity and the grievances fostered by the penal laws.[6]

Unrest in the North American colonies also had implications for the Catholic question. By not permitting the recruitment of Catholics into the military at a time of global war between 1756 and 1763, Britain had been deprived of a major source of manpower. In 1774 a new oath of allegiance was devised that was no longer unacceptable to Catholics, which permitted their open recruitment into the army (a useful change in the law, given the need for additional troops to fight the colonists). The repeal of the hated sacramental test in 1780 was a gesture of a similar kind towards Presbyterians, while in the same year restrictions on direct trade with the colonies were finally lifted—an imperative largely driven by the requirements of the Revolutionary War. This could also be said, at least in part, of the Catholic relief acts of 1778 and 1782 that had ended restrictions on Catholic landholding and worship. It was increasingly felt, especially in Britain, that such restrictions on Catholics were redundant and unjust. There were also practical considerations to be borne in mind. It made no sense not to recruit Catholic soldiers when there was a pressing need for extra troops on the other side of the Atlantic; nor was it advisable to maintain lingering sources of Catholic resentment at a time when Catholic Ireland's traditional French ally was becoming involved in the war in North America. If Irish Catholics had not gone away, then they were not to be driven into a renewed alliance with an old enemy. The fact that the Catholic archbishop of Ossory, John Troy, condemned the American revolutionaries as "rebels" in February 1779 suggests that the prospect of securing Catholic loyalty to the state, as long demanded by Catholic lobbyists, was not as unrealistic as it might once have seemed.

The most dramatic political initiative of this era, however, came from Protestants. The Volunteer movement began in Ulster in 1779 as a militia that could defend Ireland against any foreign—French— invasion, thereby freeing up troops for the American war. There was a more deliberately political undertone to the new movement that merged seamlessly with the patriot tradition. The Volunteers were offering to defend Ireland on the basis that they would receive something from the British government in return, and consequently began agitating for reform of the restrictions on Irish trade. The most famous depiction of the Volunteers is Francis Wheatley's painting *A View of College Green with a Meeting of the Volunteers on 4 November 1779 to Commemorate the Birthday of King William*.[7] But Wheatley's picture had some critical omissions: it did not depict the various placards and banners that were actually displayed outside the parliament house in Dublin that day. These included "Free trade or else" and "Relief to Ireland" draped on the statue of William III, and "Free trade or speedy revolution" on a placard hanging from a cannon.[8] The Volunteer movement was the sharp end of Irish patriotism, demanding a greater degree of autonomy for Irish affairs from the British. The popular politics of the Volunteers came in many forms; alongside assemblies and marches such as that captured by Wheatley's painting, their message was disseminated in print, at commemorations, and through material culture.

The fact that the patriot campaign of the late 1770s was happening at the same time as the relaxation of the penal laws opened the door towards Catholics reentering public life, and leading patriots like Henry Grattan, a member of parliament from Dublin, encouraged them to do so. The campaign spearheaded by the Volunteers involved many who were normally outside the Irish polity: women, the mercantile middle classes, and of course Catholics. This was not universally popular either within or without the Volunteers, but the principle was of great importance at a time when, for some at least, the traditional reasons to be fearful of Catholics were receding. Earlier in the century, when Jonathan Swift had addressed the "whole people of Ireland" in his *Drapier's Letters*, that could be taken to mean the Church of Ireland community; by the late 1770s and early 1780s, such a narrow definition was far less valid. But the question of whether or not to bring Catholics in from the cold was not the most pressing issue in Irish public life at this particular moment. In the increasingly politicised climate, Irish prosperity was increasingly perceived to be the victim of British policy. This was not a new interpretation of Anglo-Irish relations, but for it to be highlighted at this juncture gave the issue a particular potency. There were no arguments in favour of leaving the British sphere of influence, but the terms of Ireland's involvement were at stake.

1782: "Legislative Independence"

The mobilising of the Volunteers had been followed by demands for political and economic change. They fact that the new movement supported such demands made it impossible for the British authorities to ignore them. In February 1782 at Dungannon in County Tyrone, Volunteer delegates assembled as a convention to demand political reform and Catholic relief. The obvious tenor of Irish public opinion, combined with British setbacks in America and a change of government in London, prompted negotiations with patriot leaders such as Grattan and the earl of Charlemont that led to the "legislative independence" of 1782. The key provisions of these reforms amended the ancient stricture of Poyning's law (which had ensured, amongst other things, that Irish legislation first needed to be approved in London), and, more important, repealed the Declaratory Act of 1720 that gave the British parliament the right to legislate for Ireland. That said, crucial reforms did not form a part of the overall package: the viceregal government would still not be accountable to parliament, the "management" of which was still possible. The willingness of the Irish patriots to gloss over such loopholes may have hinted at a lingering awareness that Protestant security in Ireland still rested ultimately on the British connection.

Catholic involvement in the Volunteer movement was by no means welcomed by all. By 1784 the Dublin volunteers were admitting Catholics; given that the right to bear arms was often assumed to imply a full participation in public life—citizenship, for want of a better term—the symbolism was obvious. But by this time the Volunteer movement was starting to run out of steam. The patriot campaign for reform stalled and declined in the 1780s after an abortive attempt to devise a commercial union between Britain and Ireland: the so-called "commercial propositions" of 1784–85. British pressure on William Pitt (prime minister since 1783) forced him to exclude Ireland from the lucrative trade of the East India Company and to include proposals that any Irish regulations on shipping would have to follow the lead of the British parliament, which prompted an Irish outcry. The proposals were passed in parliament by such a narrow margin that they were deemed unviable and were abandoned, though some subsequent legislation on navigation and trade reflected English models. In the years that followed, British influence in the Irish parliament was to be reasserted by a more conservative clique of Protestant grandees who were wary of the politics of patriotism, led by figures such as John Fitzgibbon, earl of Clare, for whom the Irish connection with Britain was the guarantee of Protestant safety.

Demography and Politics

The rapid changes in Irish political life that came in the latter decades of the eighteenth century went hand-in-hand with major social changes. The most obvious was that the Irish population had grown in the hundred or so years since the Williamite victory of 1691. It has been estimated that there were 1.75 million to 2.06 million people living in Ireland in 1706; by 1732, the number had increased to between 2.16 million and 2.53 million. The famine of 1740–41 took a toll, as the population dropped to between 1.91 million and 2.23 million in 1744, but it then increased dramatically to 4.4 million in 1791.[9]

This was simply the latest in the series of revolutionary transformations that Irish society had undergone in the 250 years since the Kildare rebellion. But the expansion of the population had another consequence: greater pressure on available resources seems to have increased socioeconomic and intercommunal tensions in certain areas.

The activities of agrarian organisations such as the Whiteboys were becoming increasingly sectarian by the 1780s, a decade that saw the growth of Protestant organisations such as the Peep O'Day Boys in mid-Ulster (a region with a very mixed population). It would not be long before such sectarianism would return to the mainstream after being briefly challenged by some elements of the Volunteer movement. The Volunteers' major contribution to Irish life was that they left behind a politicised people; they had expanded the boundaries of political life far beyond that of the Irish parliament and its limited electorate. As the Belfast Presbyterian William Drennan put it, "history can supply us with few examples of so great a change taking place by the immediate agency of the people."[10] And some would build on this legacy; Drennan himself was, within a few years, one of the driving forces behind the formation, in October 1791, of the Society of United Irishmen.

CHAPTER ELEVEN

The French Disease
and the Union

"A Plot for the People"

The United Irishmen were one of innumerable political clubs or societies to emerge in late eighteenth-century Ireland, and like many others, it had been created and energised in the wake of the French Revolution. The society was the brainchild of Drennan, a Belfast-born physician of liberal Presbyterian stock. Educated in Edinburgh, he had lived in Newry since 1782, where he had gotten involved in the Volunteer movement. In the 1780s he conceived of an organisation that would act as a hard core of radicals within the volunteers: as he put it in 1791, it was to be "a benevolent conspiracy —a plot for the people—no *Whig* club—no party title—the brotherhood its name—the rights of man and the greatest happiness of the greatest number its end—its general end real independence to Ireland, and republicanism its particular purpose."[1]

Drennan moved to Dublin, and like many others he arrived at the conclusion that the political reforms demanded by the radicals of the 1770s and 1780s could never succeed without the involvement of Catholics. He proposed the formation of a new organisation with a secular and democratic ethos to press for such reforms. This sentiment was shared, and was most famously articulated in a tract entitled *An Argument on Behalf of the Catholics of Ireland* (1791), written by a young Anglican barrister in Dublin called Theobald Wolfe Tone. His argument for the reform of what he deemed to be a corrupt and unrepresentative government rested on the assumption that such reforms could not be achieved without the backing of the Catholic majority who also had a stake in them. The tract was hugely successful, and in the wake of its publication Tone was invited to Belfast to attend the inaugural meeting of the new society in October 1791; a Dublin branch was founded in November. At the beginning, however, the real centre of its radicalism was among the Presbyterians of Belfast: the Dublin society was relatively moderate.

The key to the significance of the United Irishmen lay in their name—the fact that they forged an alliance between some Anglicans, some Presbyterians, and some Catholics—all of whom had grievances of one kind or another with how Ireland was governed. Presbyterians and Catholics, having been on the wrong side of the law for so long, naturally felt aggrieved, but many Anglicans took issue with what they viewed as the corrupt and unrepresentative oligarchy that governed their country. The unfulfilled promise of the Volunteer movement was a further source of discontent. There were bound to be tensions within this coalition—Presbyterians were traditionally the most anti-Catholic of all Protestants—but the outbreak of the French Revolution in 1789 had injected a new, secular dimension to Irish political discourse. Throughout the 1790s Paris was a regular port of call for Irish radicals. It was this engagement with the French that led the authorities to view the United Irishmen as a threat: a pro-French group could never be acceptable after the outbreak of war between Britain and revolutionary France in 1793.

The United Irishmen were initially a radical society typical of the time, making good use of the printed word to disseminate their ideas and even establishing their own newspaper: Samuel Neilson's *Northern Star*, printed in Belfast and, for a period, the most widely circulated newspaper in Ireland. The United Irishmen sought to lobby for a radical change in the government based on what were, at least in religious terms, egalitarian ideals. They were able to tap into older patterns of radical politics left over from the 1770s and 1780s. But when war broke out in 1793 they came under pressure from the authorities, who were faced yet again with a French enemy overseas, and who sought to ensure that it stayed there. To that end the government offered a further Catholic relief act in 1793: having been permitted to practise law in 1792, Catholics were now given the right to bear arms, to attend Trinity College, and to hold some civil and military offices; plus, the right to vote in elections for parliament was extended to some Catholics, those known as the "forty-shilling freeholders." The act was intended to further secure Irish Catholic loyalty; both the British and the Catholic Church faced a common enemy in the form of the new and aggressively secularist republican government in France, and this forced them into an unlikely alliance against what one bishop dubbed a "French disease."

If Catholic relief was the carrot, there was also a stick with which to beat down any pro-French sympathies, and the United Irishmen were the most obvious target. The organisation was suppressed in 1794, but it reorganised in 1795. Having been driven underground, the natural radicalism of the United Irishmen became streamlined as it was transformed into a conspiratorial revolutionary movement, intent upon staging an uprising against what it viewed as the British government in Ireland and its Irish Protestant proxies. The ill-fated appointment of a liberal viceroy, William Wentworth, earl of Fitzwilliam, served as an example of precisely what the United Irishmen opposed: having indicated his preference for further Catholic relief and after dismissing a number of senior officials, Fitzwilliam was recalled, to be replaced by the more conservative Lord Camden. The episode was resented by Irish reformers of all faiths, as it seemed to highlight that a conservative and ultra-Protestant junta continued to exercise control over the government of Ireland.

The United Irish centre of gravity began to shift from Belfast to Dublin, especially after 1796. Wolfe Tone himself (who had previously been exiled to the United States) ended up in Paris seeking French assistance for a prospective United Irish rebellion. In December 1796 his efforts paid off when a French fleet of fifty ships carrying 13,500 troops left France for Ireland. But storms scattered them, and only thirty-five ships with 6,400 troops—still a substantial force—arrived in Bantry Bay, on the coast of Cork. They were unable to land due to bad weather, and soon returned to France. But the very presence of such a force struck terror into Irish loyalists and the government, who were painfully aware of both the relative weakness of the available military forces in Ireland and the danger that the United Irishmen could pose in alliance with the French. While there was little that could be done about the French, it was within the power of the government to grapple with their potential allies in Ireland. Government attempts to suppress the United Irishmen intensified dramatically in the aftermath, with the infamous "dragooning" of Ulster in 1797 witnessing brutal and provocative raids for weapons and suspects conducted across the northern counties.

By this time, however, the United Irishmen had morphed yet again, and had forged alliances with the so-called Defenders: the descendants of the movements for Catholic agrarian redress, such as the Whiteboys, that had existed in the latter half of the eighteenth century. The Defenders first emerged in the border zone between Ulster and Leinster, extending across into northern Connacht: areas of mixed population that were also the cockpit of a good deal of sectarian tension (the foundation of the Orange Order, a Protestant fraternity organised along masonic lines and first established in County Armagh in 1795, was one outcome of this). But the Defenders were organised on a national scale, and alongside demands for the redress of economic grievances—the traditional stock in trade of such organisations—the Defenders were more explicitly sectarian and politicised than their predecessors. Traces of Jacobite rhetoric seem to have survived in the beliefs of the Defenders, most obviously in hopes of restitution for Catholics and the overturning of Protestant ascendancy with the aid of revolutionary France.[2] The alliance between the United Irishmen and the Defenders means that contemporary claims that hundreds of thousands were involved in Ireland's revolutionary underground may not have been too far off the mark. The derogative term "croppy" was a product of this era—a reference to the fact that members of the United Irishmen allegedly cropped their hair in emulation of French revolutionaries.

The 1798 Rebellion

In the early months of 1798 the brutal repression undertaken in Ulster by General Gerard Lake was extended across the rest of the country after Lake was promoted to commander-in-chief of the army, a move welcomed by zealous loyalists, but which surely fanned the flames of what happened later in the year. Arguably this was the point: floggings, house-burnings, torture, and mass arrests were supposed to provoke a reaction and thereby bring the simmering prospect of rebellion out into the open. By March 1798 matters were rapidly reaching a head. Most of the United Irish leadership were arrested in Dublin on 12 March (apart from the colourful figure of the aristocratic Lord Edward Fitzgerald, whose military experience fighting in North America had given him a key role in formulating the military plans). In May weapons and documents were found in Dublin, and the authorities rightly concluded that a rising was imminent. The planned rebellion in Dublin was due to break out on 23 May and revolved around the seizure of a number of key locations in the city centre. On the appointed day there was still uncertainty about whether the rising was to happen, and the form it might take, but that evening the Yeomanry were called out to occupy marketplaces such as Smithfield and Newmarket that had been earmarked as assembly points for the Dublin United Irishmen; the rebellion in Dublin was stopped before it could begin. But the associated risings around the edges of the city did take place, in counties Wicklow, Kildare, Meath, and north county Dublin. Some of the mail coaches leaving Dublin were stopped, which had been the signal to rise. Fighting took place at the Hill of Tara in Meath in subsequent days, and on 29 May hundreds of unarmed prisoners were massacred on the plain of the Curragh in Kildare. The focus of the rebellion soon shifted away from Dublin.

The 1798 rebellion lasted a matter of weeks; modern estimates of the death toll usually specify an upper limit in the region of thirty thousand, but we will never know for certain. There were three principal zones in which the rebellion took place. Having broken out in Leinster in May, the epicentre of the rebellion became the southeastern county of Wexford before it erupted in the Presbyterian heartlands of eastern Ulster. The Wexford uprising began with a number of rebel victories, such as the captures of the towns of Wexford and Enniscorthy. Ferocious fighting took place in some localities (such as New Ross) before a rebel force of around twenty thousand strong was defeated at Vinegar Hill outside Enniscorthy on 21 June, and the rebellion in the southeast was crushed. Wexford was also the venue for two notorious sectarian atrocities carried out by members of the United Irishmen, when a barn filled with Protestant prisoners at Scullabogue was set alight, and seventy prisoners were stabbed to death in Wexford town with pikes (the weapons that later became the ubiquitous symbol of the events of 1798). Government forces were also responsible for widespread and bloody excesses, such as the mass shooting of untried suspects at Dunlavin in County Wicklow. Yet at the time (and in subsequent polemics) these killings in Wexford seemed to confirm the fears of loyalists that, regardless of the republican principles of the United Irishmen, the events of 1798 simply constituted another sectarian war along the lines of 1641. This belief managed to survive the fact that the second major focal point of the rebellion had been in counties Antrim and Down, where the United Irishmen who rose up were Presbyterians rather than Catholics.

The rebellion in Antrim was suppressed brutally after the United Irish forces there were defeated at the battle of Ballynahinch on 12 June. There was, however, a postscript in County Mayo in August, when a small number of French troops under Jean Joseph Humbert landed at Killala and embarked on a lightning campaign through Connacht. They scored a notable victory over British forces at Castlebar—whose retreat became immortalised as the "races of Castlebar"—and got as far as Ballinamuck in County Longford, where they surrendered to a much larger force under the Marquess of Cornwallis on 8 September. The French had been deeply unimpressed that the popular rising they were led to believe would happen never occurred; while the French were treated as prisoners, their Irish allies were decimated as rebels. The "year of the French"—*bliain na bhFrancach*—was short lived in reality, but had a long afterlife in folklore. A second French expedition was intercepted in October 1798 en route to Lough Swilly in north Donegal; it was important mainly for the presence on board of Wolfe Tone, who now held a commission in the French army. He was sentenced to death as a rebel—which meant he faced hanging—and his demand to be executed as a prisoner of war instead, by a firing squad, fell on deaf ears. Tone died after attempting to cut his own throat in captivity. His death provides a neat coda to the events of 1798. The rebellion had failed, but the tradition of republican separatism that it created would be revived again in the course of the nineteenth

century. There were other issues, however, to deal with in the immediate aftermath.

The events of the 1790s highlighted divisions between the British and the Protestant ascendancy; while their view of themselves
may have changed over time, the British view of their purpose had
not. If the Protestant ruling elite in Ireland were supposed to be
looking after Irish affairs and therefore safeguarding British interests, then the events of 1798 showed that they had failed miserably
in that task. The rebellion was a disaster from a British point of
view. It had either been provoked by heavy-handed repression, or
had been permitted to happen due to neglect. Either way, the French
should not have been offered such an inviting foothold in Ireland.
Ironically, the British held Irish Protestants partially responsible for
what had happened in 1798, and in the aftermath Prime Minister
Pitt revived an older idea: union.

The Act of Union: Motives and Methods

The Act of Union of 1800 ended Ireland's status as a separate kingdom and integrated it into the newly expanded United Kingdom.
The parliament in Dublin was abolished; Irish parliamentary representatives would sit in Westminster instead. On one hand, the union
was intended to bind Ireland closer by extending British control
over it more firmly; on the other, it was intended to offer a salve to
the persistent sectarian divisions that characterised Irish life, with
particular reference to Protestants. The fact that they remained a
minority in Ireland was to be offset by the fact that they would become part of the majority in the United Kingdom. But at the time,
many in the Irish Protestant elite were hostile to the proposals for a
union presented by Cornwallis and the chief secretary, Viscount
Castlereagh; the basis of this opposition ranged from lingering patriot sentiment to commercial considerations to a fear that the union
would ultimately threaten Protestant "ascendancy" in Ireland.

The proponents of the union were defeated in parliament in
January 1799. The second attempt to pass the union came in 1800,
complete with greater incentives for the correct vote: various in-
ducements, in terms of "compensation," patronage, and de facto
bribery being used to construct a majority. It passed on the second

attempt in 1800. The Catholic community were kept onside by a private understanding that emancipation—the granting of the right of Catholics to sit in parliament—would follow the union, an intensely symbolic move that would illustrate to Irish Catholics that they were officially part of the polity. This was, however, scuppered on sectarian grounds by the hostility of King George III; the unfulfilled promise would rankle. In the meantime, on 1 January 1801 the United Kingdom of Great Britain and Ireland came into existence, an event marked by the introduction of a new flag; the current version of the union flag was first flown in Dublin, and the union that it symbolised would remain Ireland's constitutional framework for the next 121 years.

Bold Emmett, 1803

A coda to the passage of the Act of Union came in 1803 when the United Irishmen made a second attempt at rebellion under the leadership of Robert Emmet. The Emmet family were prosperous; his father, also Robert, was the state physician. The son's older brother, Thomas Addis Emmet, was a Dublin lawyer who had joined the United Irishmen in 1792. He was close to many of the senior figures, defending them in court and providing legal advice as required. His brother Robert had joined them in 1796, and was expelled from Trinity College for his pains.

The rebellion he later attempted to plan was a direct response to the failure of 1798. As early as January 1799 the United Irishmen had begun to regroup, and to plan for a renewed offensive. In April 1799 Emmet fled to Hamburg to avoid arrest, thence to France, where he tried to get French assistance for another rebellion. But the French were uninterested, and disillusioned, he returned to Ireland in October 1802 and continued to conspire. His rebellion was intended to be a smaller but more purposeful affair, concentrated on Dublin, that would involve a much tighter and smaller band of conspirators; there was to be no repeat of the attempted mass insurrection of five years earlier. Like its predecessor, however, the rebellion of 1803 was originally to have been predicated on French assistance.

Dublin was to be the key. There were ambitious plans to decapitate the government by killing or capturing the viceroy and the privy council, and by capturing Dublin Castle itself. The preparations (with an emphasis on urban warfare, complete with folding pikes, customised guns, and logs packed with black powder with pieces of metal and nails bound to their exterior to clear troops off the streets) went largely unnoticed by the new post-union administration in Ireland. A crucial element of the plan involved insurgents from neighbouring counties flooding into Dublin. But a large explosion at one of Emmet's city centre arms depots on 16 July killed two people and forced the date for the insurrection to be brought forward to 23 July. What followed is in stark contrast to the extent of the preparations. Rebel forces did assemble at a number of points in the city, but in the end Emmet called off the rebellion by firing a rocket into the air, and most of those around the city stood down. Emmet himself led a group on an attack on Dublin Castle after reading out extracts from a proclamation. The chief justice, Lord Kilwarden, was piked to death that evening. Having hid in Wicklow, Emmet himself was captured on 25 August. His trial on 19 September facilitated one of the most famous speeches in Irish history, in which he assured his listeners that he would have fought the French as readily as the British if they had attempted to impose tyranny on Ireland, and implored his followers not to write his epitaph until Ireland took its place among the (independent) nations of the earth. Emmet was executed in Dublin the next day. His final resting place remains unknown.

Where Historians Disagree

W AS EIGHTEENTH-CENTURY IRELAND A kingdom, a colony, or a fairly typical ancien régime society? Questions of identity muddy the waters around this issue. Protestant political identity in Ireland did not automatically conceive of itself as Irish: when, in the 1690s, tensions between Protestants in Ireland and the British state came to the fore, the notion of a common origin was the basis of William Molyneux's argument that Ireland should receive equality of treatment, as it was a kingdom rather than a colony.[1] Amongst modern historians, the most compelling and sustained argument against viewing Ireland as a colony has come from Sean Connolly in his influential study of Protestant—Anglican—Ireland after 1660. Given that, as he claimed, "Ireland was not in any very clear sense a colony," he argued instead that Ireland was no different to most European ancien régime societies, and that its primary dynamics were social rather than ethnic or religious (though he later qualified his dismissal of the colonial model with regard to earlier periods).[2] The most potent critique of this has come from Vincent Morley: the argument that Ireland was an ancien régime society cannot work if one looks at the totality of relationships in Irish society, because it excludes the Catholics who made up the bulk of the population, and who had their own views on the matter.[3] If Ireland was an ancien régime society, then it was a Protestant one.

The Protestant nature of the eighteenth-century Irish state inevitably leads to consideration of the penal laws. How significant were they in reality? If the eighteenth century is indeed the period of Protestant ascendancy, then a long-running and contentious issue is the precise nature of the laws that facilitated this. Critiques of the historiography of the penal laws are nothing new, and there is some degree of scholarly consensus about their broad contours.[4] While consistent, they were hardly systematic, and their actual implementation and impact varied enormously. Even when the willingness to enforce them was there, the resources with which to do so were not; there were various loopholes by which they could be avoided, sometimes even with the connivance of liberal or friendly Protestants. The most notable (if contentious) reassessment of them in recent decades has been in relation to their objectives: Connolly argued that rather than being a repressive corpus of legislation directed at Catholics in general, as traditionally assumed, they were instead directed at "one segment of the country's natural ruling elite"—namely, the Catholic one.[5] But given what happened in the reign of James II, that segment of the ruling elite targeted by the law after 1691 was chosen precisely because of its Catholicism. The most recent exhaustive study of any of the penal laws, the laws of 1695 disarming Catholics and preventing their education overseas, concludes that they were an explicit response to the danger perceived by Irish Protestants from both the Catholic majority on the island and the newly reinvigorated (and newly Jacobite) Irish military diaspora on the continent, the Wild Geese.[6] In this interpretation, the piecemeal formulation of the penal laws was a logical continuation rather than a new departure. They may not have been systematic in their formulation and implementation, but their attempt to tackle Protestant fears of a Catholic enemy remained broadly consistent. The relationship between the Catholic community and a Protestant state is of great importance to the question, noted earlier, of whether eighteenth-century Ireland can be classed as a colonial society. Kevin Whelan's excavation of the Catholic "underground gentry" argues that their existence points to this conclusion, a view disputed by Toby Barnard, who argued in response that social and cultural barriers were far more fluid than that might imply.[7]

Some of the other major questions about eighteenth-century Ireland relate to the community that was officially discriminated against by the penal laws. In the 1920s Daniel Corkery famously wrote of a "hidden Ireland": another social and cultural world cut off from the English-speaking Protestant elite by a range of barriers, not least by language.[8] In the eighteenth century, Irish was still the most widely spoken vernacular. The Irish-language tradition remained strong, especially in Munster and south Ulster, which were also seen as hives of Jacobite activity.[9] Much, if not most, Irish Jacobite ideology would have been expressed in the Irish language. What other beliefs were articulated in Irish? Gaelic poetry makes up the only major source for the history of the mindsets and beliefs of the Gaelic world, but in the past the poems have been dismissed too readily. One historian recently claimed: "Poetry and prose in the Irish language have started to be reinterpreted. The results do not always inspire confidence that startling new perspectives will be revealed."[10] But "poetry and prose in the Irish language" has been interpreted and reinterpreted for much of the twentieth century, and scholars have mined Irish manuscripts to reveal the extent of popular politicisation and ideology. Irish was not a barrier to a sophisticated understanding of the world at large, despite arguments that the poetry is essentially devoid of any ideological significance.[11] There have been groundbreaking studies in recent years that have used Irish-language source material to great effect. Éamonn Ó Ciardha exploited Irish poetry in his study of Irish Jacobitism (which Breandán Ó Buachalla did on an even larger scale in his Irish-language work on the same subject).[12] The same is true of Vincent Morley's study of the impact of the American Revolution on Ireland's three major religious groupings.[13] And crucial events could have an afterlife: Guy Beiner wrote a pioneering study of the folk memory of 1798 in Mayo, much of which was expressed in Irish in the twentieth century.[14] Gaelic Ireland was a cosmopolitan society, tied to the wider world by links obscured by a focus on Anglophone Ireland.

Following on from this is the question of how ideas disseminated, and popular politicisation. To that end, social and cultural history has not, as yet, always been fully connected to the political, though Padhraig Higgins's work on the Volunteers demonstrates how political messages could be refracted through material culture and popular street culture.[15] Equally, Jim Livesey's study of the commercial propositions points to how political, economic, and intellectual history can usefully be blended together, rather than kept in their distinct categories.[16]

The question of popular politicisation has particular implications for studies of the 1790s. It is often assumed that the high-minded ideals of the United Irishmen collapsed in the face of the naked sectarianism of the Catholic peasantry. Sectarianism in 1798 has often been highlighted (most recently by Tom Dunne), but it cannot be the whole story of the 1790s.[17] Ó Buachalla has also examined how the continuity of ideology and rhetoric survived the end of the Jacobite cause into the era of the Defenders and United Irishmen, in terms of the overturning of Protestant ascendancy, and how such ideology mutates into a form that reemerged in the crucible of the 1790s.[18] Higgins's study of the Volunteers also indicates how political ideologies could evolve over time. Ian McBride has also written an important study of the radical political beliefs of Irish Presbyterians, who can be overlooked by concentrating on how the politics of the 1790s emerged from the earlier politics of patriotism and the Catholic question.[19]

The United Irishmen also would have used prophecy to get their message across: it was a powerful force in popular culture, and the ways in which the United Irishmen exploited popular culture in general have also been explored by Whelan.[20] That said, this is intensely subjective territory, and precise answers can be hard to find.[21] But politicization could have a material basis, with deep roots in a particular physical and cultural environment, as probed by Breandán Mac Suibhne in relation to the northwest in the last quarter of the century.[22] Ireland had, by the 1790s, a well-developed "public sphere": newspapers, reading societies, and coffee houses (not just in Dublin, though they were understandably most numerous there). The rhetoric of the enlightenment was common in public discourse. While issues such as economic improvement and the Anglo-Irish relationship traditionally loomed large, the religious tolerance of enlightenment had been invoked in support of the Catholic question in previous generations, and in favour of a union between communities that could defeat British self-interest (along lines suggested by Tone). But the dissemination of such ideas did not just involve the imposition of ideas imported from France; they evolved locally as well. If public life in Ireland was infused with the ideals of the enlightenment, as argued by Ultan Gillen, these came with a distinctive inflection created by "the governmental system, political culture and societal divisions resulting from the Glorious Revolution and Williamite Wars, and from Ireland's connection with Britain."[23]

PART IV

The Nineteenth Century

CHAPTER TWELVE

The Age of O'Connell

The Withholding of Catholic Emancipation

The Act of Union radically changed Ireland's political landscape. True, the "ascendancy" remained a crucial and significant governing class in Irish life, and would remain so for generations. But while the economic power and social status of the Protestant elite remained reasonably intact, their political power had undergone a fundamental change. The limited autonomy of the Irish parliament was gone, as Ireland was now politically integrated into the new, expanded United Kingdom. The small, embattled Protestant minority within Ireland had been converted into part of a Protestant majority in the United Kingdom; a practical expression of this was that the established churches of England and Ireland were to be united. But in purely political terms, the next logical step after the union was to complete the process of bringing Catholics in from the cold: Catholic emancipation.

The union was intended as a bulwark against revolution, but that did not mean it was impervious to reform. The demands for Catholic relief articulated since the 1750s had been met, to a large extent, by the relief acts of the late eighteenth century, but Catholics were still denied some rights. Not only were they barred from sitting in parliament, but a range of senior political and legal offices remained closed to Catholics by the necessity to swear oaths that a

Catholic would find repugnant. Most obviously, Catholics (and Jews) could not sit in parliament. It made sense, given the underlying purpose of the union, that Catholics should be fully integrated into the state; indeed, Pitt and his colleagues fully anticipated that emancipation would follow. But to assume that this would automatically happen is to underestimate the level of hostility Catholic emancipation provoked in Britain at both elite and popular levels, and in Ireland. And such hostility started at the top: the king, George III, was a vocal and resolute opponent of Catholic emancipation. The Catholic Committee remained active, but its efforts were hampered by ongoing disagreements over the terms of emancipation: most crucially the extent to which the state might play a role in the workings of the Catholic Church, as seen in a proposal in 1808 to guarantee clerical loyalty by permitting a state veto over appointments to bishoprics. Despite intermittent attempts to pass bills for Catholic emancipation through parliament, often spearheaded by liberal Irish Protestants such as Henry Grattan, such efforts foundered prior to the 1820s. In that sense at least, the union proved a bitter disappointment to the majority, and their would-be representatives.

The 1820s: Captain Rock and the "Second Reformation"

The "Catholic question" remained the dominant political issue in the decades after the union, and the continued exclusion of Catholics from high office seems to have facilitated a sharpening of sectarian self-awareness. Certainly, Catholic emancipation was discussed in a more encouraging climate by 1820 in Westminster, as the administration of Robert Peel presaged a thaw in official attitudes towards the issue. When the new king, George IV, visited Ireland in August 1821, huge and enthusiastic crowds greeted him; a popular (if mistaken) belief that he favoured Catholic emancipation probably helped. The appointment of Sir Richard Wellesley (the duke of Wellington's brother) as a pro-emancipation viceroy was indicative of a sense that Catholics were coming in from the cold. Yet this coincided with the so-called "second reformation": an evangelical drive carried out by a range of Protestant churches and organisations, and which intersected with the prolonged crisis—an economic depression, along with the famine and typhus epidemic of 1817—

that followed the end of the Napoleonic wars. Such hardships prompted waves of renewed agrarian unrest, in a combination of sectarian and class warfare directed at the landholding classes and carried out by a range of shadowy organisations, such as the Caravats and Shanvests in Munster (1806–16), and culminating in the rise of the "Rockite" movement of 1821–24. Active in counties Limerick and Cork (though spilling over into neighbouring counties), the Rockites (named after the pseudonym of "Captain Rock") were akin to previous agrarian movements such as the Whiteboys and Rightboys, with its armoury of threatening letters, extreme violence in attacks on landlords and property, and grievances over rents, tithes, and access to land. They were more obviously sectarian than their predecessors, but they also, on occasion, grasped towards a political consciousness, as one threatening notice posted in Tipperary in 1821 put it:

> We are pressed by the tyrannical laws of the English government which we cannot endure no longer, to which they crowd us up with rents, tithes and taxes which we daily sustain the burden of . . . English laws must be curbed in, for we will never be satisfied until we have the Irish parliament and king crowned in Ireland as there formerly was.[1]

Such sentiments were not unusual.

O'Connell and Catholic Emancipation

If the 1820s saw the rise of the mythic Captain Rock, they also witnessed the political coming of age of Daniel O'Connell. Amongst Irish political leaders, O'Connell looms large, not least for the manner in which he operated. O'Connell came from a prominent and wealthy Gaelic Catholic family in Kerry, one that had, like a few others, retained their wealth over the course of the eighteenth century (and added to it by smuggling). Educated in France and England, the young O'Connell had been repelled by the excesses of the French revolution. Libertarian in outlook yet socially conservative, he opposed the Act of Union and became a successful lawyer after it, and by the 1820s had become a notably more assertive voice on the

Catholic Committee. By this time the older aristocratic leaders of the committee were being been eclipsed by middle-class Catholics such as O'Connell who were opposed to any limits or restrictions being imposed on the issue of emancipation.

The foundation of the Catholic Association by O'Connell in 1823 was a new departure in the politics of Catholic emancipation. Marked by the involvement of the Catholic clergy, funded by the so-called Catholic rent (a membership fee of one penny per month), and characterized by the charisma and oratorical brilliance of O'Connell himself, the association grew rapidly, drawing in the Catholic peasantry who, if they were unlikely to benefit directly from emancipation, were enthused by the prospect of even a nominal victory on behalf of the community from whence they came. The Catholic rent was the key to mass participation, and ensured a much broader base of support than that of its fractured predecessor. The methods of the Catholic Association—mass meetings (O'Connell grasped the importance of the numbers game), petitions, propaganda—were all reminiscent of the older tactics of the Volunteers and the Catholic Committee, while they were also an early example of the mass politics that would become a fixture of Irish political life as the century wore on. The Catholic Association deftly exploited the newly invigorated and aggressively ambitious Roman Catholic Church, along with the increasing sociability of Irish life that was taking more concrete form via the expanding networks of fairs and markets. It was suppressed in 1825 (only to be replaced by the "New Catholic Association"). But O'Connell forced the issue again, in a campaign culminating in his election as a member of parliament for County Clare in 1828 (ironically, against a liberal Protestant who supported emancipation). The reality of O'Connell's being elected forced a reluctant British government to finally concede the right of a Catholic to take a seat in parliament. To not do so was to risk serious unrest, and O'Connell entered the House of Commons on 4 February 1830. Catholics could now sit in parliament, and became eligible for all but a handful of public offices (although they were still barred from ascending to the monarchy). The victory was offset by the property qualification for the franchise being raised substantially, which meant the disenfranchisement of much of the Catholic electorate: the number of Catholic voters was reduced by 80 percent. But this did not obscure the symbolic import of the victory won by the man who became known as "the Liberator": in the course of his campaigns, O'Connell had seemed to articulate the aspirations of the historically dispossessed Catholic community, and would do so again.[2]

The Impact of the Union

While O'Connell entered parliament, the state he now officially operated in was extending its reach to virtually all aspects of Irish society. Despite the introduction of the union and the integration of the two parliaments, after 1800 Ireland and Britain were to be governed in different ways. A separate administration, distinct from the Irish MPs in Westminster, remained in Dublin Castle. In the early 1800s the government began to distance itself from overtly sectarian celebrations such as the anniversary of the battle of the Boyne; St. Patrick's Day was identified as a much less divisive official occasion.[3] The Catholic question notwithstanding, there was also an economic dimension to the union: Ireland and Britain were now in a free trade area, though duties were to remain on certain key goods until the 1820s.

Against the backdrop of the Napoleonic wars, the opening years of the nineteenth century witnessed widespread food shortages and agrarian unrest. This was especially true in the west and southwest, where even before the union was passed there had been an outbreak of militant and brutally violent agitation against tithes—a form of tax payable to the established church, regardless of religious affiliation—in the aftermath of 1798. But such hardship, while widespread, was not universal; the end of the Napoleonic wars in 1815 hastened the end of an economic boom facilitated by Britain's access to the continent being cut off, and a slump in demand. Older North American markets had given way to a British market in the course of the war with France. Equally, established industries such as textiles and manufacturing were vulnerable to British competition; and when the tariff walls established by the union came down in the 1820s, to be followed by an economic downturn, the impact on the wool and cotton industries was devastating. The traditional artisan industries of Dublin's Liberties—most especially textiles—were hit particularly hard. More generally, the demographic expansion of the late eighteenth century had created newer tensions, as population growth continued even as the economy began to stagnate. On the other hand, the linen industry of the northeast underwent a revival: in short, Belfast boomed while Dublin declined. There were success stories—brewing and distilling grew to prominence, and advances in infrastructure such as railways and the steamship opened up new British markets for Irish produce—but the Irish economy after the union was not in the rudest of health. It was also subject to unprecedented demographic pressure. The Irish population jumped from approximately 5 million in 1800 to 6.8 million, according to the first census in 1821. By 1845 it stood at perhaps 8.5 million, with the highest growth rates being noted in Connacht (27.8 percent) and Munster (23.8 percent), which saw their population grow at roughly twice the rate of Leinster (12.3 percent); Ulster's population increased by 19.4 percent.[4]

The rural inhabitants were the inheritors and bearers of a rich oral tradition. And it was a sociable culture: song, dance, storytelling, sporting events, and fairs were key parts of life for the rural poor. Beliefs in the supernatural coexisted with a vernacular Catholicism infused with folk traditions, such as wakes and patterns (the latter were the traditional devotional practices, including feast days, associated with Christian saints; as time went by, these public gatherings were viewed with mounting distrust by the authorities). This rich cultural world was articulated, in much of the country, in the Irish language; there were more Irish speakers in the first half of the nineteenth century than ever before. While this was an overwhelmingly oral culture, remnants of the scribal tradition survived, but this was a society undergoing a sure but steady linguistic transformation. The threatening letters of the Rockites, for example, were written in English, albeit often imperfectly—a concrete sign of the penetration of English amongst the peasantry. Such was the world of the Irish peasant, marshalled by O'Connell and scrutinised by its imperial masters.

As for those at the top of the social pyramid, the old ascendancy retained a great deal of power and influence, and continued to occupy many of the offices of government at the local and national levels. Yet the 1820s and 1830s saw the state reach into hitherto undisturbed corners, as the expansion of its coercive and adminis-trative capacity slowly but surely eclipsed the local notables who traditionally dominated Irish society. Ireland was minutely exam-ined by a plethora of parliamentary inquiries (such as the Poor In-quiry of 1833–36), and the 1830s saw the creation of a fledgling national education system, the extension of the Poor Law to Ire-land, the establishment of the Ordnance Survey, and the creation of a formal Irish constabulary, along with new local administrative units such as grand juries and boards of works. Major developments in infrastructure also took shape in this increasingly commercialised economy; networks of mail cars were established, providing the first public transport in the country, via horse-drawn carriages, followed by railways in the 1830s.

The growth of mass literacy amongst the Irish population dates from the second half of the eighteenth century.[5] There were a num-ber of reasons for this. During a time of relative stability, Ireland's commercial economy began to expand rapidly; the records of com-merce were usually written down. The same was true with regards to politics: the turbulence of the 1790s saw both urban and rural Ireland being flooded with tracts, posters, handbills, books, and newspapers. Organisations such as the United Irishmen used words as a key tool in their attempts to turn the world upside down, but their opponents did likewise in order to maintain the status quo. In addition to such earthly conflicts, words had a role to play in spread-ing messages about worlds to come. The "second reformation" of the 1820s saw both Catholic and Protestant churches use the printed word as a tool to win converts to their creeds. The rapidly expand-ing bureaucracy of the British state in Ireland also depended on the written word for its administration. It can be debated whether these developments reflected a literate population that already existed, or whether they created one. The statistics for literacy that we have for this period need to be treated with caution, and the very notion of literacy can have a wide range of meanings. But the fact remains that by the middle of the nineteenth century the printed word had as-sumed a role in Irish society that it had never possessed before.

What is less contentious is that literacy in English very obvi-ously went hand in hand with education. In 1824, out of a popula-tion of 6.8 million there were as many as 560,000 attending a wide range of primary schools, mostly locally based unofficial "hedge" schools, so-called because they assembled wherever they could, even outdoors. Political impulses could sometimes be discerned within these. Thomas Crofton Croker's pen portrait in 1824 of the archetypal hedge-school master, to whom parents would pay a modest fee, depicted him as the propagator of historical consciousness characterised by firm belief in the existence of British oppression, the strength of Irish patriotism (apart from the occasional traitors), and the utter rejection of the legitimacy of British rule in Ireland; he was "frequently the promotor of insurrectionary tumults" to boot.[6] In 1831 the national school system was created, complete with a set curriculum, in an attempt to standardise the education system. The hedge-school master, as defined by Crofton Croker, would presumably have been unwelcome in the new system.

The Repeal of the Union: Arguments For and Against

Following the success of the campaign for emancipation, O'Connell directed his attention to a greater target: the Union itself. "Repeal of the Union" became the catch-cry of his second great campaign, and from 1832 O'Connell was insisting that prospective members of parliament who wanted his support would have to take a pledge that they would back repeal; thirty-nine Irish MPs were subsequently elected having subscribed to this idea. The precise meaning of repeal was always ambiguous, but the broad thrust was clear: in 1800 the British had deprived Ireland of its parliament, and in the decades since then, British rule had been the font of injustice and hardship. The restitution of a parliament to College Green was to be the panacea for such ills. But it was evident by 1834 that there was little appetite for such a measure in Westminster. The demand for repeal was offset somewhat by a loose alliance that O'Connell entered into with the Liberal government in the 1830s, resulting in a limited number of reforms. Opposition to the hated system of tithes had prompted major unrest during the "Tithe War" of 1830–33; such agitation was defused somewhat in 1838, when tithes were combined with the rent due to landlords, who then became responsible for their payment. The reform of Irish local government in 1840 paved the way for O'Connell's election as lord mayor of Dublin in 1841: the first Catholic to hold the office since 1691.

In 1840 O'Connell founded the repeal association and in 1843— the "repeal year"—orchestrated massive rallies in support of the objective. He also began to demand the calling of a "council of 300"; an embryonic assembly to press forth the cause of repeal. Those rallies at which the Liberator himself was present became huge theatrical spectacles: "monster meetings," often held at sites of symbolic importance, such as Tara in County Meath. As one anonymous balladeer commented on the meeting at Tara:

Hurrah for Dan and noble [Thomas] Steele,
The pride of Erin's nation,
In spite of Wellington and Peel,
We'll gain our liberation

And as he concluded:

God bless our Queen, long may she reign,
What foe dare to offend her?
Granua's [Ireland's] sons, with swords and guns,
Are ready to defend her.
Long live each man that joins with Dan,
No matter what communion,
But in spite of all the Tory clan,
We will repeal the Union.[7]

"Repeal" did not mean republican separatism; the message was one of self-government. And at these vast gatherings, the spectacle was as important as any speech. Estimates of attendance at the monster meetings of 1843–45 depended upon the sympathies of the observers: the numbers reported present at the meeting held at Castlebar in County Mayo in July 1843 ranged from fifteen thousand to three hundred thousand.[8] O'Connell could hardly be heard by such a huge throng, but music and visual accompaniments such as decorations and even elaborate physical displays would be used to drive the point home; those watching would also get the message. There were official restrictions on flags and banners that could be deemed provocative, but these could be circumvented by the brandishing and wearing of ribbons or plants (conveniently green in colour), which also served to display support for O'Connell and his cause while evading formal restrictions. Processions and parades would usually be followed by the actual meeting, and eventually by a smaller celebratory banquet, in what amounted to an elaborate piece of sustained political theatre. But not every place was prepared to bear witness. Only one of O'Connell's monster meetings was held in Ulster (in Monaghan in 1843). Protestant Ulster was not receptive to the message being put forth by an overwhelmingly Catholic mass movement.

But a confrontation with the authorities was inevitable, and it came at Clontarf, outside Dublin, in October 1843. The prime minister, Sir Robert Peel, declared the meeting illegal; O'Connell declined to force the issue and, by backing down, did massive damage to his reputation. He sought to explore a new alignment with the Whigs, but his career was in decline thereafter. He died in 1847, but events the following year hinted at a different vision of how Irish nationalists might articulate their objectives.

Young Ireland and the Rhetoric of Nationalism

In 1842 a loose coalition of younger nationalists aligned with the repeal movement had begun to publish a newspaper called the *Nation*. Inspired by the Italian nationalist movement of Giuseppe Mazzini, they became known by a similar name: Young Ireland. They were firmly non-sectarian in outlook; as the first editorial of the *Nation* put it, "There are, in truth, but two parties in Ireland: those who suffer from her national degradation, and those who profit by it."[9] The group consisted of such individuals as Thomas Davis, John Blake Dillon, George Gavan Duffy, and John Mitchel, and they initially enjoyed good relations with O'Connell, but things became strained as O'Connell adopted a more stridently Catholic attitude toward educational reform. He had often proclaimed that he did not wish to replace Protestant ascendancy with a Catholic equivalent, but his firm alignment with the Catholic Church forged a potent and enduring nexus between Catholicism and constitutional Irish nationalism (a combination that the Protestant population of the northeast found particularly repugnant). When Peel proposed to establish a network of universities in Belfast, Cork, and Galway, it met with ferocious opposition; figures as diverse as the evangelical Tory MP for the University of Oxford, Sir Robert Inglis, and the Roman Catholic archbishop of Tuam, John MacHale, both denounced the scheme as "godless." O'Connell aligned himself with the Catholic hierarchy, much to the distaste of the Young Irelanders.

A final breach came in 1846 over the question of whether to abjure the use of force in pursuit of political objectives such as repeal, or even Irish independence. Young Irelanders wanted to keep this door open and, in 1848, inspired by the French revolution of that year, they carried through on the commitment. That summer, against the backdrop of famine and an increasing level of government repression of perceived political dissent, a small revolt broke out in late July in County Tipperary spearheaded by William Smith O'Brien. It lasted a matter of days and resulted in two deaths. In the aftermath, its leaders were convicted of treason, but their death sentences were commuted to transportation to Australia. Yet the significance of Young Ireland did not lie in their abortive insurrection. In the pages of the *Nation*, they had articulated a new form of Irish cultural nationalism, one that emphasised the particular history and culture of Ireland in a way that could be shared by all across sectarian divides, just as some Protestant and Catholic antiquarians had attempted in the eighteenth century. They also propounded a language and symbolism in which such ideas could be adequately expressed. This was to be a very different, and longer lasting, successor to the patriot belief of the preceding century. But the death of O'Connell in 1847 and the Young Ireland rebellion of 1848 were overshadowed by events that saw the immediate exigencies of life and death take priority over the relative abstraction of political demands.

CHAPTER THIRTEEN

Famine and Diaspora

People and Potatoes

The famine of the late 1840s—*an gorta mór*, or "the great hunger"—is the most important event in Irish history between the union of 1801 and the achievement of independence in 1922. The Irish population went from 8.2 million in 1841 to 6.5 million in 1851; on the eve of the famine, in 1845, the Irish population may have been in the region of 8.5 million. Within that drastic loss of population, a death toll of one million people from malnutrition, starvation, and disease is hardly unrealistic.[1] Emigration accounted for the remainder. Central to the famine was the failure of a single crop, the potato, which seems to have been introduced to Ireland in the late sixteenth century. Initially used as a garden crop, by the end of the eighteenth century it was a fixture of Irish life, with the high-yield "lumper" potato (which had arrived in Ireland via Scotland) soon to become the staple diet for the poorest section of a rapidly expanding population, as poor land was colonized by potatoes; Ireland's moist climate and acidic soil offered the perfect conditions for its widespread cultivation, especially along the Atlantic seaboard. The massive expansion of dairy had forced many of the rural poor to shift towards the potato, and to physically move onto upland areas. The potato displaced "whitemeats" (dairy) and pulses in the Irish diet.[2]

Those people most dependent on the potato were the impoverished small farmers and landless labourers at the bottom of a complex, stratified system of landholding. A recurring theme in the accounts written by visitors to Ireland in the pre-famine era is the appalling material deprivation of that vast underclass. The former slave Frederick Douglass, who visited Ireland in 1845, told his fellow abolitionist William Lloyd Garrison: "I had heard much of the misery and wretchedness of the Irish people, previous to leaving the United States, and was prepared to witness much on my arrival in Ireland. But I must confess, my experience has convinced me that the half has not been told." Douglass was horrified by the squalor of Dublin's streets, and the wretched villages that skirted the city. He who had seen the slave's cabin wrote that "of all the places to witness human misery, ignorance, degradation, filth and wretchedness, an Irish hut is pre-eminent."[3] While such impressions may have been shaped by travels in summer months, between harvests when work was scarce, the sheer extent of Irish poverty was no illusion: the 1841 census recorded that 51 percent of dwellings were fourth class, officially described as "mud cabins having only one room."[4] Yet the census could not tell the whole story, and the complex and multifaceted nature of pre-famine rural society often passed observers by, and more positive features of Irish society often escaped attention. Indeed, visitors arriving during the summer came at a time of underemployment and food scarcity before the harvest, so they were seeing the country at its worst.

At the bottom of Ireland's social pyramid were the cottiers: labourers who rented a cabin, and possibly a small subsistence plot, from farmers or landlords, often in exchange for their labour rather than a cash payment. At the top of the pyramid was the Protestant landed elite. But between these two extremes was a multilayered land system, and throughout this segment subletting and subdivision were prevalent. Within this system, the potato played a key role. Its high yield and dietary qualities ensured its importance as a foodstuff as much as a fodder crop; indeed, the same visitors who were appalled by the poverty of the Irish could also be bemused at the fact that they were healthy physical specimens. The height of Irish recruits to the East India Company in the late eighteenth and early nineteenth centuries, for instance, shows them to have been in good physical shape.[5] The potato was a remarkably complete foodstuff, being a valuable source of carbohydrates, proteins, and vitamins B and C. When consumed in large quantities—as much as ten to fourteen pounds per adult male per day—and combined with dairy products, it made for a highly nutritious (if unvaried) diet. Before the famine of the late 1840s fully one-third of Irish agricultural output was devoted to potato tillage. The colonisation of marginal ground unsuited to either tillage or livestock was successfully managed by the potato; whether this was a cause or a consequence of the rapid population growth of pre-famine Ireland is unclear, but the two were surely connected.

The famine itself had a straightforward cause. A strange disease that attacked potato plants was noted in Belgium in June 1845. It had reached Dublin by August and was observed nationwide by early September. The fungus that caused it, *phytophtera infestens*, devastated potato crops in Ireland in 1845 with frightening rapidity and effectively eradicated them in 1846. The impact of "the blight" was not confined to Ireland: potato crops were devastated across the continent in the mid-1840s, but no segment of the population of any other European country depended upon the potato to the extent that the Irish poor did; the consequences were disastrous, as famine was the result.

Famine

There had been periods of dearth due to poor potato harvests in the 1820s and 1830s. But the failure of the 1840s was on a different scale. The collapse in the potato crop was catastrophic. In 1845, 2.4 million acres were devoted to growing potatoes in Ireland; by 1847, thanks to the ravages of the blight, that number had collapsed to 284,000 acres. In 1845 perhaps a third to a fourth of the crop failed, prompting emergency relief measures by the Tory government of Sir Robert Peel, who, to circumvent the protectionist Corn Laws that restricted cereal imports to the United Kingdom, ordered the surreptitious purchase of maize in North America and the opening of food depots along the west coast of Ireland. But the partial failure of 1845 was followed by a complete failure in 1846, as the spores of the fungus were washed into the ground in the course of a wet winter, to reemerge the following year. This major crop failure saw the first reports of fatalities, and relief works began; the 130 workhouses established under the Poor Law of 1838 were under pressure by the end of the year. The workhouse system was infused with a moralistic purpose: the strictly regimented rules to be found within their walls were intended to deter all but the most genuinely destitute. But these, and such public institutions as existed (such as dispensaries), were never designed to cope with a crisis of the kind they now faced.

Unrest manifested itself from an early stage. A particular source of anger was the continued export of cash crops in the early years of the famine, which prompted food riots in coastal towns and cities; by the end of the crisis, the British garrison in Ireland had nearly doubled in size, from 15,000 troops in 1843 to 29,500 in 1849. Strikingly, more money was spent on security throughout the period of the famine, £14 million, than on famine relief: £9.5 million. Yet even as official coercion was readily deployed, government relief measures did have an impact: by the end of 1847, seven hundred thousand people were employed on public works, with soup kitchens feeding huge numbers between January and October 1847. But in 1847 the burden of relief was shifted onto the Irish Poor Law under the new Whig-Liberal government of Sir John Russell. Irish resources were to pay for what was deemed to be an Irish problem, despite the fact that Ireland was a part of the United Kingdom, and public works were to justify the administration of relief. There were limits to official charity, and despite the obvious effectiveness of the soup kitchens, they were phased out. Senior treasury officials such as Charles Trevelyan articulated a myopic vision that the famine was the unavoidable consequence of various Irish social evils, which needed urgently to be reformed; in this reading, the famine was a symptom rather than a cause, and offered an opportunity for re-moulding Irish society. The view of the British government was that the relief of the famine was a responsibility that should fall upon the shoulders of Irish landlords, as they were responsible for the plight of their tenants. While some landlords behaved responsibly and humanely, others—and many strong farmers—used the famine as a pretext for widespread evictions, or profiteered from the crisis.

On the whole, the official reaction, in terms of the deployment of the state's resources, was inadequate: an additional £50 million may have been required to replace the food that had been lost. But even that expenditure might not have offered a full solution.[6] Private charity went some way towards plugging the gap. Quakers, for example, organised charity drives across the United Kingdom and North America to alleviate, to some degree, the desperate human reality of the famine. A harrowing account of a visit to Belmullet in Mayo—the county most badly ravaged by the famine—was left by the English Quaker William Bennett:

> The scenes of human misery and degradation we witnessed will haunt my imagination, with the vividness and power of some horrid and tyrannous delusion, rather then the features of a sober reality . . . perhaps the poor children presented the most piteous and heart-rending spectacle. Many were too weak to stand, their little limbs attenuated—except when the frightful swellings had taken the place of previous emaciation—beyond the *power of volition when moved.* Every infantile expression entirely departed; and in some, reason and intelligence had evidently flown. Many were *remnants of families,* crowded together in one cabin; orphaned little relatives taken in by the equally destitute, and even strangers . . . they did but rarely complain. When inquired of what was the matter, the answer was alike in all—*"Tha shein ukrosh"* —*indeed the hunger.* We truly learned the terrible meaning of that sad word, *ukrosh.*[7]

It is only through such testimonies that the voices of famine victims can be heard.

While deaths from starvation were widespread, malnutrition opened the door to the most assiduous killers: diseases such as typhus, dysentery, and cholera. The precise death toll was almost certainly higher than that suggested by the 1851 census, on which details of deaths outside the public institutions were to be recorded by family members. But what if an entire family was dead, or had emigrated?

Racist and sectarian attitudes can be discerned in some British responses to the famine. What was deemed to be the callous stance of British officialdom was roundly condemned by Irish nationalists, and indeed by many other British and Irish contemporaries. The highest death rates during the famine were to be found in the south and the west, the areas that also saw the highest confirmed deaths from outright starvation. Massive migration into major coastal ports such as Belfast, Cork, and Dublin provoked unrest in the form of riots over work and food, while also placing great pressure on the existing infrastructure of the cities: in Dublin, disease seems to have been a bigger killer than outright starvation. The impact of the famine mirrored the east-west divide between a relatively literate, Anglophone, mixed economy and a largely illiterate, Irish-speaking agricultural region. The western half of the country had the worst dwellings, the lowest rates of literacy, and the highest proportion of people employed in agriculture; areas with more mixed economies, such as the northeast, were better equipped to deal with the crisis. But the sheer scale of the catastrophe and its repercussions—the depopulation, the subsequent shift in land use, the triggering of emigration and its consequences—had a profound and irreversible effect on Irish society. Nowhere was left untouched.

The Irish Diaspora

Between 1801 and 1921 perhaps as many as 8 million people emigrated from Ireland. Even before the famine, the Irish were the major source of overseas labour for both Britain and the United States. The vast majority of these migrants were under thirty, and between 1820 and 1845 migration by families was relatively low. Yet this changed dramatically during and after the famine: between 1845 and 1852 perhaps 1.4 million people left Ireland. There was occasional state assistance for emigrants from the 1820s to the 1890s, and landlords sometimes paid for emigration in order to free up land occupied by unprofitable tenants. But the bulk of the financial aid that facilitated emigration came from those who had already left: perhaps £34 million was sent to the United Kingdom, mostly to Ireland, between 1848 and 1887.[8] The famine migrants were drawn largely from the poor; more of them were Irish speakers than not, and more were Catholics than Protestants. The poorest areas of the country along the western seaboard, from Mayo to Cork, were the most drastically affected by the famine, yet they had strikingly low rates of emigration; the inhabitants were too poor to leave. Assisted passage, whether by public or private means, accounted for only a small number of migrants. Their impact in their destination was huge, though there were common denominators within the experience of famine emigrants in their various destinations: they lived in poor conditions, tended to find employment as manual labourers, and were often the victims of prejudice. The majority of emigrants, like the majority of famine victims, were from the lower social classes. Seasonal migration now hardened into permanent departure.

Britain was a crucial and often unavoidable destination for Irish emigrants: in 1846, of 301 ships carrying Irish migrants to New York, 214 had come from Liverpool, though as time went by the necessity to travel via British ports to the United States and Canada lessened, as direct crossings from Ireland became more common. In the decades after the famine, ongoing emigration ensured that British cities such as Liverpool and Glasgow acquired substantial and prominent Irish communities; the existence of Celtic Football Club in Glasgow today is an enduring legacy of this. For those who kept going, the northeastern United States was a key destination, with port cities like Boston, New York, Philadelphia, and Baltimore acquiring an enduring Irish complexion. New York received 900,000 Irish immigrants between 1845 and 1855, and eventually had more Irish born residents than Dublin, with districts such as Five Points and institutions like Tammany Hall, the headquarters of the Democratic Party in the city, becoming dominated by the Irish. It should also be noted that the Irish language became part of the vernacular of the American cities to which the Irish flocked. The impact of the famine was registered within the dwindling Gaelic scribal tradition, and large numbers of such manuscripts emigrated with their owners.

The massive rates of emigration witnessed during the famine were never replicated, but mass emigration had begun and did not cease. Although the scale of emigration might fluctuate—a recession in the United States in the 1870s resulted in a dip—it remained a fact of Irish rural life that was impervious to the views of priests and politicians. One consequence of the famine was a change in the manner in which land was inherited: there was a definite shift away from the subdivision of smallholdings into even smaller, uneconomical units. This lessened the options available to members of the next generation in rural Ireland who would normally have expected to inherit something; the fact that they were now faced with the prospect of inheriting nothing helped to push people out. Emigration became an integral part of Irish life in the second half of the nineteenth century, and the Irish population declined at a remarkable rate.

In the aftermath of the famine the widespread migration of children was noted from western counties like Cork, Galway, and Kerry. In the forty years before the First World War, the United States was the main destination for emigrants from the west of Ireland; emigrants from the north and northwest favoured Canada, and the phenomenon of "chain migration" saw families, and sometimes whole communities, slowly move en masse. The Irish migration to the states coincided with the expansion of many U.S. cities that now became homes to the new arrivals, who mainly became labourers and servants in their new land; domestic service accounts for the very high rates of female emigration to the United States in the decades after the famine, and also the prominence of Irish women in those occupations. When the incendiary English author James Anthony Froude travelled to America on a lecture tour in 1872 after publishing a history of Ireland that many deemed to be little more than a extended diatribe against the Irish, it was noted that Irish servants refused to deal with him on his travels, a small indication of how prevalent they had become on the eve of the gilded age.

The Irish in the Empire

There was, however, another obvious destination for Irish migrants: the British empire itself. The empire received its share of Irish migrants during and after the famine: 70,000 Irish settled in Australia in 1845–55 (many of whom, including the Young Irelanders George Gavan Duffy and William Smith O'Brien, were transported as convicts); an additional 175,000 emigrants arrived in Australia from 1855–60. Even aside from deported convicts, there was another factor that meant migration within the empire was not always a person's choice: very often it was an unavoidable requirement of the particular jobs that many Irish people were doing, as soldiers or administrators. One consequence of the repeal of the eighteenth-century penal laws was that Catholics could now enter the service of the state, and for the majority of those Catholics, the most obvious state institution to offer employment was the army. In 1830, 42.2 percent of the British army—40,979 soldiers—were Irish, when Ireland made up only 32.2 percent of the United Kingdom's population (though by 1898 the number had dropped to 26,376). The Irish were also overrepresented in the armies of the East India Company prior to 1857. They were most common in the infantry (many emigrants enlisted outside Ireland), though the famine affected both the quality and quantity of recruits.[9] The army offered a path out of poverty, and sometimes perhaps an alternative to judicial punishments.

Even aside from the rank and file, the Irish Protestant elite was well represented amongst the officer class: Arthur Wellesley, duke of Wellington, was born in Dublin (though he reputedly dismissed his place of birth on the grounds that being born in a stable did not make one a horse). Religious division was an issue that the army sought to avoid in the nineteenth century, and sectarianism in the ranks was not encouraged; the Orange Order was banned from the army in 1822, and Catholic chaplains were gradually accepted. By the second half of the nineteenth century any lingering wariness about the loyalty of Irish soldiers had to be reconciled with basic military requirements. If stationed in Ireland, the army was obliged to deal with law and order. The foundation of the Irish Constabulary in 1836 had taken the army off the front line, but soldiers remained a vital adjunct to the civil power.[10]

Military service was not just confined to Ireland; there was also an empire to be fought for. In the Indian mutiny of 1857, perhaps half of the East India Company's army of 14,000 strong was Irish. The Irish remained prominent in the British army after the company's rule in India was ended—reflected in the fact that the eponymous hero of Rudyard Kipling's famous novel *Kim* (1901) was the son of an Irish soldier—and also in the new Indian Civil Service, which opened the door to new applicants on a meritocratic basis. In 1857 one-third of all recruits to the Indian Civil Service were Irish, a proportion that made the government in London sufficiently uneasy that it rigged the recruiting procedure in favour of Oxbridge and away from the Queen's Colleges in Ireland, all of which, alongside Trinity College, were offering courses in Indian languages and history. Between 1886 and 1914, 80 percent of such Irish recruits to the bureaucracy of the Raj were Catholic.[11]

Catholic (and, to a much lesser degree, Protestant) missionary activity also took place under the auspices of the empire; Catholic missions were especially important in sub-Saharan Africa, though the Irish presence did not restrict itself to the jurisdiction of the British empire.[12] At home, the material culture of British rule became increasingly evident in Irish cities and towns; the British empire was an essential backdrop to Irish life, but the traffic went both ways. British rule in Ireland became an important reference point for British rule in India; the office of the Indian viceroy, established in 1858, was apparently based on the Irish version.[13] Likewise, the application of scientific techniques to imperial rule followed precedents set in Ireland; the Irish Ordnance Survey of the 1830s was the model for the Great Trigonometric Survey of India conducted between the 1850s and the 1870s. Yet this transmission of people and ideas within the empire does not mean that the Irish population was reconciled to membership of it. Some Irish nationalist commentators were critical of the British response to the Indian mutiny and were sympathetic to what they interpreted as a revolt against oppression; they also drew unfavourable comparisons between British rule in Ireland and imperial rule elsewhere.[14] The widespread and understandable assumption that the catastrophe of the famine was the product of British misrule left a potent legacy at home and abroad; a legacy that, at the same time as the Irish were becoming prominent in the British Raj in India, began to manifest itself in militant and influential ways.

CHAPTER FOURTEEN

New Departures

Socioeconomic Change

In the generations after the famine, Ireland underwent a series of profound cultural, economic, and social transformations: mass emigration and population decline; increased urbanisation (most obviously seen in the massive expansion of Belfast into an industrial city of global significance); and changes in the structure of rural society, as the cottiers were virtually wiped out and a new Catholic middle class began to emerge in both town and countryside.

Emigration was perhaps the single most important driver of change at all levels of Irish society. The Irish population halved in the sixty years after the famine, as emigration whittled away at the numbers living on the island and the birth rate declined (immigration was the exception rather than the rule). Rents did not increase at the same rates as prices, but due to the modernisation of farming practices in an increasingly commercialised economy, agricultural labourers lost out in post-famine Ireland. Such labourers can be difficult to fully differentiate from the farmers they worked for, as many engaged in farming themselves. But the rural labouring class was undoubtedly shrinking in the post-famine era; the shift in Irish farming from tillage to pasture saw the demand for labour decline, and the labouring classes were further eroded by emigration. Livestock was more profitable, and the proportion of Irish farmland

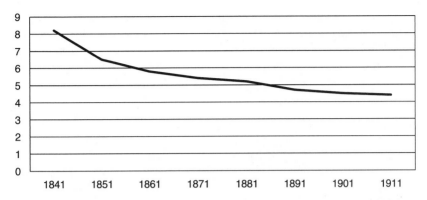

The decline of the Irish population (in millions) from the 1840s to the eve of the First World War. The natural rate of population increase was consistently over-taken by higher rates of emigration in the decades after the famine. (Source: A. J. Fitzpatrick and W. E. Vaughan, eds., Irish Historical Statistics: Popula-tion, 1821–1971, *Dublin: Royal Irish Academy, 1978)*

given over to meadows and pasture jumped from 68 percent in 1851 to 79 percent by 1876.[1] Munster saw the greatest shift (pasture al-ready predominated on the poorer lands of Connacht). Land was now at a premium, and less became available to sublet to labourers. A shift away from the tradition of partible inheritance also pushed up the age of marriage; if fewer landholdings existed to be distrib-uted, there were also fewer opportunities for either marriage or a livelihood on the land. The numbers of those who never married increased, and the alternative to a celibate life was emigration (though in the post-famine era admissions to the new system of dis-trict lunatic asylums, established to deal with the mentally ill, also increased substantially).

Farmers now took over as the dominant component in Irish rural society. The overall number of farmers in Ireland declined from 732 out of every 1,000 of the male population in 1831 to 547 by 1911. But whereas in 1841 there were 271 labourers for every 100 farmers, by 1922 that number had declined to 131, a decline that may have eased class tensions by draining away many of the "have-nots" in Irish life.[2] Wages and life expectancy went up in Ire-land between the famine and the First World War, but emigration

Table 2. Social change in post-famine Ireland, as reflected in changing farm sizes. The decreasing number of farms under 30 acres corresponds to an increasing number of farms over 30 acres, as land holdings were consolidated, a phenomenon that contributed to emigration and the rise of the rural middle classes.

Year	1–5 acres	5–15 acres	15–30 acres	30–50 acres	50–100 acres	100–200 acres	over 200 acres	Total over 1 acre
1860	82,800	181,400	140,900	72,400	54,000	21,700	10,100	563,200
1870	74,300	171,000	138,000	72,400	55,300	21,700	9,800	542,500
1880	64,300	161,300	136,500	72,900	56,200	22,400	9,900	523,600
1890	60,800	155,800	134,200	73,700	56,600	23,000	10,000	514,000
1900	62,200	154,800	133,500	74,000	57,600	23,100	9,800	514,900
1910	62,100	154,100	136,700	75,900	58,700	22,800	9,400	519,800

Source: Central Statistics Office (http://www.cso.ie/en)

may have played a part in this by reducing demand for resources and competition for employment.

A new rural middle class began to emerge in the form of the larger farmer. The proportion of the rural population living in a house with five or more rooms went from 17 percent in 1841 to 27 percent in 1851, and to 56 percent in 1901; this was a testament to the social changes that had come in the wake of the famine, as the old cottier class was eradicated from Irish life and the middling farmer became the most numerous and vocal constituency in the Irish countryside. These farmers were matched by the rise of a new urban middle class in Irish towns, often tightly bound to the farming classes by familial and marital ties and shared economic interests. People increasingly purchased their food rather than growing it themselves, and the Irish diet also changed during these decades, though not necessarily for the better: white bread, for instance, became much more common, but was a far less nutritious alternative to potatoes.

The necessity to purchase extended to a wide range of goods: clothing changed too, due to changes in leisure practices, fashion, and the standardising of styles arising from commercial production. Shopkeepers and publicans thus became increasingly important as many Irish towns began to reorient themselves to cater to the farming community that was developing. By decimating the rural under-class, the balance of cultural influences—such as language and religious practice—shifted decisively in favour of the newer Catholic middle classes.

Rural labourers were not the only ones to lose out in the post-famine era; rates of female employment (in occupations such as labouring, spinning, and weaving) declined from 28 percent in 1851 to 19.5 percent in 1911). But industries such as brewing, milling, and food processing did well. The industrial heartlands of the north-east boomed—shipbuilding became a huge industry in Belfast—and this economic growth attracted British migrants to the northeast. The most distinctive cohort of immigrants included eastern Euro-pean (especially Lithuanian) Jews who began to settle in Belfast, Cork, Dublin, and Limerick. Leopold Bloom, the protagonist of James Joyce's novel *Ulysses* from 1922, was the product of a mixed marriage between a Jewish immigrant and an Irish Protestant mother, but as created by Joyce, his background, language, and even his politics would almost certainly have made him an outsider in the Yiddish-speaking world of Dublin's "Little Jerusalem." Nonethe-less, Bloom remains an enduring (if not quite accurate) representa-tion of Dublin's once thriving Jewish community.[3]

Religious and Cultural Change

The sectarian struggles for hearts and minds of the 1820s did little for conversion but had an impact on interdenominational relations. In 1834, 80.9 percent of the Irish population were Catholic, 10.7 percent were Anglican, and 8.1 percent were Presbyterian. By 1901, 74.2 percent were Catholic, 13 percent were Anglican, and 9.9 per-cent were Presbyterian (from the 1850s on, evangelism had become more pronounced in all the mainstream Protestant churches).[4] The Protestant community was strongly concentrated in Ulster and more thinly dispersed elsewhere; outside Ulster, the Anglican strong-holds were Dublin and Wicklow. Anglicans were overrepresented in the Irish landowning classes; and while there were major Presbyte-rian landowners, Protestants of all denominations were well repre-sented within the commercial and professional classes. That said, the gradual erosion of Anglican privilege culminated in the disestablish-

ment of the Church of Ireland in 1869. This loss of status can be
contrasted with the fact that its Catholic rival was technically going
from strength to strength. Both major churches had been reformed
and streamlined in the early nineteenth century, but in the post-
famine era the Catholic Church became notably more disciplined
and efficient. The ratio of Catholic priests to people in 1840 was
one priest per 2,750 people; by 1900 it had shifted to one priest per
900.[5] The population declined, but the ranks of a newly assertive
Catholic clergy were swollen; the new Catholic middle classes provided the bulk of the new clergy, as the hegemony of "respectable"
Catholic society became increasingly secure.

The Roman Catholic synod held in the Tipperary town of
Thurles in August–September 1850 was a seminal event; it served to
streamline trends that were already under way prior to the famine,
while providing the institutional framework within which the Irish
Catholic Church became markedly more energetic and efficient in
the decades after the famine. The convening of a national synod
formed part of the specific instructions issued by the Vatican to the
newly appointed primate of all Ireland and archbishop of Armagh,
Paul Cullen, who had been given the status of apostolic delegate for
the very purpose of convening it. The synod was the first of its kind
since the middle ages. Amongst its recommendations were the condemnation of the "godless" Queen's Colleges established in Cork,
Galway, and Belfast in the 1840s; renewed demands for a Catholic
university; the administration and discipline of the clergy who would
be trained at the seminary in Maynooth was to be improved, with
the sacraments to be brought into appointed places of official worship; and conversion to Protestantism was to be resisted. The emphasis on discipline reflected Cullen's authoritarian and ultramon-
tane view of the church; its influence would be felt for a very long
time indeed. Roman Catholic bishops such as Cullen presided over
what was, in many ways, a new Catholic Church. The "devolutional
revolution" in Irish Catholicism superseded many traditional customs; indeed, the rich vernacular culture of Ireland was seen by
many observers to have been devastated by the famine. Connacht
had relatively low rates of mass attendance, but a strong attachment
to vernacular religion could be seen in the region. The latter was hit
hard by the famine.

It seems reasonable to assume that these Catholic reforms intersected with the aftermath of the famine in a way that aided their
acceptance. The institutional Catholic Church presided over by
Cullen may well have filled a void. The dramatic increases in the
number of its clergy, and the expansion of teaching orders such as
the Christian Brothers testified to its increasing power and influence, reflected in higher rates of mass attendance, and an increasing
inclination to adopt a role in policing public morality. The vernacular architecture of Ireland after the famine also reflected the new
prominence of the Catholic Church. The ending of penal restrictions on Catholic landowning had opened the door to a new wave of
church building in the eastern half of Ireland in the generation prior
to the famine. Thurles crystallised these existing trends; they may
have helped to facilitate the imposition of the church's new discipline, as there were now more formal venues for worship established across the country. Yet this new post-famine Catholicism also
had a cultural and social impact. The church was hostile to unregulated, allegedly immoral gatherings; this hostility had an impact on
traditions of music and dance. Equally, traditional games such as
hurling (which was already disliked by graziers intent on using their
lands for cattle rather than as venues for sport) attracted the ire of
the clergy who deemed such sporting contests to be unregulated,
overly boisterous gatherings. The Catholic Church was also profoundly hostile to a new organisation that had emerged in the aftermath of the famine in both Ireland and North America: the Fenians.

The Fenians

On 17 March 1858—St. Patrick's Day—James Stephens, Thomas
Clarke Luby, and John Denieffe founded a secret, conspiratorial
group in Dublin that was intended to secure Irish independence
through force. A veteran of 1848 who had since spent time in Paris,
Stephens had come into contact with Irish-American elements interested in orchestrating another rebellion. The origins are obscure,
as is the original name, but at some point the group became known
as the Irish Republican (or sometimes Revolutionary) Brotherhood.
The term "republican" had, by this time, come to mean a separatist;
if Ireland was to break away from British rule, it would do so in the

form of a republic of some kind. The following year John O'Mahony founded a sister organization in New York, the name of which soon came to used for both branches: the Fenians.

It was a popular movement, and it grew rapidly on both sides of the Atlantic. Outside of Ireland it garnered support from the embittered emigrants who had left during and after the famine, many of whom found their way into the ranks of both the Confederate and the Union armies in the American Civil War. Indeed, 38 of the 86 federal troops present at Fort Sumter in South Carolina when it was attacked in the opening engagement of the war were Irish, and perhaps 150,000 Irishmen fought in the Union army over the next four years, with another 20,000 in the Confederate forces.[6] Therefore, there were large numbers of hardened Irish troops who might be cajoled into fighting in the uprising that the new organization was dedicated to fomenting. It also made headway within ranks of the British army, with its large Irish component. The IRB was an oath-bound secret society, organized along cellular lines into hierarchal "circles" that were meant to be difficult to infiltrate. Conversely, the group was not averse to orchestrating major public events, such as the funeral of the Young Irelander Terence Bellew McManus, whose body was repatriated from the United States to be buried in Dublin in 1861. However, the Catholic Church was deeply hostile to secret, oath-bound conspiracies in general, and the Fenians in particular; one Catholic bishop famously stated that hell was not hot enough, nor eternity long enough, for the punishment of its members.

In 1863 Stephens established a newspaper, *The Irish People*, dedicated to spreading the gospel of republican revolution. It was written and administered by senior figures in the movement—Stephens, Luby, Jeremiah O'Donovan Rossa, and Charles Kickham—and, at the time of its suppression in 1865, had a circulation in the region of eight thousand. It was distributed quite widely in Ireland, and also in British cities with substantial Irish communities like Liverpool. It made no secret of its politics. The final issue, dated 16 September 1865 (the day after its offices were raided), carried a militant editorial that commented on the hostility of Catholic clerics to the Fenian movement, but which openly stated that "our beautiful and fruitful land will become a grazing farm for the foreigners cattle, and the remnant of our race wanderers and outcasts all over the world if English rule in Ireland be not struck down. Our only hope is in revolution."[7] Comments such as these were used as evidence by the prosecution at the trials of John O'Leary, Luby, and O'Donovan Rossa in December 1865 and January 1866. As the American movement operated in the open, the name Fenian Brotherhood was generally associated with the IRB by both the government and the press after the arrest of the leadership. The movement had been infiltrated, and the newspaper was suppressed.

In 1866 the Fenian brotherhood attempted the first of three abortive attacks on Canada, aimed at creating a bargaining chip for the Irish cause should an Anglo-American war break out and in the hope that the movement in Ireland might be emboldened by events across the Atlantic. The invasions failed, but pointed to the fact that this new organisation, like its republican predecessor in the United Irishmen, was prepared to exploit international affairs in order to further its objectives.

On 4 March 1867 the Fenians embarked upon their planned rebellion in Ireland. It proved to be a miserable failure. Despite elaborate attempts at organization, including a proposed raid on Chester Castle and the transfer of its weapons to Ireland, the Fenian rebellion of 1867 was badly prepared and was easily dealt with as skirmishes broke out in the Dublin mountains and counties Tipperary, Limerick, Clare, and Waterford. The Fenians were also poorly armed: their American supporters had been able to muster a shipment of weapons that arrived off Sligo only in May 1867, and turned back when it became obvious that the moment for rebellion, in that year at least, had passed. The Irish Constabulary were given the honorary prefix "Royal" in tribute to their role in suppressing the rising, and new, fortified police barracks began to be constructed around the country in response to the lingering Fenian threat.

But although defeated, they did not go away. In September 1867 two Fenians—Thomas Kelly and Timothy Deasy—were arrested in Manchester. While being transported from court to jail, the van they were in was attacked by a large group who shot dead the horses and broke open the van, killing a police sergeant in the process. Police raids on the Irish communities of Manchester resulted in a wave of trials and arrests, and five men were sentenced to death. One conviction was quashed, another death sentence was commuted to transportation, but three of the five—William Allen, Michael Larkin, and Michael O'Brien—were hanged for murder. The "Manchester Martyrs" were the first Irishmen executed for political crimes since Robert Emmett; theirs became a cause celebre, and their fate generated vast public sympathy for the Fenian ideal along with an enormously popular song, "God Save Ireland," that served as an unofficial Irish national anthem up to the outbreak of the First World War in 1914. Another member of the organization was executed for planting a bomb at Clerkenwell Prison in London to aid a jailbreak the following December. The global reach of the group was later illustrated by the rescue of six Fenian prisoners from captivity in western Australia by the whaler *Catalpa* in April 1876. Organised by a new American Fenian group, Clan na Gael, the ship evaded capture and deposited the former detainees in New York the following August. The Fenian threat remained a potent bugbear in the 1870s and beyond. It soon intersected with other strands of Irish life.

The Emergence of Home Rule

Isaac Butt was a lawyer in Dublin from a Protestant unionist background who had defended a number of Fenian prisoners in the late 1860s. Having apparently become sympathetic to the Irish nationalist cause, in 1870 Butt established the Home Government Association and subsequently, in 1874, the Home Rule League.

Home Rule was in some ways a rerun of what O'Connell had been proposing in the 1840s: not republican separatism, not revolution, but instead the rather modest and moderate demand for Irish self-government. By this time, British fears about the integrity of the empire militated against any concession of independence to Ireland, which might be seen as setting a very dangerous precedent to other parts of the empire. Home Rule thus operated on a simple principle—Ireland would remain within the United Kingdom, and the integrity of the empire would thereby be kept intact. The British would agree to establish a parliament in Dublin with limited powers, but a parliament nonetheless that would give Irish nationalists some control over the running of their country.

However, the Irish MPs whom Butt had attracted to the cause

were a diverse assortment with varied commitments, and Butt, with his deep respect for the institution and traditions of parliament, was ill equipped to marshal them into a cohesive force. That would be left to the enigmatic figure of the Wicklow landlord Charles Stewart Parnell. Elected to Westminster in 1875, Parnell soon came to Irish prominence and British notoriety by aligning himself with the more militant "obstructionists" amongst Butt's followers who sought to force Irish matters on to the parliamentary agenda by deliberately exploiting procedural issues to disrupt its business. For Parnell, his burgeoning reputation as a man who meant business reached a peak when he claimed, referencing events in 1867, that there had been no murder in Manchester, a contention that provoked outrage in Britain, but which also brought him to the attention of the dormant Fenian movement. The statement foreshadowed an enduring element of Parnell's career: a studied ambiguity that enabled him to yoke together the disparate elements of Irish nationalism. He certainly had some contacts with the IRB, and became a focal point for those Irish parliamentarians who had become disillusioned with Isaac Butt. By the end of the decade the circumstances were in place for Parnell to succeed him. Butt's successor would be able to tap into deeper and more potent energies.

The Land League and the Land War

In the decades after the famine the Irish landlord class had come under increasing pressure. Many landlords had already been in precarious financial straits even before the famine, and had been bankrupted by the relief obligations placed upon them by a British ruling elite who were increasingly unsympathetic to their plight after the famine, and had few compunctions about replacing them with a more efficient alternative. The Encumbered Estates Act of 1849 was established to sell indebted estates to prospective investors, usually Irish, and did so on a very large scale (perhaps a quarter of Irish land was sold off in this way). There were perhaps no more than ten thousand landlords in 1851, and their world was shaped by rapid and extensive post-famine changes. There had been a major shift towards more profitable livestock farming in the years after the famine, and often, as notoriously happened on the Derryveagh estate in

Donegal, the space used for livestock was made available by evicting the previous human inhabitants. By the 1870s, perhaps 50 percent of Irish land was held by a thousand major landlords. But vast patrimonies such as the Downshire estate, consisting of 115,000 acres stretching across five counties, were the exception; 20 percent of the landlords presided over estates of between 2,000 and 5,000 acres. Some of those at the top were amongst the wealthiest in the British empire, and their political power remained largely unchallenged until the 1880s.[8]

An Irish farmer at this juncture, of whatever status, was most likely a tenant, and the extent of sectarian, ethnic, and class tensions between landlords and tenants in Ireland should not be underestimated. The process by which the landed elite were slowly but surely eclipsed began in earnest from the 1870s onwards, and the catalyst for that change was the organisation established by a returned emigrant: Michael Davitt, who was born in the impoverished Atlantic county of Mayo and whose family later emigrated to the industrial heartland of Lancashire in England. Having lost an arm in a factory accident, Davitt received an education and returned to Mayo in the late 1870s. What he saw there led him to conclude that Ireland's unresolved economic conditions, most especially those pertaining to land ownership, were laying the foundations for another famine during a global economic downturn. Davitt canvassed support for Fenian involvement in a new approach to tackle these problems and toured the United States to get Clan na Gael support for his new initiative. This proved decisive. The outcome was the creation of the Land League, a movement pressing for action on the most important issue in Irish life between the famine and the First World War: the ownership of Irish land. The so-called "new departure" of June 1879 saw the Fenians, land reformers, and Home Rulers—represented, respectively, by John Devoy based in New York, Davitt, and Parnell—forge a loose alliance that would achieve at least some common aims (though the ultimate goals of Fenians and Home Rulers were quite far apart). It set the stage for the "Land War" of 1879–82.

In the absence of written agreements, the standard assumption in the Irish countryside was that a tenant renting a holding from a landlord would remain in place for a year—hardly an incentive to think in the long term. The threat of eviction lurked in the shadows, and could be used as a tool of coercion to guarantee the payment of rent. In the 1850s there had been tentative demands for greater rights for tenants to be enshrined in law, with the so-called "Ulster custom" providing a model. This was encapsulated in what was known as the "three f's": a fair rent, the right to a fixed tenure, and the right of free sale to another tenant if circumstances dictated or allowed it. The distinction between landlord and farmer that opened the door to the articulation of these demands may have become more pronounced after the famine, and demands for economic justice were an issue that affected not just farmers: between the 1850s and 1880s labourers engaged in breaking machines in Munster lest these threaten their livelihoods. But agrarian issues always had the potential to mobilise people on a much wider scale, and secret agrarian movements such as Ribbonmen remained vibrant on either side of the famine and even overseas: the "Molly Maguires" of Pennsylvania's coalfields in the 1870s were the Ribbonmen of Donegal transplanted across the Atlantic. And in Ireland, by the 1870s the old spectre of Captain Rock was replaced by that of Captain Moonlight (the cover name often used by more militant agrarian agitators when delivering threats to their targets). Agrarian unrest continued to simmer as a fact of Irish life until at least the 1920s.

It can be hard to define agrarian crime. Between 1848 and 1880 there were 16,579 incidents in that broad category, but only 206 were homicides, and of the 100 homicides between 1858 and 1878 perhaps only a quarter can be directly linked to disputes between landlords and tenants.[9] The Land War began as a campaign to demand fairer rents from landlords; where these were refused, the rents would simply be withheld altogether, and the tenants in question could depend upon the Land League to support them. The league would interfere with evictions, and would also make it difficult for the landlords to replace evicted tenants with new ones. More violent activities were also unleashed, as landlords were attacked and intimidated; the worst counties for "outrages" during the Land War were Kerry, Tipperary, Offaly, Westmeath, Leitrim, and Galway. The Land War saw a huge spike in both unrest and evictions—there were 11,215 in 1882 alone—but the law had, slowly but surely, slipped from the landlords' grasp. The rhetorical power of the land question should not be underestimated, for it touched upon the very basis of British rule in Ireland.

Parnell himself often walked a tightrope between moderation and extremes. Indeed, this was a useful strategy when presenting himself as an Irish leader at Westminster; for if British politicians refused to deal with him adequately, who could say what would take his place? But Parnell could hardly advocate an open revolt against landlords, so he suggested a new form of collective action in a speech in County Clare in September 1880, when he posed the following question from the platform:

> Now, what are you to do to a tenant who bids for a farm from which another tenant has been evicted?
> Several voices: Shoot him.
> Mr Parnell: I think I heard somebody say, "shoot him" (cheers). I wish to point out to you a very much better way—a more Christian and charitable way, which will give the lost man an opportunity of repenting (laughter, and "hear, hear"). When a man takes a farm from which another has been evicted, you must shun him on the roadside when you meet him—you must shun him in the streets of the town—you must shun him in the shop—you must shun him in the fair-green and in the market place, by leaving him alone, by putting him in a moral Coventry, by isolating him from the rest of his country as if he were the leper of old—you must show him your detestation of the crime he has committed.[10]

The first victim of the new tactic bequeathed his surname to the English language: the Mayo land agent Charles Cunningham Boycott.

The Heyday of Home Rule

The nationalist coalition forged by the land question coincided with the premiership of a British prime minister who was inclined to take a conciliatory interest in Irish affairs: the Liberal leader William Ewart Gladstone, who had already overseen the "disestablishment" of the Church of Ireland a decade previously, when it had lost its unique but deeply unpopular status as the state church in 1869. Meanwhile, Parnell had been imprisoned in 1881, and issued an abortive manifesto from captivity demanding the non-payment of rent, which resulted in the Land League being officially suppressed. Gladstone, however, was prepared to make overtures to the Irish leader; Parnell was released, and under his leadership a disciplined political movement began to emerge in Ireland, and began to operate in Westminster in the 1880s; his primary focus now shifted away from the land question towards the political issue of Home Rule.

Arguably, Parnell simply used the land question as a means to this end. His treatment of the Ladies Land League, founded by his sister Anna as an adjunct to the main organisation, is a case in point. Its militancy, in encouraging aggressive action and supporting evicted tenants and Land League prisoners, came to be seen as an embarrassment; Parnell had it dissolved in the course of his alignment with the British Liberals, and his sister never spoke to him again. By 1882 the Home Rule movement was firmly allied with the Liberals, who committed themselves to both land reform and Home Rule. Indeed, Gladstone adopted the cause of Home Rule enthusiastically.

The same could not be said of the Conservative opposition, however, or of a sizeable wing of Gladstone's own party, who vehemently opposed Home Rule. Parnell's movement had, after all, pushed it on to the British agenda at a time of imperial crisis in the 1880s, in which Boer victories and German incursions threatened British imperial rule in Africa.[11] Attempts to pass Home Rule legislation through Westminster in 1886 and 1893 failed, as Gladstone's Liberal party split over the issue and some of his followers sided with the Conservatives who opposed it; indeed, the Liberals never fully recovered from their espousal of a cause that was deeply unpopular in Britain. But their subsequent dependence on approximately eighty parliamentary votes offered by Parnell and his MPs meant that they were in no position to disavow it. Given the Liberal commitment to Irish Home Rule, the Conservatives saw no need to follow suit, and perceived greater electoral advantage in unyielding hostility towards it. Home Rule would remain a divisive issue in British political life until the outbreak of the First World War.

The "Uncrowned King" and the "Long Gestation"

By the time Gladstone introduced a second Home Rule Bill in 1893, the party that Parnell constructed had collapsed into disarray and he himself was dead. Parnell had been in a relationship with Katherine O'Shea, the wife of one of his fellow MPs, William O'Shea, since the early 1880s. Having successfully weathered an attempt to implicate him in the Phoenix Park murders—the 1882 assassinations of a newly appointed viceroy and chief secretary in Dublin by a Fenian splinter group—Parnell was named in the eventual divorce between the two O'Sheas, which had been delayed as William O'Shea hoped to benefit from an inheritance due to his wife. Gladstone stated that his party would not tolerate any dealings with a party led by a man many viewed as an adulterer. After Parnell refused to relinquish his leadership of the Home Rule party, it split, and an acrimonious electoral campaign was fought between the rival Home Rule camps throughout 1890 and 1891. The split was sufficiently toxic to prompt the chief secretary, Arthur Balfour, to discreetly discourage anti-Home Rule—unionist—candidates from standing for election, lest they provide a distraction for rival wings of a party that was now tearing itself apart.[12] As for Parnell himself, he married Katherine O'Shea in June 1891, and he died near Brighton on 6 October 1891.

Despite the public acrimony that marked the final years of his life, Parnell's funeral was an extraordinary public pageant. His coffin was met near Dublin at Kingstown (now Dun Laoghaire) on 10 October, and it was brought to Dublin's City Hall to lie in state. The funeral cortege to Glasnevin Cemetery north of the city was led by the hearse followed by, amongst a vast crowd, members of the parliamentary party and the Fenian brotherhood (including James Stephens and John O'Leary). In line with his professed desire to be interred with the people of Ireland, Parnell's tomb consisted of a single piece of Wicklow granite resting over a cholera pit housing thousands of victims from the famine. The image of Parnell as a lost leader would appear within a generation in James Joyce's *Dubliners* and *A Portrait of the Artist as a Young Man*. But it was the poet William Butler Yeats who best put a spin on it, claiming with the benefit of hindsight that the death of Parnell and the disarray into which his party fell marked the beginning of the "long gestation" of the events that would, within a generation, lead to Irish independence. Yeats's claim was tendentious. But it is certainly true that after Parnell's death, Home Rule lost much of its potency, and other forms of cultural and political activity began to assume a greater prominence.

CHAPTER FIFTEEN

Culture Wars

Changes in Land Ownership

Aside from emigration, the most profound changes in Irish social life in the post-famine era took place outside the towns and cities: the revolution in land ownership that happened in the decades after the Land War of 1879–82. The sequence of Lands Acts passed by the Westminster parliament in 1881, 1885, 1891, 1903, and 1909 permitted tenants to buy their holdings from the landlords with loans from the British exchequer (which also resolved to top up the sale price as an inducement to landlords to sell). The net result was a social revolution in the decades before independence, as millions of acres of land changed hands. This broke the power of the Irish landed class, established in the seventeenth century, and created a new class of "proprietors." It also facilitated the increasing dominance of the urban and rural middle classes that had emerged in the decades after the famine. The Ireland that Parnell had sought to rule and Davitt had hoped to transform was transforming anyway. Others would attempt to keep remoulding it.

Sporting Change

Sporting events had been important social occasions in Ireland for centuries. But some sports were deemed to be better than others.

Sports involving horses, such as racing and hunting, were often associated with the gentry and upper classes more generally; they had the means to engage in them, and such sports had a distinct social cachet. On the other hand, the social and moral status of hurling—a sport of considerable antiquity which had evolved over time—had declined in the nineteenth century, and in the decades after the famine became confined to pockets in counties such as Galway, Cork, and Wexford (the shift to livestock farming deprived the game of suitable venues in many areas). Ireland was by no means impervious to the Victorian sporting revolution, and by the 1880s games such as soccer, rugby, cricket, and golf were very obviously becoming increasingly popular and better organised across a wide social spectrum. This was not a development welcomed by many nationalists; often the spread of British games was influenced by the location of military bases (hence the pejorative term "garrison games"). These could be viewed as, at worst, agents of British cultural influence, or at best as pastimes unsuited to Irish conditions. The Gaelic Athletic Association (GAA) was founded in 1884 to provide a distinctively Irish alternative.

The key figure in its creation was the Clare civil servant Michael Cusack, an athlete in his youth (and an aficionado of cricket and rugby) who was nonetheless alarmed by the decline of "native" games and the increasingly rapid penetration of soccer, rugby, and cricket in Ireland. The impetus for founding the GAA was, however, as much practical as ideological. Athletic contests were an established element of Irish rural life, but Cusack and his associate Maurice Davin worked off the assumption that the British rules which were increasingly used in Ireland were simply not suitable for Irish conditions; the British emphasis on holding meetings on a Saturday, for instance, clashed with the more traditional Irish emphasis on sporting contests on a Sunday. Alongside this was a concern with the increasing elitism of sports that were conducted under such rules; the GAA was conceived of as a broad church.

It codified rules for the games under its aegis by 1885—initially hurling and athletics—and grew rapidly, using counties as an organizing framework from an early stage. Eighty-four clubs were represented at its annual meeting in 1886, which officially established the county boards and all-Ireland championships, which first took place in 1887. There were tensions with other bodies such as the Irish Amateur Athletics Union (the GAA was originally athletic in orientation), which boycotted the GAA. Hurling and football soon eclipsed athletics within the new association, and, in a move with far reaching consequences for its later development, individual parishes were chosen as the basic unit of organisation. It also sought to expand overseas. In 1888, fifty athletes and hurlers travelled to the United States. After a gruelling voyage (especially so due to many being from inland counties) they toured in the states for a month; but seventeen of them remained there, and a number of others only returned to Ireland to settle their affairs before emigrating, much to the chagrin of Davin.[1]

The GAA had a broadly nationalist inflection from its inception, which ensured that the IRB had a presence within it from an early stage. The authorities rapidly infiltrated the GAA, and members of the national police force, the Royal Irish Constabulary (RIC), were banned in 1887 (though members of the armed forces were initially permitted to join). The GAA was effectively controlled by the IRB by the end of the 1880s, which backfired disastrously when the association was the only major national organisation to back Parnell in the split. It thereby incurred the wrath of the church and was forced into disastrous retreat in the 1890s before recovering in the first decade of the twentieth century. Its growth was also facilitated by the development of Ireland's extensive rail network, which enabled the transport of substantial numbers of spectators to and from matches. The tensions evident in the early incarnation of the GAA were probably unavoidable in a group that aimed at having a broad appeal, though ultimately this did not impede its growth in any fundamental way.

Language and Literacy

The shift from Irish to English as the most widely spoken vernacular language accelerated in the post-famine era. Statistics for language proficiency were first incorporated into the 1851 census, and these revealed that Ireland in the immediate aftermath of the famine was a predominantly English-speaking country. This had clear implications for literacy, as the ability to read and write increasingly took the form of being able to do so in English. The creation of the national school system in the 1830s had been followed by an observable increase in literacy levels in English in the second half of the nineteenth century (though equally, the impact of the famine might have skewed this proportion by wiping out a largely illiterate Irish-speaking underclass). The ability to read and write was first quantified in the census of 1841. In that year, 47 percent of the Irish population over the age of five declared that they could read. In 1911, the figure was 88 percent. These figures concealed as much as they revealed; literacy levels varied according to region, class, gender, and occupation. But a straightforward conclusion can be drawn: throughout the nineteenth century and into the twentieth, more Irish people gained the ability to read and write. The remarkable growth of the provincial press from the 1850s onwards had almost certainly aided this process. Equally, the success of novelists such as Gerald Griffin, and even the Fenian Charles Kickham (whose 1873 novel *Knocknagow* was a huge success) suggest that literacy was not always a purely functional matter.

But this increase in literacy in English was happening at the same time as the usage of Irish was declining. The relationship between literacy in English and the decline of Irish is open to debate: for example, in west Galway literacy went hand in hand with the spread of English, whereas in northwest Donegal it did not.[2] Ireland had been a multilingual society for centuries; the impact of the famine accelerated the shift to English. By 1851, according to the census, less than 25 percent of the population spoke Irish: 319,602 (4.88 percent) were monoglot speakers, and 1,204,683 (18.38 percent) were bilingual. The majority of Irish speakers were concentrated in the poor rural west, with pockets elsewhere: in 1851, 3.54 percent of the population of Leinster spoke Irish, as opposed to 50.77 percent of Connacht.[3] Clearly, Irish was in decline, but this process accelerated in the post-famine era. By 1891 approximately 15 percent of the population spoke Irish, and it was slowly but surely retreating westwards. The English involvement with Ireland over the centuries had guaranteed that Ireland had become a bilingual country, with a population split between bilinguals and monoglots in either language, but Irish-speaking areas tended to be more impoverished, and these areas bore the worst brunt of the famine and were ravaged by emigration in the aftermath (though on the other hand, emigrants' remittances also sustained the communities of the western seaboard).[4]

Official attitudes to the Irish language had veered from wariness to hostility for centuries. The Church of Ireland had displayed an intermittent interest in it, and there was a considerable degree of antiquarian interest in Irish language and culture in the eighteenth century. This was sometimes harnessed to politicised debates about the true nature of the Irish past and the possibilities of the Irish future (language, after all, was a less divisive badge of identity than religion); sometimes it was undertaken for genuine scholarly reasons. While the language of power in Ireland from the early modern period onwards was English, in the eighteenth century English had also become the language of opposition to power, as political movements operated through English regardless of their cultural or ideological programmes. The same was true of the expanding organs of the state—especially educational institutions and the law—and, for the most part, the revitalised Catholic Church under Cullen. English, after all, was also the language of commerce, and thus of prosperity. But the decline of the Irish language, and the loss of the vernacular culture and worldview that this implied, increasingly came to be seen as a loss understood best in qualitative rather than quantitative ways.

Attempts to revive Irish as a vernacular did not constitute a single coherent movement. Members of the Young Ireland movement had displayed an interest in Irish; there were sporadic attempts to revive it in the 1860s, and even in the 1870s some western newspapers carried columns in Irish. Various preservationist societies and publications were formed from the 1870s onwards, and Michael Logan of Galway published an Irish-language newspaper in New York in 1881. But was Irish to look backwards or forwards? Was it a relic of the past, or did it have a value in a rapidly modernising world and, if so, how was it to meet the challenge? The Gaelic scholar Douglas Hyde attempted to answer at least some of these questions in an lecture he gave in 1892 titled "The Necessity for De-Anglicising Ireland." Hyde argued that the decline of Irish pointed towards a more general cultural malaise, that the Irish people were in "a most anomalous position, imitating England and yet apparently hating it." Furthermore, the loss of the language was the key: "The losing of it is our greatest blow, and the sorest stroke that the rapid anglicisation of Ireland has inflicted upon us."[5] The subsequent founding of the Gaelic League (*Conradh na Gaeilge*) in 1893 proved to be a seminal moment in the history of the Irish language in intellectual and ideological terms. On a more pragmatic level, in response to pressure by activists, Irish was on the schools curriculum by 1878 and, despite being viewed dismissively in some quarters, in 1908 Irish became an admission requirement for the National University of Ireland. The revival of Irish, alongside the increasing popularity of the GAA, was to become one of the most obvious markers of the Irish cultural revival of the late Victorian era.[6]

Revivalism and Politics Outside the Mainstream

The GAA and the Gaelic League were the most prominent contemporary manifestations of a potent trend in late-nineteenth- and early-twentieth-century Ireland: the myriad attempts to foster a regeneration of Irish cultural, economic, and social life. The most famous manifestation, however, was the coterie of literary figures, such as W. B. Yeats and Lady Augusta Gregory, associated with the Irish Literary Theatre established in 1899. But there were other groupings: the "Irish Ireland" movement exemplified by the reactionary journalist D. P. Moran; the economic nationalism of Arthur Griffith's Sinn Féin; and even the Co-operative movement of Sir Horace Plunkett. All of these initiatives were arguably responses to a fin de siècle fear that Ireland was being relegated to a second-rate, indeed provincial status. The idea of regeneration had a natural appeal to a younger generation, though it was never a homogenous movement and the motivations of the various individuals and organisations differed, and could lead to clashes that might be personal as much as ideological.

The most famous examples of such discord were the "riots" prompted by J. M. Synge's satirical drama from 1907, *The Playboy of the Western World*. Synge's depiction of life in an impoverished community in the west of Ireland was denounced as a condescending and immoral depiction of the Irish peasantry. The west was increasingly idealised by cultural nationalists as a repository of Gaelic culture surviving in its purest form. Synge was intimately familiar with the western seaboard; he had become fluent in Irish whilst living on the Aran Islands, and had proven himself a sensitive and sympathetic chronicler of life along the Atlantic coast. Yet as his play explored the gap between the real and the ideal, it outraged some strands of nationalist opinion. The opening run of the play in Dublin's Abbey Theatre was continually disrupted, and Yeats was famously disgusted. Disputes over the content of literary works such as the *Playboy of the Western World* were mirrored by concerns about their form, as the medium of artistic expression was also contested: was the literary expression of a new Irish identity to be in Irish or in English? Such questions were never fully answered with any degree of consensus, but the very fact that they were asked is testament to the intellectual vitality of the scene from which they sprung.

Alongside the cultural revival that took place from the 1880s onwards, there was a remarkable proliferation of political movements on the fringes of the mainstream. The IRB had engaged in a dynamiting campaign in British cities between 1881 and 1885, and had declined thereafter. The centenary of the 1798 rebellion in 1898, however, gave separatist republicanism a shot in the arm; the IRB was revitalised, and began to be quietly repopulated with a new generation of activists. Yet this was still a fringe concern, as indicated by the miserable fate of what was supposed to be one of the set-piece projects for 1898. A campaign had been established to raise money for a memorial to Wolfe Tone in Dublin, yet only £561 was raised, rather than the £14,000 required.[7]

The revival of overt republicanism, however modest in scale, was aided by the outbreak of the Boer War, as fringe nationalists expressed solidarity with South African settlers in their own struggle against British imperial power. The pro-Boer Irish Transvaal Committee drew in a wide variety of activists—W. B. Yeats, the socialist James Connolly, and the veteran Fenian Thomas Clarke were all involved. The Boer War gave a renewed impetus to the Irish Party, which also opposed it.[8] Equally, there was an attempt to raise a force to fight alongside the Boers from amongst Irish emigrants in South Africa, although the four hundred members of this "Irish Brigade" have to be contrasted with the twenty-eight thousand Irishmen who fought as British soldiers in the same conflict. St. Stephen's

Green in Dublin was intended to house the aborted memorial to
Wolfe Tone; instead, by 1907 the entrance to the Green had been
adorned with a large memorial arch to commemorate members of
the Royal Dublin Fusiliers—the principal regiment in the British
army to recruit from Dublin and its hinterland—who had been killed
in South Africa.

Other political ideologies had a presence in late Victorian Ireland. The question of educational and political rights for women, so
prominent in Britain in the same era, made itself felt in Ireland. As
early as 1825, William Thompson made the case for women's rights
in Ireland, and women did, in fact, become involved in political organisations such as the Ladies Land League. In terms of socioeconomic and educational rights, major advances had been made by the
Married Women's Property Acts of the 1870s, and the Universities
Act of 1879 that permitted women to receive a university education
—a process completed when women were finally admitted to Trinity College in 1904, much to the disgust of its incumbent provost,
George Salmon.

Organisations demanding the vote for women were founded in
the 1870s by such women as Isabella Todd and Anna Haslam (female suffrage activists tended to be drawn from the middle classes).
Women got the vote in local elections in 1898 and by 1911 could sit
on county councils. But Irish women, like their British counterparts,
were not yet permitted to vote in parliamentary elections. The
foundation of the Irish Women's Franchise League in 1908 marked
a new, more militant departure in pursuit of that objective. Mainstream Irish nationalists in the Home Rule party tended to be quite
hostile to the idea of giving women the vote; on occasion, suffragists
repaid this hostility. Over time, some Irish women felt that their
own liberation as women was intertwined with the broader struggle
for Irish independence.

The politics of labour were also evident in this period. Craft
unions had existed in Ireland throughout the nineteenth century,
and many Irish unions gravitated towards the British Trade Union
Congress (TUC), but in 1893 the Irish Trade Union Congress
(ITUC) was founded. At its first convention in June 1894, 119 delegates met, representing 60,000 workers both directly and indi-
rectly. There had been small socialist groupings in Dublin from the

1880s, but inevitably, it was the industrial northeast that saw major labour organisation. Irish unions changed rapidly, most especially due to the influence of the Liverpool-born James Larkin, who in 1907 orchestrated a major dock strike in Belfast before turning his attention to Dublin. The arrival of Larkin heralded a new and more overtly political era in Irish labour organisation; not least because the union established by Larkin in 1909—the Irish Transport and General Workers Union (ITGWU)—sought to expand the base of union organisation in Ireland from skilled to unskilled labour.

The most famous manifestation of labour activism in Irish history came in 1913 in Dublin, a city that officially had a greater proportion of its population living in poverty than anywhere else in the United Kingdom—87,000 out a population of 304,000—due to its relatively small industrial base and higher levels of casual employment. Dublin employers claimed to have no problem with unions in the traditional sense, but Larkin's attempts to organise amongst the vast ranks of the unskilled labouring poor met with a ferocious response. After one of Dublin's major employers, the transport magnate William Martin Murphy, banned his employees from membership of the ITGWU in August 1913, Larkin called his union out on strike. After Murphy galvanised other Dublin employers into a collective opposition to "Larkinism," the members of Larkin's union were barred from employment, resulting in the traditional name given to the dispute: the Dublin "lockout."

The strike and lockout snowballed into an industrial dispute that lasted until early 1914. It highlighted potent and enduring class distinctions in Ireland that the focus on British rule often caused to be overlooked. By the end of September, English trade unions attempted to get involved in order to resolve the dispute, troops were being drafted to protect property and guarantee supplies to government agencies, and shipments of food, organised by English unions, began to arrive in Dublin. What is remarkable is the degree of solidarity that was shown: while the authorities and Home Rule nationalists proved deeply hostile to the strikers, the British TUC raised £106,000 in relief funds to alleviate distress in the city. The impact was felt hardest in the slums where the vast majority of Dublin's unskilled labour force lived. The sum of monies raised by the TUC can be contrasted with the £6,400 raised by the relief fund established by the lord mayor of Dublin, two-thirds of which had been pledged by the Catholic bishops of Dublin and Derry. By December workers had been starved into submission, and the lockout petered out in the early months of 1914. The employers insisted that those returning to work sign a pledge repudiating the ITGWU. They claimed to have broken the strike, but in reality they discreetly ignored their own demand lest they face a second, disastrous period without a workforce; it would have been difficult to weather another storm. And so the ITGWU survived: by 1920 it was the biggest union in the country, with 120,000 members.

Home Rule and Constructive Unionism

These various organisations—the GAA, the Gaelic League, and the ITGWU—all existed in the shadow of Home Rule, which remained the dominant political issue for nationalist Ireland. That said, there was little sympathy for Home Rule in the main channels of British political life. The Conservatives were in power for most of the period from 1886 to 1906, and while profoundly hostile to the idea of Home Rule, they did have a pragmatic attitude to Irish matters. While the unpopularity of Home Rule was a useful stick with which to beat the Liberals at election time, the Tories offered both carrot and stick. Ironically, in the 1890s and the first decade of the twentieth century, Conservative governments implemented a number of strikingly progressive policies in Ireland. There was a certain element of self-interest to this, as the passage of reforms in Ireland would hopefully neuter the demand for Home Rule, most obviously through the continuation of land reform against the backdrop of intermittent agitation. The introduction of elected county councils (1898) devolved at least some measure of power into local hands. The establishment of this limited form of local democracy effectively destroyed the remaining localised power of the landlord class, which was already being whittled away under the land acts. In 1891 the Congested Districts Board had been established to tackle chronic poverty and underdevelopment in the regions under its jurisdiction; by 1909 the remit of the Congested Districts Board came to cover the entire Atlantic seaboard, and even extended into parts of east Connacht.

This policy of "constructive unionism" was intended to forestall the prospect of Irish Home Rule, and to deflect the threat to the empire it was seen to pose. Assuming that the Irish were capable of governing themselves (there was often a racist undertone to this debate), should they be granted Home Rule, might they not demand more? And might the sight of Ireland gradually extricating itself from the rule of the imperial parliament set a dangerous precedent for other parts of the empire? The Tories were not prepared, under any circumstances, to travel down this road. A second Home Rule Bill had been rejected by the Conservative-dominated House of Lords in 1893. Gladstone's eventual resignation as prime minister, and the return of the Tories to government in 1895, ensured that Home Rule became an irrelevance—a situation that was not helped by the fractious and fragmented condition of the Irish party after the Parnell split. The reunification of the party under the relatively moderate and broadly imperialistic leadership of John Redmond after 1900 gave it a degree of renewed momentum, though Irish Home Rule was an impossibility as long as the Tories remained in power. But given that one of the great British political parties was committed, albeit reluctantly, to the cause of Irish Home Rule, there seemed little reason for Redmond and his followers to turn to any rival ideology; all that they required for success was patience and a certain combination of circumstances, and these were bound to come with time. Home Rule politicians were capable of fiery rhetoric that was wholly at odds with the limited measure of self-government that they demanded. It was vague enough to satisfy all kinds of aspirations, which perhaps explains the mass support it enjoyed in Catholic nationalist Ireland.

Yet despite the unpromising prospects for Home Rule in this era, one can discern a Catholic ruling class in waiting: the children of the new Catholic elite that had slowly but surely emerged throughout the nineteenth century, often from business and the legal and medical professions. This younger generation visible in late Victorian Ireland was often shaped by schools such as Clongowes Wood and Mount Anville (not to mention elite schools overseas); yet in 1911 only 6 percent of the Irish school-going population progressed beyond primary school.[9] Their families were Catholic constitutional nationalists who were securely middle class, who had become more visible in Irish life from the 1870s onwards, and who were firmly anchored in the professions and educational system. Figures such as the academic and politician Thomas Kettle (born in 1880) were perceived as the potential rulers of a Home Rule Ireland that might soon come to pass. At the turn of the twentieth century the Home Rule cause was in the doldrums, but in little over a decade it seemed to be on the brink of success. In less than two decades it would be dead.

Where Historians Disagree

THE NINETEENTH CENTURY HAS perhaps not been subject to fundamental reinterpretation in recent years, but new approaches have begun to shed light into neglected corners. Just as the study of popular culture and popular politics has illuminated the eighteenth century, it has paid dividends with regards to the early nineteenth century. The extension of British state power in the 1820s and 1830s meant that the "condition" of Ireland was examined in unprecedented detail, and this accumulation of information has been exploited by historians such as Niall Ó Ciosáin, whose recent study of the "poor inquiry" of the 1830s examines the popular culture of pre-famine Ireland.[1] Likewise, the lurid and murkily violent world of pre-famine Ireland, as conjured up by many contemporary commentators, might not reflect the reality: pre-famine Ireland does not seem to have been unusually violent in terms of homicides.[2]

The most significant reassessment of the pre-famine era relates to the social and economic impact of the Act of Union. Many contemporaries and later historians assumed that the union ushered in a sustained period of poverty and underdevelopment (issues that were highlighted in the nineteenth century as evidence of British neglect and misrule), and the decline of Dublin was seen as a particularly obvious marker of this. Both of these propositions have been modified: Cormac Ó Gráda's major study of Irish economic history suggests that the real turning point for Irish economic decline came with the ending of the Napoleonic wars in 1815.[3] Equally, David Dickson's examination of Dublin has painted a picture of a capital city that remained reasonably prosperous and vibrant for decades after the union.[4] Neither of these studies disputes the existence of poverty and underdevelopment; they simply challenge the time frame within which it should be interpreted.

This does, however, bring us to the most significant event of the nineteenth century: the potato famine of the 1840s. Ó Gráda has examined the socioeconomic background, demographics, and cultural legacy of the famine in very sophisticated ways.[5] But debates over the famine can often dwell on two questions. The first is the question of British culpability; or, to paraphrase the Young Irelander John Mitchel, regardless of whether God created the blight, did England create the famine? Underpinning a great deal of commentary and scholarship on the famine is the lurking question of responsibility. Ireland was, after all, part of the United Kingdom. So how could the famine have been let happen by the U.K. government? Why did they not do more to alleviate it? Or was the famine precisely what they wanted to see happen? Did the British embark on genocide in the Ireland of the 1840s? No serious historian would accept the latter proposition (even the limited provision of relief was inconsistent with a desire to wipe out the Irish). That said, there would be a broad scholarly consensus that Ireland's British rulers must bear a great deal of responsibility, that British officials, commentators, and politicians operated within particular ideological, racial, sectarian, and political frameworks that coloured their response, and that more could have been done.

A second issue relates to the question of food exports: did the British deliberately export food during a time of scarcity, thereby letting the Irish starve? A more detailed examination of Irish rural society indicates that much of the responsibility for the export of Irish cash crops rests with Irish farmers, albeit with the assistance of the state, and that by the end of the famine more food was being imported than exported. These can often prove to be emotive issues. But scholarship on the famine since its 150-year anniversary in the mid-1990s has not detracted from its overall importance; quite the opposite. Much of the vast quantity of scholarship generated since then has been synthesised in the enormous *Atlas of the Great*

Irish Famine, which deploys a detailed analysis of Irish society at a local level and examines the catastrophe from a remarkable range of angles, in terms of its long-term origins, nutrition, the structure of the society that it affected, the impact of emigration on both Ireland and the destinations of emigrants, along with cultural and social legacies.[6] The famine is thus confirmed as *the* seminal event in modern Irish history.

The post-famine era throws up some intriguing questions. The American historian Emmet Larkin devised the influential thesis that Irish Catholicism underwent a "devotional revolution" after the famine, with profound consequences for social and cultural life in the Catholic community.[7] Arising from this are questions relating to the ways in which official morality engaged with sexuality: as the Catholic Church became a more prominent and assertive institution, in a society where changes in inheritance patterns caused broader social changes, did a concentration on sexual morality dovetail neatly with the requirements of that society? The Victorian era saw an emphasis on marriage as an institution of sexual control, but in post-famine Ireland the option of marriage became increasingly unavailable. In other words, if there were fewer farms to inherit, and if that restricted the chances for marriage, did an emphasis on sexual morality serve to police Irish rural society?[8] Marriage, it can be argued, thus became an institution that was seen as necessary for social stability, which in turn led to the enduring conservatism of that society. Another consequence of this might be the prevalence of infanticide, a crime associated with single and poor women, many of whom were single domestic servants.[9]

Another major issue is the shift from Irish to English, a shift that was happening in the seventeenth century but that became irrevocable in the nineteenth century.[10] Did this lead to the loss of a particular worldview and culture? It can be difficult to isolate any single overarching factor that led to the loss of the language, though it is not automatically the case, however, that English was seen as a superior language of modernity; a pragmatic bilingualism was also a component of language shift.[11] The cultural difference implied by the use of a language other than English also points to the manner in which some English commentators and politicians viewed the Irish in profoundly negative terms: was this based on racism, class prejudice, morality, sectarianism, or a mixture of all of these?[12] Like many of the issues flagged above, this question can defy an easy answer.

Finally, the political narrative of the late nineteenth century has not been challenged in any fundamental way in recent years, but the cultural revival of the late nineteenth and early twentieth centuries has been reassessed. Philip O'Leary has explored how attempts to revive Irish had deeper roots than is often assumed, and continually tackled the question of the place that Irish was to have in Ireland's future.[13] And one of the most important works on the revival in recent years has been that of P. J. Mathews, who has explored how it was about much more than either language or literature.[14] These do not automatically constitute disagreements among historians, but they point to the fact that new questions are continually being asked —and answered—by scholars. Many of those questions remain relevant for the history of twentieth-century Ireland as well.

PART V

The Twentieth Century

CHAPTER SIXTEEN

Revolution

The Ulster Crisis

Unionism—the demand to maintain the union between Britain and Ireland, as established in 1801—was the political ethos that most of Ireland's Protestants subscribed to by the beginning of the twentieth century. It had begun to crystallise during the 1880s in response to increasing demands for Home Rule and became more formally organised in the northeast with the formation of the Ulster Unionist Council in 1905. There was an obvious distinction to be made between the thinly spread unionists of Ireland's southern counties, and the far more densely settled unionist majority in the northeast. What gave Irish unionism an added impetus after 1906 was that the Liberals returned to power that year with a landslide victory. The dominance of the Tories in the House of Lords ensured that Home Rule remained an impossibility, but Ireland benefited from the reforming zeal of the new government: the extension of the old-age pension to Ireland in 1908 was perhaps the most notable of these reforms. But in 1911 Liberal patience with Tory obstructionism snapped, and the government restricted the right of the lords to veto legislation passed by the Commons; from an Irish point of view, the last and greatest obstacle to achieving Home Rule was thereby removed. Given that Herbert Asquith's Liberal government ruled with the support of John Redmond's eighty-four Irish nationalist MPs, it was inevitable that they would demand a third Home Rule Bill. This passed through the House of Commons in 1912, but now the lords were in no position to halt its progress, and it was passed amidst great jubilation in Ireland. The lords could, and did, delay it for two years, but that was seen as a technicality: Home Rule had finally been secured. It became obvious over the next two years, however, that the 26 percent of the Irish population who could be classed as Protestant unionists wanted nothing to do with Home Rule and were prepared, quite literally, to fight against it.

Protestant hostility to Home Rule was fuelled by a number of factors. The industrial prosperity of Ulster proved to many Protestants that British rule was working; so if it was not broken, then why fix it? There was a real fear that the industries of the northeast would be disregarded by the hypothetical new government in Dublin. Belfast was an industrial city of global significance: just prior to 1914 its shipyards accounted for 8 percent of the world's shipping tonnage, including the *Titanic*. Yet the overwhelmingly agricultural emphasis of Irish nationalism seemed to have little room for industry; unionist propaganda often depicted poverty as the handmaiden of Home Rule, and the squalor of Dublin's tenements could be held up as a microcosm of what Ireland might face under the rule of a Home Rule parliament.

Alongside the concerns for their livelihoods were very real fears that the Protestant minority would be victimised by the Catholic majority, for, to paraphrase one of the most famous slogans of this era, Home Rule was deemed to be Rome rule. So, in September 1912, over 237,000 Protestant Ulstermen signed a "Solemn League and Covenant," declaring their willingness to resist "the present conspiracy to set up a Home Rule parliament in Ireland." Over 234,000 Protestant women signed a declaration to the same effect. The leaders of this new unionist movement were the Dublin-born lawyer Edward Carson and the Belfast businessman James Craig. Unionism existed all across Ireland to some degree, but it was obvious that it was strongest in the Protestant heartlands of Ulster. It was there that unionism made its stand, with the formal creation, in April 1913, of the Ulster Volunteer Force.

The UVF was founded to resist Home Rule by force. The threat of violence was implicit in the stance of Carson and Craig, who had even drawn up elaborate plans to establish a provisional government to take control of Ulster should Home Rule come into being. The UVF was in a position to benefit from the experience of Ulster Protestants who had served in the British army. The unionist cause also attracted a great deal of sympathy in Britain (up to and including the Conservative leader Andrew Bonar Law). But if one group in Ireland could arm itself in a way that seemed to threaten the will of parliament, why couldn't another? In November 1913 Irish nationalists emulated their unionist counterparts by arming themselves to defend Home Rule, with the foundation of the Irish Volunteers. This new nationalist militia was larger than the UVF, perhaps numbering 182,000 at its peak, though it was not as well equipped or well trained. But in 1913 two large paramilitary armies had sprung up in Ireland.

Underpinning this burgeoning crisis was a sense that the British authorities were more inclined to favour the cause of unionism over that of nationalism. In March 1914 came the so-called Curragh Mutiny (or "incident"), when fifty-seven cavalry officers at the largest military base in Ireland offered to resign their commissions rather than face the prospect of being ordered to act against the UVF. The officers in question got a written assurance that they would not be expected to do this. A month later, in April, the UVF successfully landed twenty thousand rifles at the northern port of Larne without hindrance from the authorities. The Irish Volunteers followed suit in July on a much smaller scale, landing nine hundred rifles just outside Dublin, but an attempt by the authorities to seize them culminated in troops shooting dead three people in the centre of Dublin (a fourth died later). The UVF had faced no such sanction. To Irish nationalist opinion, the double standard seemed obvious.

There were genuine fears in the summer of 1914 that the Irish Volunteers and the UVF would take up arms against each other; the biggest problem facing the British military was the prospect of a sectarian civil war in Ireland between the rival militias (both of whom, they felt, had been tolerated for far too long). If that happened, the British army would be forced to intervene, but if this came to pass, the government would be unable to commit itself to any European war. It was no coincidence that Germany kept a close eye on events in Ireland. The outbreak of war on the continent in August 1914 soon overshadowed all else.

The Great War and the Easter Rising

Ireland went to war in August 1914 along with the rest of the United Kingdom. Over the next four years, over 200,000 Irish men served in the British armed services, and perhaps as many as 35,000 were killed. All were volunteers: Ireland was the only part of the United Kingdom not to have conscription.[1] The outbreak of war defused the burgeoning conflict in Ireland, as all parties agreed that this was not the time for internal divisions to remain a running sore, so a compromise was cobbled together. Home Rule became law on 18 September 1914, but was postponed for a year (or until the war was over), and some separate provision for Protestant Ulster would also be made. But these were issues for another day: once Home Rule was officially on the statute books, John Redmond, speaking in County Wicklow, exhorted members of the Irish Volunteers to enlist and serve "as far as the firing line extended," as the war was being "undertaken in defence of the highest principles of religion and morality and right." Given that Germany had invaded (Catholic) Belgium, should Irishmen not fight, argued Redmond, it would be "a disgrace forever to our country" and "a denial of the lessons of her history."[2] Redmond also hoped that service in the war might be rewarded with Home Rule, and that the shared burden of combat might break down barriers between Catholics and Protestants.

The outbreak of the war saw the creation of three explicitly Irish divisions: the 36th (Ulster) Division, drawn largely from the ranks of the UVF; and the 10th (Irish) and 16th (Irish) Divisions. Large numbers of recruits joined from the ranks of both the Irish Volunteers and the UVF; indeed, the 36th Division was virtually the UVF in a different uniform. However, the War Office was wary of creating a division along similar lines from the ranks of the Irish Volunteers, despite Redmond's demands for one. The perception lingered that, once again, Britain had favoured unionism over nationalism. But Irishmen enlisted in the British armed forces for a variety of reasons. There was perhaps a certain degree of idealism, reflecting

Redmond's call and driven by a sense that Germany was the enemy. As ever, poverty and unemployment, especially in Dublin, also played a part: the army could offer a job. Principle was also a factor: one of the groups most likely to enlist were Protestant shipworkers from Belfast, who were politically unionist and who worked in one of Ireland's most prosperous industries. Yet a touch of ambiguity was neatly encapsulated by the Irish poet Francis Ledwidge, who observed: "I joined the British Army because she stood between Ireland and an enemy common to our civilisation and I would not have her say that she defended us while we did nothing."[3] Ledwidge was killed at Ypres in 1917.

Having enlisted to fight in the war, Irish soldiers did not escape the consequences. The 10th Division was involved in the Gallipoli campaign, landing at Suvla Bay in August 1915 and suffering massive casualties; half of its numbers were listed as killed, wounded, and missing over the next two months. Over two days in July 1916 the Ulster Division lost over a third of its men—dead, wounded, and missing—when it became one of the first units "over the top" at the battle of the Somme. Their nationalist counterparts in the 16th Division also suffered huge casualties at the Somme. The cost of the war was keenly felt, as it impinged on virtually all aspects of domestic Irish life. But the war provided an opportunity for those on the radical fringe of Irish politics to make an enduring mark.

On 24 April 1916—Easter Monday—a small group of militants seized a number of buildings around Dublin, most notably the General Post Office (GPO) on the main thoroughfare of Sackville Street (later O'Connell Street). Outside the building, the teacher and Irish-language activist Patrick Pearse read out a manifesto proclaiming the existence of an Irish Republic as a "sovereign independent state." Over the next five days perhaps as many as twenty thousand British troops (many of whom were in fact Irish) occupied Dublin, and much of the city centre was devastated by artillery. The Great War had finally come to Irish shores.

The Easter Rising would not have happened had the war not been ongoing, nor would the British have responded in the way they did had they not been at war themselves. The conspiracy that led to the rising was the work of the IRB, most especially the veteran militant Thomas Clarke and the Machiavellian Sean MacDiarmada.

The bulk of those involved in its execution were members of the Irish Volunteers; or more precisely, of a substantial faction of the original volunteers who had dissented from Redmond's call to support the war effort. Having split from the main body of the Irish Volunteers, this more militant group managed to hold on to the name and had perhaps ten thousand followers by 1916. At a later stage the conspirators were joined by James Connolly's Irish Citizen Army, a trade union militia originally formed during the 1913 lockout. Both organisations took part in the rising, along with members of Cumann na mBan (Society or Association of Women), which was founded as an adjunct to the Irish Volunteers in 1914, and had remained aligned with those opposed to John Redmond's call to support the war effort.

The Easter Rising was planned in secrecy, but the rebellion that broke out was quite different to the one that seems to have been intended. Some senior figures in the volunteers did not share the enthusiasm for insurrection; Eoin MacNeill, their commander, was prepared to support a rebellion only if it stood a reasonable prospect of success, and he sought to call off the rising that was being planned behind his back after an abortive attempt to obtain weapons from Germany. Clarke and his cohorts were thereby deprived of both weapons and numbers. They were also faced with the prospect that the attempt to import weapons might trigger a British crackdown on the militants. And so the rebel leaders went ahead with their plan. Figures such as Pearse, who became the public face of the rising, did indulge in rhetoric glorifying sacrifice (not unusual in the context of the war), but it seems that the overwhelming sentiment amongst those who took part in the rising was that it was better to do something, no matter how foolhardy, than nothing.

The Easter Rising was mainly a Dublin affair, and perhaps as few as two and a half thousand men and women took part in it. There were some skirmishes in counties Meath and Galway, and members of the volunteers assembled in Coalisland in Tyrone, Cork City, and the Wexford town of Enniscorthy. The British, however, took the rising extremely seriously, not least because the rebel proclamation spoke of the assistance allegedly provided by "gallant allies in Europe." Hence the massive mobilisation of troops; events happened so quickly that soldiers disembarking from ships in Dublin supposedly thought that they were in France. Martial law was declared on Tuesday, and from Thursday the rebel positions were being pounded by artillery. The insurgents surrendered on 29 April; after six days, the rising was over. During (or because of) the rising, 488 were killed, 2,600 were wounded, and much of Dublin's city centre was laid waste.

Public opinion most definitely seemed stacked against the rebels, and this hostility cut across boundaries of politics, religion, and class; the families of serving soldiers were particularly outraged at what had happened. There was also the more straightforward fact that the rebels had brought war to the streets of Dublin, with the disruption that entailed. Outside the capital, even where there was no fighting, hostility could be discerned as local authorities across the country passed resolutions condemning the rising; Dublin, however, was a notable exception. Equally, an uprising against British rule resonated with many. Some Irish soldiers involved in suppressing it were quite ambivalent about the rising, and this was also evident amongst some Irish soldiers at the front. But on balance it looked as if the rising had been defeated and could be disregarded, as the United Kingdom pressed on with the war effort. Approximately ninety rebel prisoners were sentenced to death by court-martial, and between 3 and 12 May, fifteen men (including the ringleaders) were shot, all but one in Dublin. Such figures as Clarke and Pearse seem to have felt that their executions might serve to galvanise Irish opinion in favour of their cause; they may have had a point. Regardless of public feelings about the rising, the sight of the British army shooting Irish prisoners struck a chord. Redmond's deputy, the veteran Home Ruler John Dillon, gave a ferocious speech in the House of Commons on 11 May where he indicted the British government for "washing out our life's work in a sea of blood," and that "it is not murderers who are being executed; it is insurgents who have fought a clean fight, however misguided, and it would be a damned good thing for you if your soldiers were able to put up as good a fight as did these men in Dublin."[4]

Asquith's government intervened to commute the remaining death sentences. But the damage was done. The extension of martial law across the entire country in response to an event that was essentially confined to Dublin and the detention of more than thirty-five hundred suspects (far more than had actually taken part in the rising) also seemed to indicate that the British were holding the Irish population guilty as a whole. Such insensitivity and heavyhandedness added to the backlash, and over the next two years, Irish people switched their allegiance from the modest objective of Home Rule to a more radical demand for independence being espoused by the organisation that was blamed for the Easter Rising: Sinn Féin.

The Rise of Sinn Féin and the War of Independence

Sinn Féin was originally founded in 1905 by the pugnacious Dublin journalist Arthur Griffith, advocating a blend of protectionist economic nationalism (the name Sinn Féin meant "Our Selves") and the novel political position of "dual monarchy," based on the model of Austria-Hungary. As formulated by Griffith, this was a step beyond Home Rule, in which Ireland would enjoy de facto independence, but would retain the British monarch as head of state. While many of Griffith's ideas were influential, Sinn Féin itself never commanded much support. But by 1916 the name had been adopted by Home Rulers, unionists, and the authorities as a catch-all term to describe radical nationalists; the Easter Rising was erroneously declared to be the "Sinn Féin Rebellion" almost as soon as it had broken out. As Irish opinion began to shift towards the separatism of the rising, the separatists who survived now had a banner under which to regroup.

The remarkable rise of Sinn Féin after 1916 was also related to the collapse of the Home Rule cause. The rising had prompted a hasty attempt to reach a negotiated compromise between nationalists and unionists to hasten the implementation of Home Rule, resulting in the so-called "Irish Convention," held at Trinity College Dublin in 1917 and boycotted by Ulster unionists. But this effort failed, and throughout 1917 Redmond's party haemorrhaged support to Sinn Féin, which was officially reorganised in October 1917. The most senior of the 1916 survivors, the New York–born maths teacher Éamon de Valera, was installed as its president. Sinn Féin reconstituted itself as a political party committed to the pursuit of an independent Irish republic (subject to the self-determination of the Irish people). To this end, it planned to lobby for recognition of Irish independence at the peace conference that would follow the war. Its specific aims were somewhat vague; when one journalist asked a senior member what its policy was, the answer came back as "vengeance, bejaysus."[5] It aimed to be as broad a church as possible; potentially contentious stances on social issues tended to be fudged or avoided.

Sinn Féin received its greatest boost in the spring of 1918, when German breakthroughs on the Western Front raised the spectre of conscription being extended to Ireland. Virtually all shades of nationalist opinion were outraged. Conscription was opposed by the Catholic Church, by Home Rulers, by the labour movement (which organised a general strike in protest against it), and above all, by Sinn Féin, who reaped the benefits. There was also another cohort of activists who were prepared to support the revamped Sinn Féin: the republican prisoners who had been detained after the Easter Rising, and who were released by 1917. In the internment camps in England and Wales a new generation of militant leaders had emerged, and as they were released they also began to throw their weight behind the reorganisation of the Irish Volunteers, who were increasingly referred to as the Irish Republican Army and who benefited hugely from the wave of popular unease that accompanied the threat of conscription in 1918.

Sinn Féin took 73 of Ireland's 105 Westminster seats at the first postwar election, in December 1918, effectively wiping out the Home Rulers, who were left with six. The franchise had been expanded, and many first-time voters, including women over thirty, seemed to cast their lot in with the new party. The direction of women's votes may have been influenced by the very visible activities after 1916 of Cumann na mBan. Prior to 1916 it had become more militant in both theory and practice, and many of its members participated in the Easter Rising, though some male republican activists (such as Éamon de Valera) disapproved of the idea of Irish women fighting. After 1916 Cumann na mBan became prominent in propaganda and fund-raising activities for republican prisoners and, by extension, Sinn Féin itself. Its profile may have been out of all proportion to its numbers, but the existence of Cumann na mBan ensured that Irish women had a presence and some degree of representation within the independence movement. The first woman ever

elected to Westminster as an MP was from Sinn Féin: the exotic
figure of Constance Markiewicz, a republican member of the Anglo-
Irish gentry who had married a Polish count.

But neither she nor her colleagues ever took their seats. Sinn Féin
candidates had campaigned on a vow that, if elected, they would
boycott Westminster and instead set up an assembly of their own in
Dublin (although many of these new members of parliament were
in no position to go anywhere, having been elected while imprisoned). On 21 January 1919 the newly elected members from Sinn
Féin still at liberty carried out their promise: they assembled at
Dublin's Mansion House under the banner of Dáil Éireann (loosely
translated as "Irish assembly") and declared Ireland independent.
But the same day as the Dáil met, in an unconnected development,
two RIC officers escorting a load of gelignite to a quarry in Solo-
headbeg, County Tipperary, were killed in an attack led by Dan
Breen and Sean Treacy. The attackers went under the name of the
Irish Republican Army: the IRA.

The IRA was a somewhat amorphous and localised organisation, and had its origins in the remnants of the Irish Volunteers. On
paper its headquarters was based in Dublin, in which the key figures
were two 1916 veterans: the chief of staff, the Gaelic Leaguer Richard Mulcahy, and the energetic director of intelligence, the Cork-
man Michael Collins. But very often IRA units on the ground led
the way. One consequence was that some areas were more active
than others, with Dublin and the southern county of Cork emerging
as particular hotbeds of IRA activity.

The IRA was a young man's organisation, with many of its
members drawn from the Catholic lower middle classes, and it
fought the war of the flea, using guerrilla tactics. Their stock in
trade was ambush and assassination—a far cry from the set-piece
fighting of the Easter Rising, and a pragmatic solution to the fact
that their enemy was far more formidable than they were. The British had difficulties getting to grips with this type of fighting, which
was far removed from their experience of the open warfare of 1914–
18. British rule in Ireland became noticeably more coercive in the
years after 1916, a trend which continued as the IRA campaign
swung into gear. Trade unions and the labour movement also acted
as a third party in the movement for independence: between May

and December 1920 the ITGWU refused to allow British troops and munitions to be transported on the Irish rail network. Sympathy for the republican cause was not confined to republicans only. Class tensions often came to the surface as well, and agrarian unrest remained a fixture in some parts of Ireland throughout the period.

The republican campaign was not just about waging a guerrilla war. Sinn Féin established a form of guerrilla government, in part to fulfil the requirements of their own propaganda but also because they were successfully undermining British rule. They established arbitration courts to defuse local disputes (especially over land) and administer such justice as they could, with the IRA sometimes acting as police. By 1920 Sinn Féin had taken over most of the local authorities in the country and proved remarkably successful at running the machinery of local government themselves.

In 1920 the IRA also became noticeably more audacious and active. Particular targets for the republicans were the police and the judicial system, which by the summer of 1920 seemed to be on the brink of collapse. The British compensated for this with draconian legislation (by the end of the year eight southern counties were officially under martial law) and the recruitment of paramilitary forces drawn from demobilised former servicemen (such as the Auxiliary Division and the special constabulary nicknamed Black and Tans, so-called due to their mixture of police and army uniforms). The new forces acquired an unenviable reputation for indiscipline and reprisals against civilians, some of which had official sanction yet virtually all of which were condoned. Their activities prompted unease among elements of the regular British army along with condemnation in Britain, replete with comparisons to the German invasion of Belgium in 1914. The war in Ireland was not popular.

The increasing repression also led to a major shift in the IRA's tactics. As more and more members were forced "on the run," they were organised into "Flying Columns": mobile units that would roam the countryside, often quite independently, staging ambushes and attacks wherever possible. The tit-for-tat war continued, and soon the most notorious incident of the entire conflict occurred, in November 1920: Bloody Sunday. For a number of years the IRA in Dublin, under the direction of Collins, had been involved in assassinating police officers and civil servants. On the morning of Sunday,

21 November 1920, fifteen current or former British officers (some of whom were Irish by birth) were killed in Dublin. Reprisals followed that afternoon, as twelve spectators were killed when British forces opened fire on a Gaelic football match at the GAA headquarters ground of Croke Park. Later that evening three prisoners were killed in custody in Dublin Castle; one was a civilian detained after a raid on a hotel. On 28 November, seventeen auxiliaries were killed in an IRA ambush led by Tom Barry (a former British serviceman) in Kilmichael in County Cork; parts of Cork City were subsequently burnt down in reprisal attacks. Despite this increasing viciousness, from late 1920 the British put out feelers to determine if there might be a way out of this intractable conflict. But before any negotiations could take place with the independence movement, one outstanding issue received a drastic solution.

In early 1920 new legislation—the Government of Ireland Act —permitted the establishment of two Home Rule parliaments, one in Belfast, and the other in Dublin, though the southern assembly never met. This effectively partitioned Ireland into two jurisdictions, which was plainly meant to cater to Ulster unionists rather than Protestants in the rest of Ireland. Ironically, having started the decade being militantly opposed to Home Rule, Protestants ended it with a Home Rule parliament of their own, and James Craig became its first prime minister. The jurisdiction of the new Belfast parliament—Northern Ireland—was confined by the British government to six of the nine counties of the historic province of Ulster (counties Antrim, Armagh, Down, Fermanagh, Londonderry, and Tyrone). Northern Ireland was essentially intended to be a Protestant enclave, and since only four of the counties had Protestant majorities, it made no sense to extend its jurisdiction across the entire province. But a mere four counties was considered too small to survive, and the British accepted the Ulster unionist argument that six was a happier medium, as this would permit the maintenance of a Protestant majority in the new parliament. The existence of a substantial Catholic minority was deemed an unavoidable necessity. More than five hundred people were killed in the sectarian violence that accompanied the establishment of the new jurisdiction; easily the most violent region in Ireland was Belfast, where more than 450 were killed in the intercommunal violence between 1920 and 1922.

Once Ulster unionist sentiment had been placated by the new constitutional arrangement, the road was clear for the British to open
negotiations with the independence movement in the south. On 11
June 1921, the IRA and the British agreed to a truce.

The Irish War of Independence ended in a stalemate. Even
though it had become increasingly violent in its later stages, the
numbers killed in the years after the Easter Rising were relatively
small. In total, just over twenty-one hundred people were killed in
Ireland between January 1917 and December 1921; to put this in
perspective in terms of excess mortality, perhaps thirty-five thousand Irishmen were killed between 1914 and 1918 in the course of
the First World War, and twenty thousand Irish people were killed
by the Spanish flu epidemic of 1918–19.[6] The British had become
more effective in the months prior to the truce. The IRA had also
become more active, even as they were increasingly stretched; on
the eve of the truce they were trying to secure a large shipment of
the new Thompson submachine gun from the United States. Thanks
to Sinn Féin's campaign of political resistance and the IRA's guerrilla
war, the twenty-six counties that became the Irish Free State in December 1922 had been rendered ungovernable from a British point
of view. Equally, the British army could not, at this juncture, spare
the resources that its high command felt would be required to crush
the "rebellion," and the level of repression that would be required
was likely to be politically disastrous. If the war was over, then negotiations were the next step.

Truce and Treaty

In August 1920, Prime Minister David Lloyd George told the
House of Commons that "the authentic representatives of the Irish
people demand something which Britain can never concede except
as a result of disaster or defeat, and that is secession. We cannot accept it. It would be fatal to the security of the empire."[7] This remained the British bottom line, which perhaps explained why de
Valera (who had spent most of the previous two years on an extended fund-raising trip in the United States) went to London for
exploratory talks in the summer of 1921, but controversially declined to be present at the actual negotiations. It may also explain

the hard line that the British ultimately took at the end of the proceedings. The Irish delegation that went to London was led by Arthur Griffith and Michael Collins. The treaty that they negotiated
with a British delegation that included Lloyd George and Winston
Churchill was signed in the early hours of 6 December 1921, following a dramatic ultimatum from Lloyd George that the alternative was
"immediate and terrible war." If this was a bluff, it succeeded.

The Anglo-Irish Treaty of 1921 was undoubtedly far more substantial than the Home Rule on offer in 1912. It established the
Irish Free State as a dominion within the British Commonwealth,
based on the Canadian model. Members of its parliament were to
swear to be "faithful" to the British monarchy. Ireland had already
been divided into two distinct jurisdictions, though the treaty gave
Northern Ireland the fig leaf of an opt-out clause that would make
its exclusion permanent. In the aftermath of the First World War,
the principle of creating new borders was not unique to Ireland:
after 1919 a defeated Germany lost a large proportion of its national
territory. It is striking to bear in mind that so did a victorious United
Kingdom. But nobody seriously expected Northern Ireland to add
to that proportion by opting out of its union with Britain. Instead, a
council of Ireland would enable the governments in Belfast and
Dublin to discuss matters of common interest, most strikingly,
"safeguards for minorities in Northern Ireland."[8]

Collins openly admitted that he would have gladly defeated the
British were it possible; he did not think that it was, and this in-
formed his decision to sign. He and Griffith brought immense pressure to bear on their fellow delegates to follow suit. Yet Collins's
subsequent observation that in doing so he may have signed his
death warrant left no doubt as to the possible consequences in Ireland. The treaty split the independence movement in acrimonious
fashion. The partition of Ireland was not the main bone of contention
—an indication, perhaps, that it had been accepted as a fact on the
ground, or that it was an issue to be dealt with at another time. The
key issue was Ireland's constitutional status. The IRA and Sinn Féin
had sought a republic, but the Irish Free State was nothing of the
kind, and the fact that the British monarch would remain the head
of state proved particularly obnoxious. Collins famously argued that
the treaty offered "not the ultimate freedom that all nations desire

... but the freedom to achieve it."[9] However, the other side of the argument was that it did not, and that the struggle for full independence was not over. When the Dáil voted on the treaty in January 1922, sixty-four members voted for it and fifty-seven against. The latter group, led by de Valera, walked out. Interestingly, de Valera had himself put forward an innovative compromise whereby Ireland would voluntarily associate itself with the commonwealth, but this proposal was withdrawn in the face of great hostility. Collins and Griffith became the leaders of the pro-treaty faction, while de Valera became the political figurehead for those who opposed the treaty.

Of far greater significance than the split in Sinn Féin was the split in the IRA: those who had actually fought for a republic were particularly unimpressed, and from an early stage it was obvious that the bulk of the active IRA opposed the treaty. The organisation split three ways. One segment followed Collins and became the nucleus of the new National Army. A minority of purists declared their wholesale opposition to the treaty from the outset, and in April 1922 occupied the Four Courts complex in Dublin. But the hardened southern units of the IRA, led by the Cork commander Liam Lynch, held off, and in the early months of 1922 attempts to reach a compromise were initiated. These revolved around the possibility that the new Irish Free State could have a constitution that was republican in all but name; Lloyd George and Churchill, however, made it clear that such a manoeuvre was unacceptable. The first election to the Free State parliament, held in June 1922, also clearly showed that only 20 percent of the electorate were prepared to support parties that unequivocally opposed the treaty. If the British were unwilling to go beyond the boundaries of the treaty, in early 1922 Irish voters in the twenty-six counties were prepared to accept it.

Civil War

The Civil War broke out after Sir Henry Wilson, the former chief of the Imperial General Staff (the most senior position in the British army), was shot dead on his doorstep in London by two members of the IRA (both of whom had served in the British army during the First World War). As a die-hard Irish unionist, Wilson had since become an adviser to the new government in Northern Ireland.

The IRA had been carrying out attacks in Britain since 1920, but none so bold as this. British patience snapped, and the Provisional Government led by Collins and Griffith were told in no uncertain terms that it was time to deal with the anti-treaty republicans whom they blamed for the killing of Wilson.

On 28 June the Free State's new military force, the National Army, began to bombard the Four Courts using artillery borrowed from the remaining British garrison. The buildings remained relatively intact until a massive explosion destroyed the Irish Public Record Office. The fighting in Dublin was over within days, but it also destroyed any remaining hope of compromise. Over the next six weeks the National Army attacked towns held by their opponents, sometimes even landing troops by sea, and soon the Civil War had taken the familiar form of guerrilla warfare. But crucial differences existed between this and the war against the British. At the core of the National Army were members of the IRA, who had been experienced guerrillas themselves. They knew how to fight their former colleagues, and the British ensured that they would not be short of weapons to do so. The Irish Free State received a double blow in August, when Arthur Griffith died of a brain haemorrhage and Michael Collins was killed in an ambush in his native county of Cork. Still, in the following months, their successors proved ruthless in crushing their opponents.

The government and army of the Free State, led now by the Sinn Féin politician and Easter Rising veteran William T. Cosgrave and the former IRA chief of staff Mulcahy, took the view that they were in a war for their very survival, and as a result went further than the British in terms of the measures they were prepared to impose. At least seventy-seven republicans were officially executed during the Civil War, some without trials in reprisals for republican attacks; there was also a large number of unofficial reprisal killings by Free State forces. Despite the mounting ruthlessness of the Civil War, by April 1923 the republican cause was lost, and at the behest of Eamon de Valera (who was quite marginal to events during the Civil War), they laid down their weapons, with the defiant statement that "military victory must be allowed to rest for the moment with those who have destroyed the republic."[10] With that, the Irish Civil War, and Ireland's "revolution," ended with a whimper rather than a bang.

CHAPTER SEVENTEEN

Two Irelands

State Building

The Irish Free State officially came into existence on 6 December 1922—a milestone overshadowed by the killing of a member of the new Free State Dáil by the IRA and the subsequent reprisal execution of four prominent republicans who had been in custody since the previous June. The six counties of Northern Ireland promptly exercised their right to opt out of the jurisdiction of the new twenty-six-county Free State. By the time the Civil War ended in April 1923, the new southern government was faced with its legacy of enormous destruction and disruption. The pro-treaty elements of Sinn Féin coalesced in March 1923 into Cumann na nGaedheal (Society of the Irish), and from the beginning the new government set out its responsibilities under the treaty while cleaving to Collins's notion that it offered a freedom that could be built upon.

With regards to the new state that they ruled, there was major administrative continuity from British rule, which may have contributed to the surprising stability of the state. Most of the civil service, for instance, remained unchanged. The new regime fell back on British institutions rather than the republican ones of the revolution. This may have been an understandable and pragmatic decision in time of war, but it may also have built in a degree of stasis as well as stability. An obvious innovation was the new police force, the

Civic Guards (later renamed An Garda Siochána, or Guardians of the Peace). But this was the exception rather than the rule. The creation of the Irish Free State—Saorstát Éireann—was accompanied by a certain disillusionment after the bitter end of the revolutionary period. The state's premier, W. T. Cosgrave, lacked the charisma of Collins or de Valera; he was perhaps more manager than visionary. But he and his colleagues, such as the steely minister for justice, Kevin O'Higgins, seemed to take the view that the time for visions was past, as they were the ones now tasked with the messy and unromantic job of constructing a viable independent state.

The first task was to guarantee that the government was in charge, which meant dealing with the existence of the huge National Army, nearly fifty thousand strong; this was not an unusual problem in Europe following the war. Collins had been unclear on the question of whether or not the army was the institution that was really in control of Ireland in the early months of 1922, and the subsequent preeminence of the military in terms of conducting the Civil War did little to clarify this. The "army mutiny" of March 1924 brought tensions about its role to a head: a number of former IRA officers in the National Army complained that the new regime was betraying the legacy of Collins. They were faced down by O'Higgins, and Mulcahy was forced to resign (though he later returned to political life); another victim was the IRB, which was finally stood down. By the summer of 1924 the civil power had asserted its authority over the military, and the army was reduced from its peak of more than forty-eight thousand soldiers during the Civil War in 1923 to fewer than six thousand in 1932; it never became integral to the self-image of Irish society. This may have been one reason for the political stability of the Free State. Another was undoubtedly that the most obvious challengers to that stability began to reconcile themselves to coming in from the cold at some stage.

The IRA had been defeated in the Civil War, which left Sinn Féin as the obvious alternative vehicle for republican ambitions. The defeated anti-treaty republicans had, in line with the traditional Sinn Féin policy, boycotted the Free State parliament, Dáil Éireann, which left the Labour Party to provide the only meaningful opposition for the first few years of its existence. But in 1926 Sinn Féin had split over the issue of whether or not to continue abstaining from the Dáil. The majority (including significant elements of the IRA) followed Eamon de Valera to form a new party: Fianna Fáil (generally translated as Soldiers of Destiny). Although the IRA remained a prominent force in Irish life in the 1920s and 1930s, the creation of Fianna Fáil formed an alternative outlet for republican political allegiance. It was an admission that republicans would not achieve their objectives by military means alone, though they would not actually enter the Dáil until 1927.

A striking allegory of the end of the revolution was unveiled in Dublin in 1925: a painting by the Limerick-born painter Sean Keating, entitled, unsurprisingly, *An Allegory*. This was Keating's own response to the Civil War and its aftermath. Two men—one a member of the IRA, the other a member of the National Army—bury a coffin draped in the Irish tricolour flag, and the warring sides in the Civil War thus bury the dreams of the struggle for independence. In the background there is the burnt out shell of a "big house"—a hint of the passing of the old ruling gentry. Many of these ancestral homes were attacked and destroyed during the revolution, and many more fell into decay as the lands that previously sustained them were stripped away by the Land Acts. In the foreground is a woman with a child (based on Keating's wife May) and an exhausted man, and waiting in the wings are a priest keeping an eye on the proceedings and a businessman: representatives of a new, conservative order. Keating's image of a dream that had died can be taken as a representation of the disillusionment that followed the war. O'Higgins notoriously described himself and his colleagues as "conservative revolutionaries"; the two figures on the edge of the painting hint that, in some ways, it was to be business as usual in the Irish Free State.

Economy and Society

The Free State under Cosgrave is often characterized as highly conservative. Arguably this simply reflected some of the elements of Irish society who supported Cumann na nGaedheal, such as former home rulers and southern unionists. There can be no doubt, however, that Cosgrave's government was extremely conservative in economic terms from an early stage, being committed to low taxation and low government expenditure. There was little emphasis on industrialisation, though the impressive Shannon electrification scheme of the late 1920s was an ambitious exception. But continuity rather than change could be seen in the structure of the Irish economy after 1922: the link to the British pound sterling was retained, and livestock grazing continued to occupy pride of place in terms of economic output. It was certainly true that full economic independence from Britain was not feasible at this point, but no attempt was made to explore the possibility. Such complacency found notorious expression in a remark made in 1924 by the minister for industry and commerce, Patrick McGilligan: "It is no function of government to provide work for anyone . . . people may have to die in this country and die through starvation."[1] That this was uttered at a time when the recurrence of famine was feared in the aftermath of the Civil War is striking, to say the least.

One radical social change that did become evident in the Free State was the absence of the Protestant ascendancy. The Land Acts had finally broken the remaining economic power of the landlord class, whose roots could be traced back to the seventeenth century, and the wholesale transfer of Irish land into tenant ownership constitutes the social revolution that preceded the political revolution of the early twentieth century. In the 1920s, in a curious echo of the settlement of the 1660s that had confirmed the existence of the Protestant landed elite in the first place, the Land Commission was established to complete the enormous task of land redistribution under the terms of the Land Acts, which had been suspended on the outbreak of the First World War. The commission redistributed 2.34 million acres, affecting 248,000 families, between 1923 and 1987, easily making it one of the most important drivers of social change in independent Ireland.[2] Yet this did not translate into economic change; the ownership of land seemed to take precedence over the uses to which it might have been put.

Institutional conservatism could also be discerned in the Irish educational system, which was dominated by the Catholic Church (as the majority faith), and which placed relatively little emphasis on innovation. In part, this was due to the fact that independent Ireland was so poor: a lack of money guaranteed that the level of investment in the educational infrastructure following independence would be low. But equally, the state did not seem to attach much importance either to getting more children into the educational system, or keeping them in it for lengthy periods. Attendance at primary school was mandatory for children from six to fourteen years old, beginning in 1926, but secondary education remained out of reach. The deep social conservatism of Irish society meant that education was viewed in purely functional terms. There was a very strong sense, even prior to 1922, that "a limited education in literacy and numeracy was deemed sufficient" for the "poor and working classes."[3] The existing order of Irish society was to be the natural order.

Free State Morality: Public and Private

Sexual morality continued to preoccupy the Catholic Church in independent Ireland, especially due to a suspicion that the upheaval of revolution had weakened the boundaries of public morality. Catholic moral teaching was reflected in restrictions on divorce and the availability of contraceptives, not to mention in the regime of literary and cinematic censorship that was in place by the end of the 1920s. Vigilance was required to counter new threats that might emerge: dance halls were obvious homes for sin, while the music played in them could be seen as even more pernicious; jazz, for example, was often condemned as not merely immoral but un-Irish, and often in explicitly racist terms. Concerns were also voiced about sexual diseases, which could no longer just be blamed on the presence of the British army. In the 1920s an emphasis on the family as a unit could be seen in public discourse, along with punitive attitudes towards unmarried mothers and the provision of welfare. Extramarital sex was seen as a crime in a society where singlehood and celibacy were accepted as necessary choices, and in which women were often painted as little more than temptresses.[4] The participation of women in Irish public life was increasingly restricted from the 1920s onwards; their natural place, according to church and government authorities, was to be in the home, amongst a family. This emphasis on morality may have served to provide a marker of identity: to paraphrase Joe Lee, the Free State might yet prove to be a beacon of light in a naughty world.

But a more sordid reality lurked beneath the veneer of official respectability. The Carrigan committee, set up to devise legislative responses to sexual crime, reported in 1931 that "gross offences are rife throughout the country"; one estimate, based on the low numbers actually reported, is that ten thousand sexual assaults took place in Ireland between 1924 and 1960, with 80 percent of victims under the age of eighteen. Yet in the subsequent debates on the findings, the emphasis was on the necessity to protect men from female blackmailers. The report was suppressed and its recommendations were ignored.[5] The public morality of the Irish Free State was explicitly, if not officially, Catholic. The remarkable spectacle of the enormous international Eucharistic Congress hosted by the Free State in 1932 illustrated the vigour of Catholic lay organisation and belies any notion that the Catholic Church simply imposed its moral authority upon the Free State; in an overwhelmingly Catholic society, it was to be the obvious arbiter of public and private morality.

Northern Ireland and the Boundary Commission

The essential reason why the Free State was an overwhelmingly Catholic society is that most of Ireland's Protestants had remained within the United Kingdom. Even before the Civil War, Collins had been involved in attempts to destabilise Northern Ireland by supporting the IRA there. But there was little appetite to continue this after his death, and the Cosgrave government had to face the fact that there was no easy and obvious Irish nationalist answer to the existence of Northern Ireland. The Free State's erection of customs barriers along the new border in April 1923 can be taken as confirmation of this.

There was, however, another possibility. The treaty of 1921 had contained provisions for a "boundary commission" to adjudicate upon the possible line of a new border between north and south that would reflect demographic realities on the ground; in other words, it would recommend land transfers to permit Protestant regions within the Free State to be transferred to Northern Ireland, and Catholic areas in the north to become part of the south. The nationalist assumption was that the commission would recommend radical changes that would strip the six counties of so much territory that Northern Ireland would be rendered unviable. But in the event, only minor changes were recommended. The leaking of this embarrassing fact resulted in the border being secured as it stood, and the prospect of a "council of Ireland" to enable cooperation between north and south was abandoned. Nothing was or would be done to change the border, and the two Irelands went in largely separate directions for the next four decades.

North of the border the new prime minister, James Craig, consolidated the unionist position. In the 1920s Northern Ireland established armed constabularies, such as those known as the "B Specials," which essentially became an exclusively Protestant force, and enacted special legislation that could be used to quash political dissent that was most likely to come from a Catholic minority who, from an early stage, were reluctant and unwilling to engage with a regime that they viewed as hostile, and vice versa. But that same regime did little to stop this alienation; quite the opposite. In the 1920s unionist hegemony was extended by abolishing proportional representation at elections and redrawing electoral boundaries to favour Protestant voters: Derry became a notorious example of such gerrymandering. These changes squeezed out not only Catholic representatives, but Labour and independent unionist candidates who might gain support in a time of economic turmoil (the northeast had seen a downturn in the years after the Great War). Craig ensured control by a one-party system, and he had no compunctions about conjuring up the image of a nationalist bogeyman to stiffen the resolve of unionist voters who might be tempted to support anyone other than his Ulster Unionist Party, a tactic that would be repeated by his successors. In the 1930s Craig famously observed that if the south was a Catholic state for a Catholic people, then the regime he presided over was a Protestant parliament for a Protestant people. The casual blindness of this observation bespoke its fatal flaw.

Official Identities and the Wider World

One possible venue in which cooperation between north and south was mooted was within the broader arena of the British Commonwealth. The Cosgrave government always had issues with questions of identity. An official commitment to the Irish language had been

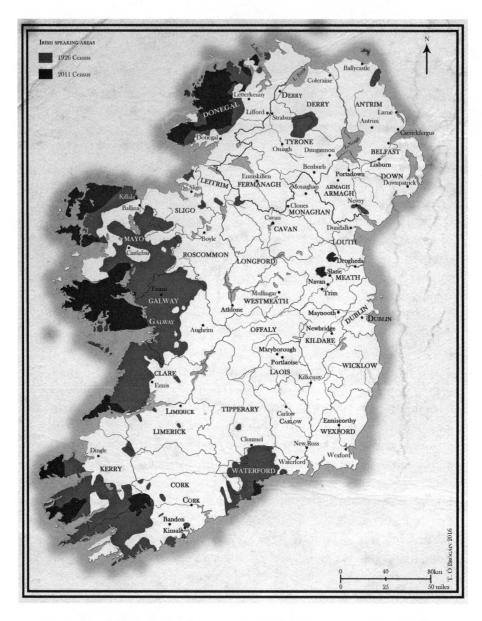

The decline of the Gaeltacht, those areas in which Irish was, or had been until recently, the primary spoken language of a substantial proportion of the population. Despite the Irish state's official commitment to the language, the geographical extent of the Gaeltacht shrank inexorably throughout the twentieth century. By 2011 the total Gaeltacht population was 100,716. While Irish is understood and spoken by sizeable numbers outside the Gaeltacht, English remains the dominant vernacular. (Map by Tomás Ó Brógáin; source, Central Statistics Office, http://www.cso.ie/en)

enshrined in law by the 1920s, which pointed to a degree of fidelity
with the ideals of the Gaelic revival that had preceded the revolution
(though this was perhaps more symbolic than real, given the continued decline of Irish-speaking communities—the "Gaeltacht"—
throughout the twentieth century).

More explicitly political markers of identity were, however,
problematic: the commemoration of Armistice Day (marking the
end of the First World War) at home and abroad, and even the
choice—or lack—of a national anthem all touched upon the uncomfortable fact that the constitutional status of the Free State was anchored within the British sphere of influence. After all, less than a
decade previously, men like Cosgrave and O'Higgins had been involved in a struggle for national liberation against the British. Yet
they did try to carve out a distinct international identity for the state
that would push against the limits set down in 1921 without formally breaking them. In 1923 the Free State was represented at the
League of Nations, and the treaty of 1921 was registered as an international agreement. Diplomatic legations in Washington, D.C.,
Paris, Berlin, and the Vatican followed. Links were forged with
other dominions, and the Irish Free State became an active player in
the process by which the dominions began to assert and obtain their
autonomy. But this cut little ice with an Irish electorate who found
Cumann na nGaedheal's opponents to be an increasingly attractive
prospect.

Fianna Fáil and the Republican Revolution

The repression of republicans during and after the Civil War, most
especially the executions of IRA members during the conflict, ensured that the Free State's minister for justice, Kevin O'Higgins,
was a particular hate figure for Republicans. In July 1927, three
members of the IRA spotted O'Higgins by chance, on his way to
mass in the Dublin suburb of Booterstown, and shot him dead. The
assassination had major political ramifications, as Cosgrave's government rapidly introduced a range of legislation giving it additional
coercive powers and, crucially, closing off the loopholes by which
political opposition in the Free State could remain detached from
the institutions of the Free State. New laws stated that those elected

to the Dáil were obliged to take their seats or else they would forfeit them. This meant, in practice, taking the hated oath to the monarchy. Fianna Fáil, which had continued to abstain from the Dáil, now changed course, took the oath while loudly proclaiming that it was merely an empty formula, and finally entered the new Irish parliament. Once inside the system, the party grew rapidly. Its candidates campaigned on a more radical and attractive platform that was more assertively republican, with a definite appeal to land issues—many Irish farmers were still making substantial payments to the British exchequer for monies lent under the Land Acts—and they gained major support once they entered the Dáil. Fianna Fáil won 26 percent of the vote in June 1927, and 44 percent when they came into government in 1932. Despite attempts at scaremongering by Cosgrave's Cumann na nGaedheal party, who sought to paint their opponents as communists and gunmen, Irish voters opted for Fianna Fáil, memorably described by Seán Lemass, one of its future leaders, as a "slightly constitutional" party. Yet considering that only a few years earlier figures like Lemass had been fighting the government they were now challenging in parliament, the relatively swift transition from insurgency to participation in formal politics was remarkable.

Fianna Fáil were dominant in the 1930s, and began to roll back the original treaty of 1921. Their particular brand of populist republicanism painted itself as being on the side of the worker and the small farmer, though the party was a broad church. Certainly, in the 1930s it proved itself quite progressive (though not radical) on social issues. It initiated housing programmes (twenty-nine thousand new urban dwellings were built between 1932 and 1942, as a genuine response to horrific slum conditions across the state), and introduced legislation to improve social welfare and working conditions. De Valera's government seemed to be holding out the prospect of completing most of the unfinished business of 1921–22, albeit within the confines of the twenty-six-county Free State.

If the economic orthodoxy of the 1920s tended towards free trade, that of the 1930s tended towards protectionism, and de Valera's government took to this with enthusiasm. Large numbers of additional jobs were created in new industries by the end of the 1930s (ironically, many of these depended on British raw material).

On the other hand, Irish farmers were badly hit by the "economic war" waged between Ireland and Britain from 1932 to 1938. It originally began as a dispute over the continued repayment of monies owed to the British exchequer under the land acts. Fianna Fáil refused to pay them, and the British response (which was not so much punitive as an attempt to get the money somehow) was to impose tariffs on a wide range of Irish agricultural produce, especially live cattle and beef, the import of which to the United Kingdom was severely restricted by quotas imposed in 1934. While symbolically important as a marker of independence, the economic war inevitably affected Irish farming producers more than the British consumers of their products: the United Kingdom was, after all, the market for 90 percent of Ireland's exports.

There were also internal problems. The IRA remained an active force, and often came into conflict in the early 1930s with the quasi-fascist Blueshirt movement aligned with Fine Gael (the successor organisation to Cumann na nGaedheal, the name of which could be loosely translated as Family of the Irish), though the threat posed by these faded over time in the face of government repression. External events such as the Spanish Civil War also had the potential to cause unrest. Militant lay Catholicism was exercised by the existence of left-wing republican fringe groups such as the breakaway Republican Congress, and the Catholic Church itself took a very strong line in support of the regime of Francisco Franco, a stance that had significant popular support, but was not shared by de Valera.

Where the government and the Catholic hierarchy did find some common ground was in the drafting of a new constitution that came into effect in 1937, after it was approved in a referendum. In that year the Irish Free State effectively ceased to exist in constitutional terms, due to the passage of the new constitution, largely devised by de Valera. It placed great emphasis on the popular basis of sovereignty, and removed any remaining official links to the commonwealth as it did so; the official name of the state was changed to "Éire," or Ireland. Yet the influence of Catholic social teaching infused the document (which, interestingly in the context of 1930s Europe, extended a degree of official recognition to Judaism). Catholic clerics had been consulted as it was drafted, though they did not always get their way; opposition from within the cabinet ensured the dilution of the original article 44, which in its published version gave Catholicism a special position due to its status as the majority faith. But Catholic social thought could be seen in the articles relating to education, private property, and social policy, amongst other things; the constitution's emphasis on the family unit and the prohibition on divorce were certainly in line with Catholic doctrine and were seen—correctly—as having major implications for the prospects of Irish women. The new constitution was roundly criticised by contemporaries such as the journalist Gertrude Gaffney, who satirically juxtaposed its "reactionary clauses" with sections of the 1916 proclamation that promised equality of treatment for women before caustically concluding that "Mr de Valera has been driven to this by the nightmare of unemployment that has been hanging over him for the last few years, and as I have already stated, by his own innate prejudice against women anywhere outside the kitchen."[6]

The Emergency

Ireland had been an active participant in the League of Nations prior to the outbreak of the Second World War, and de Valera's assumption was that on the outbreak of war between major belligerents, the only realistic option for a small country such as Ireland was to stay outside the conflict as best it could. This was the rational choice, though many other European countries declared themselves neutral only to see this violated brutally by the Nazi regime. But there was a broad domestic consensus in favour of Irish neutrality, and the state of emergency declared at the outbreak of the war gave its name to the period as a whole. Where other countries experienced the Second World War, Ireland experienced "the Emergency."

Enthusiasm for Irish neutrality was not a sentiment shared by the British, who in 1938 had returned three naval bases to Ireland, but still viewed Irish cooperation as vital for their own strategic interests. As head of the U.K. government, Winston Churchill particularly sought to persuade the Irish prime minister (officially termed "Taoiseach," meaning "leader," since 1937) to enter the war by promising Irish unification, but de Valera did not feel the promise would, or could, be delivered on (the British also exerted pressure on Ireland by refusing to permit the export of crucial agricultural goods on occasion). De Valera scrupulously denounced the German invasion of the Low Countries in May 1940, but his overall attitude was one of pragmatic calculation: Great Britain could keep Germany at bay, and could be mollified by surreptitious cooperation. This could only go so far, however; there was a German plan to invade Ireland in the event of an invasion of Britain, and a parallel British invasion plan in order to confront the Germans. The battle of Britain inadvertently spared Ireland from this fate.

Neutrality was certainly no luxury. The Germans dropped bombs on Dublin and elsewhere on numerous occasions, and Belfast, as a major industrial city, was devastated by the Luftwaffe during the Blitz, with the loss of more than a thousand lives in bombing raids in April and May 1941. There was no mistaking what might happen to the southern state should Germany view it as necessary to attack it. It was only after the failure of the German invasion of Russia that the Irish stance shifted: while remaining officially neutral, de Valera's government favoured the Allies and provided unofficial support to them, although both Great Britain and the United States made no secret of their displeasure at the official Irish position. The treatment of combatants who ended up in Ireland is a case in point. Germans were interned, whereas Allied personnel were discreetly taken to the border to eventually return to their units. Indeed, Northern Ireland held a substantial U.S. military presence for much of the war; American soldiers were by no means uncommon on the streets of some Irish towns and cities during the Emergency.

It does seem that public sentiment in the early phases of the war favoured Germany; given the recent history between Ireland and Britain, this was perhaps to be expected. One striking report dated 12 June 1940 tells of two school inspectors in County Mayo, one of whom "indulged in loud and long arguments with members of the public in favour of Germany and he advocated the advent of the German Nazi Party to this country," while the other "conversed with the children as to their views on the belligerents in the present war and advocated that they should favour Germany."[7] There were also pro-fascist and anti-semitic elements in Irish society who were favourable to the Nazi programme. And some of these sentiments were also to be found in the ranks of the IRA. While some republicans had fought against Spanish fascism in the International Brigades during the Spanish Civil War, proof that Irish republicanism was a broad church can be found in the fact that other members of the IRA forged links with the Nazi regime on the grounds that, as the enemy of Britain, it was an obvious ally of the Irish. The dangerous naivety of this position was recognised by the Fianna Fáil government, which took a very harsh line towards potential collaboration. IRA members were interned; five were executed by a government containing men who, two decades previously, had been members of the same organization, while a number of other IRA members died while on hunger—and in one case, thirst—strike.

The war took a toll on everyday life. A rigorous regime of censorship was imposed (which may have helped to hide any cooperation with the Allies); imports were severely restricted, and the war years saw an unprecedented supply crisis and a remarkable level of state intervention to alleviate this, alongside a thriving black market. The government implemented compulsory tillage schemes to grow cereal crops, the better to ensure food self-sufficiency, and massive efforts to harvest turf as a substitute fuel took place. This somewhat authoritarian approach may have been necessary, but it was unpopular. The economic blow was tempered in many cases by emigration to Britain and across the border to Northern Ireland, where war industries and military bases provided employment. As well as this, perhaps as many as seventy thousand Irishmen enlisted in allied armies, usually the British army, and were generally permitted to do so without hindrance, though the fact that some members of the Irish Defence Forces deserted in order to enlist elsewhere proved a thorny issue after the war.

In 1943 de Valera gave a subsequently much maligned radio broadcast in which he outlined a pastoral vision of a simple, rural society unsullied by materialism (though the promotion of this rural-style folk culture at an official level should not be taken as indicative of reality, especially in relation to urban Ireland).[8] Towards the end of the war, in 1945, in a moment of extremely questionable judgement for which he was widely condemned, de Valera observed normal diplomatic protocol by extending condolences to Germany on the death of Adolf Hitler. If public utterances such as these were the image of neutral Ireland that the Irish leader presented to both the country and the wider world, then it should be obvious that the reality of the Emergency was very different indeed. The ultimate rationale for Irish neutrality came in May 1945, when Churchill, in his victory broadcast following the end of the war in Europe, went out of his way to criticize the de Valera government while at the same time praising British restraint in not violating Irish neutrality in time of war. In a thoughtful and dignified response, de Valera argued that a world in which the rights of small nations were subordinate to the aggressive requirements of more powerful neighbours was a world doomed to war. It struck a chord with Irish listeners and helped to justify the legitimacy of his government's stance. Neutrality thus became a benchmark for Irish independence.

CHAPTER EIGHTEEN

The Second Republic

Into the Light

The end of the Emergency did not automatically herald a bright new dawn. Ireland remained an impoverished society with significant social problems. A lack of progress in alleviating enduring issues of poverty and public health could, to some degree, be put down to the exigencies of the war years, but it could also be construed as an indictment of Fianna Fáil rule. The progressive inclinations of Fianna Fáil in the 1930s were now a memory, and by 1948 the party that had been denounced as communists and gunmen in 1932 were being accused instead of corruption. Fianna Fáil was replaced in 1948 by a so-called "inter-party" government, a coalition composed of Fine Gael, Labour, and a number of smaller parties, including Clann na Talmhan, representing farmers, and the new republican party Clann na Poblachta, led by the colourful figure of Sean MacBride. The new taoiseach was John A. Costello of Fine Gael, whose most notable act was his seemingly unilateral decision to declare Ireland a republic in 1949, after which the last links with the commonwealth were severed. The British responded with the Ireland Act of 1949, which confirmed a principle that had been obvious since the 1920s: that the status of Northern Ireland would remain unchanged until such time as its parliament decided otherwise.

For most of its first decade, the new republic was governed by a succession of interparty coalitions and short-lived Fianna Fáil governments. Yet official deference to the Catholic Church remained a factor in Irish public life, and was highlighted by the "mother and child" scheme of 1951. The crusading minister for health, Noel Browne from Clann na Poblachta, announced a scheme to provide free medical care to mothers and children under the age of sixteen. This was denounced by the Catholic hierarchy as unwarranted state interference in the family, and the scheme was abandoned. Browne was forced to resign, having been disowned by his party leader Mac-Bride, who displayed a remarkable degree of deference to the church, as did Costello as taoiseach. The abandonment of the scheme was also a victory for powerful vested interests: the medical profession was firmly opposed to an initiative that would have deprived its members of an important stream of income. But it was generally assumed that the Catholic Church won the victory, and the "mother and child" controversy is an indication of the power and influence it wielded, as epitomised by the authoritarian archbishop of Dublin, John Charles McQuaid. A willingness to accept the dictates of the majority church was shared across the political spectrum.

Catholicism continued to pervade the culture of the new republic. This might, at times, take eye-catching forms, such as vocal and enthusiastic opposition to the "godless" doctrine of communism. Devotion to the cult of the Virgin Mary also became a notable focal point for anti-communism and public piety in the 1950s, one that left an enduring physical manifestation in the form of statues and grottos devoted to her scattered across the island. A more stultifying example of Catholic influence was to be found in the restrictive censorship regime that had been established in the 1920s, and which was applied to a veritable who's who of Irish and international literature. The maintenance of censorship can be interpreted as an attempt to enforce the Catholic moral code, especially in relation to sexuality. Christopher J. O'Reilly, for example, who enthusiastically served as a censor from 1951 to 1956, was particularly exercised by sexual morality, and recommended a wide range of fiction (including works by John Steinbeck, F. Scott Fitzgerald, Truman Capote, Emile Zola, Saul Bellow, Bertrand Russell, Samuel Beckett, Henry Miller, Raymond Chandler, Ian Fleming, and Dylan Thomas) and non-fiction for prohibition. Of 1,294 books he examined, 994—

over 75 percent—were banned (although the scale of his influence cannot be fully discerned). The emphasis on literary greats should not obscure the fact that many other works were banned. Medical books dealing with contraception, for instance, were also struck down. A typical entry in O'Reilly's notebooks recorded the reason for banning Martin M. Goldsmith's *The Miraculous Fish of Domingo Gonzales* (1951) as "indirect references to contraceptives," while *The Next Two Years* (1951) by Peter de Polnay was to be banned due to the presence of "very passionate scenes minutely described." On the other hand, mercy could be shown, which hints at a potential pragmatism: having noted that the contents of Manning O'Brine's *Killers Must Eat* (1951) included "prostitutes. Nudes. Girl dressed in a comb and garters," O'Reilly also noted that it was a "good spy story," and replaced his original stricture to "ban" with a recommendation for "no action."[1]

Despite the official dominance of a Catholic ethos, however, Irish society was not exclusively Catholic. The treatment of the Protestant minority was highlighted by an egregious event in Wexford in 1957, when members of the Protestant community of Fethard-on-Sea, in Wexford, were boycotted at the insistence of a local Catholic priest. The pretext was a dispute within a couple of mixed faith over whether to have their children educated as Catholics, an idea that their mother opposed. This contravened the papal decree *Ne temere*, and the subsequent attempt at economic intimidation (which was eventually condemned by de Valera, who had returned to power) was seen to send out a message that Protestants in the republic might not be treated in the manner befitting a republic. It also confirmed the prejudice towards the supposedly priest-ridden south held by many in the unionist community in Northern Ireland.

The Economy and Emigration

The southern economy after the war was stagnant and depressed; this did not change markedly in the 1950s. Having avoided the devastation of the war, Ireland did not enjoy the benefits of the postwar boom, and the great marker of Irish economic underperformance in the 1950s was the same as it had been a century earlier: emigration, which reached massive levels in the 1950s. The Irish economy diversified throughout the twentieth century, and shifted away from its historic dependence on agriculture. This would have squeezed out many opportunities for manual labour. But there was also a burgeoning awareness that there were other futures with brighter prospects than farming. Young Irish men and women in the 1940s and 1950s were quite unwilling to commit to the drudgery that could characterise life on a small farm; the emotionally barren vista painted in Patrick Kavanagh's poem *The Great Hunger* in 1942 reflected a cold reality. In 1931, one in every four Irish-born people lived overseas, but from the 1930s onwards the major destination for emigrants had been Britain rather than the United States: postwar reconstruction and economic expansion offered plenty of opportunities, and for many young men and women the bright lights of British cities offered an attractive alternative to what was still a conservative society. But the primary motivation was economic, and the impact of emigration, as always, took its toll. In the late 1960s the journalist John Healy looked at where his twenty-three classmates in the local school had ended up since they left it in 1944, and offered this withering, if dramatic, assessment of the toll taken by emigration on his hometown of Charlestown in Mayo: "Out of a random class of 23, 3 remain in the town itself and have given it a renewal of four children. That class has renewed North America with the gift of 24 children; it has renewed Britain with 10 children and Dublin with 7. In any permutation, Ireland loses heavily . . . does one need the symbolism of a truncated tree, standing outside the town, to point up the message?"[2]

By the late 1950s it had become obvious that the protectionism of the 1930s had failed. This was particularly apparent as Ireland was becoming worse off compared with other European states that were shifting towards an emphasis on free trade and manufacturing. De Valera was replaced in 1959 by his deputy Seán Lemass, who duly took on board the radical suggestions of T. K. Whitaker, the (relatively) young secretary of the Department of Finance, who in 1957 had devised a new scheme for economic expansion, based on the principle not of protectionism, but its polar opposite: opening up the Irish economy to global trade in an increasingly intercon-

nected postwar world. The severity of the situation ensured that
Lemass, who had been an advocate of protectionist policies throughout the 1930s and beyond but was less hidebound by ideology than
his predecessor, adopted this approach enthusiastically.

External Affairs

The opening up of the Irish economy had other implications.
Lemass and Whitaker realized that for their new departure to succeed, Ireland would have to come in from the cold in which it had
languished since the end of the Second World War. Ireland's neutral
stance during the war had not been appreciated by the British or by
the United States. Ireland received a limited amount of Marshall
Plan aid—as a Catholic country, it was an obvious candidate for the
western nations to keep on their side in a world where communism
had emerged as a new enemy—but made its international presence
felt outside the North Atlantic Treaty Organization (NATO). Ireland joined the United Nations in 1955, and under the aegis of the
minister for foreign affairs Frank Aiken (a former IRA chief of staff),
the Irish delegation at the U.N. aligned itself firmly with nation-
states emerging from the inexorable breakup of the European empires.
Alongside this diplomatic voice, U.N. peacekeeping also offered a
means by which Irish troops could engage in military operations,
although the deaths of Irish soldiers on U.N. duty in the Congo in
November 1960 was a stark reminder of the potential costs.

In 1961 Lemass and Whitaker identified membership of the European Economic Community (EEC) as an essential strategic goal.
In part, this reflected the realisation that if the Irish economy was to
diversify, it would have to break its traditional dependence upon the
British market. U.S. investment was to be encouraged and facilitated, including through the visit in 1963 of President John F. Kennedy to Ireland, which could be seen in purely symbolic terms as the
return of the descendant of Irish emigrants to his ancestral home-
land. But it was also a sign that, having remained neutral in World
War II and having remained outside NATO, by the 1960s Ireland
was still part of the western fold. The economic implications of this
were of particular importance.

Rising Tides

Economic progress may have depended on attracting foreign investment, but there was also a recognition that the state had a role to play in creating the conditions to make Ireland an attractive destination. As a result, the period of economic growth in the later 1960s also became a time of considerable educational reform, with a great emphasis on modernising an outdated system and making it as widely accessible as possible. Alongside a massive investment in the education system, the most well known consequence was the provision of free secondary schooling beginning in 1967. The issue became a telling source of public friction between the state and the Catholic Church (though ultimately the church retained control of schools while the state committed itself to paying the teachers). This expansion of educational opportunity was simply one of a number of crucial changes that Ireland underwent in the 1960s, not least in a basic material sense: widespread rural electrification and the provision of sanitary facilities occurred in the 1960s as well. This was also a period in which the leadership that had dominated Irish life since independence began to give way to a newer generation. Lemass himself was a prime example. He retired as taoiseach in 1967, but not before appointing a number of younger and talented individuals to key government positions, such as Donogh O'Malley and his own son-in-law, the future taoiseach Charles Haughey.

The relatively new medium of television also played a role in the liberalisation of Irish society in the 1960s. A state radio service—Raidió Éireann—had existed since 1926, but in 1955 television transmissions from the BBC were being relayed from Northern Ireland, and by 1958 there were as many as twenty-eight thousand TV sets in the republic. It was perhaps inevitable that an expansion of the Irish broadcasting service into television would follow. The establishment of Raidió Teilifís Éireann, broadcasting TV as well as radio, introduced a new dimension to Irish life, opening up fresh vistas on the wider world while acting as a forum where the manner in which Irish life was changing could be debated.[3] It also ushered in more prosaic changes: the advent of TV had a detrimental effect on the number of people going to the cinema in the 1960s and attendance at League of Ireland football games from the early 1970s, when the BBC's *Match of the Day* programme made soccer played at a higher level in England available for Irish audiences to view.

The arrival of television and its implications for the future were reflected in a notable programme that sought to apply the techniques of the new technology to an iconic event from the past. The RTÉ production *Insurrection* in 1966 adopted the novel conceit of reporting on the Easter Rising in the manner of rolling news reports. This was the state broadcaster's flagship contribution to the fiftieth anniversary of the rebellion, which was to be used as an opportunity for the Republic of Ireland to put its best foot forward by presenting an optimistic and modern image of itself to both its own citizens and the rest of the world. The Lemass government had very consciously tried to foster community participation in the pageantry that marked the anniversary (though they also tried to ensure that the message they sought to convey would not be marred by what were deemed to be discordant notes). But despite the best efforts of the state to control and direct the process of remembrance, the anniversary of the rising was also an opportunity to articulate a critique of a state that, for many, was an abject failure when judged by the benchmark of the principles of the rising (at least as contained in the famous proclamation). Republicans, feminists, Gaeilgeoirí (Irish speakers), the left: all could take issue with the state that had emerged in the twenty-six counties since 1921, and in 1966 even some visiting journalists reached rather critical conclusions about the country they were being invited to admire.[4]

The juxtaposition of pious tradition with a more ramshackle and messier modernity was the central theme of Peter Lennon's documentary film in 1968, *Rocky Road to Dublin*, which posed the question of what one was actually supposed to do with a successful revolution, and it remains a striking snapshot of a society in flux. Much of this tension arose from a perceived generational clash. As international youth culture arrived on Irish shores, and the dance music played by clean-cut "Showbands" of the 1950s gave way to the slicker (or hairier) representatives of beat culture and the folk revival, inevitable concerns about how the youth of Ireland were being corrupted by music, drink, drugs, or even just city life in Dublin did not stop young people from enjoying themselves, and taking advantage of the greater potential opportunities that the Lemass era seemed to offer. How their elders perceived all this was a different matter entirely.[5] The 1960s were a period of change across the western world, as, rightly or wrongly, youth culture became synonymous with revolt internationally. Ireland was no exception.

CHAPTER NINETEEN

Between Boston and Berlin

Northern Ireland and the Birth of the Troubles

Between the late 1960s and the mid-1990s Northern Ireland became the principal venue for the conflict fought between British state forces and both republican and loyalist paramilitaries that became known as "the Troubles." For twenty-five years, violence defined international views of Ireland. The ultimate origins lay in the treatment of the Catholic minority in Northern Ireland since the 1920s under what James Craig once described as the Protestant parliament, based at Stormont outside Belfast, as the unionist regime was inclined to treat Catholics as second-class citizens in a number of ways. In one notorious incident from the 1930s, a Catholic gardener at the grandiose parliament buildings at Stormont was dismissed on explicitly sectarian grounds; the fact that he was a veteran of the British army, one of whose references for the job had been provided by the Prince of Wales—the heir to the British throne—cut little ice. As a Catholic he was suspect, and was dismissed. The incident served as a microcosm of attitudes towards Catholics in the northern state, and of the official and unofficial discrimination that they routinely faced.

In the aftermath of the Second World War, sectarian outbursts were not encouraged by Northern Ireland's ruling Ulster Unionist Party (the Stormont regime was even held up as a possible model for

Scottish devolution in the late 1940s). But the unchanging hegemony of unionist rule, given an explicitly Protestant complexion by
its links to the Orange Order, ensured that there was no need to
conciliate Catholics, who were not going to vote for them anyway;
so the absence of sectarian rhetoric did not match the reality. In any
event, by the 1960s the unionist regime seemed to be in a reasonably
secure position. Northern Ireland's traditional heavy industries were
in decline, but the supposed threat posed by the rump of the IRA
had fizzled out after an abortive campaign it conducted in 1956–62,
which had been crushed on both sides of the border. As for the government in Dublin, in 1963 the ever pragmatic Lemass had met his
Belfast counterpart, Terence O'Neill, in what seemed to be a historic thaw in north–south relations.

But such overtures were furiously denounced by more conservative elements in unionism, most obviously the militant evangelical
preacher Ian Paisley. The unionist establishment would have to
tread carefully about taking a conciliatory attitude towards Catholics, to avoid alienating Protestant hard-liners. The catch was that,
by later in the 1960s, an increasingly assertive generation of young
Catholics—"baby boomers" who had benefited from the educational opportunities offered by the postwar welfare state in the
United Kingdom—were demanding meaningful reform and an end
to discrimination. The movement that subsequently emerged to
press for these changes adopted much of the rhetoric of the civil
rights movement in the United States (slogans like "One man, one
vote" were applicable to elements of Northern Ireland's electoral
system). But the protests organised by the Northern Ireland Civil
Rights Association (NICRA) met with a furious and violent response
from Protestant loyalists and, disturbingly, members of the overwhelmingly Protestant police force, the Royal Ulster Constabulary (RUC).
Footage of RUC men beating unarmed civil rights protestors—who
were mainly Catholic—at a march in Derry on 5 October 1968
caused outrage after being broadcast on RTÉ in the republic. August 1969 saw concerted loyalist attacks on Catholic areas of Belfast
and Derry, as the situation began to spiral out of the control of the
unionist government of James Chichester-Clark.

The outbreak of widespread unrest in the north had repercussions in the south, and generated a great deal of public sympathy for

beleaguered northern nationalists. This could take a militant form.
Lemass had been succeeded as Fianna Fáil leader and taoiseach by
Jack Lynch, a former hurling and Gaelic football star from Cork, who
eventually dismissed two of his own ministers—Charles Haughey and
Neil Blaney—on suspicion of being involved in gun-running to nationalists in Belfast. By 1969 nationalists in the north were coming
under increasing attack from loyalists and the RUC, and some of
them undoubtedly expected the government in the south to come to
their aid in some capacity. The increasing gravity of the unrest in
Northern Ireland led to British troops being deployed there beginning in mid-1969. Yet the British army, following the orders and the
lead of the Stormont government, soon alienated Catholic opinion
through one-sided and heavy-handed measures. Two of these stand
out: the Falls Curfew of July 1970, when troops carried out brutal
raids looking for weapons in nationalist districts of Belfast, being
attacked as they did so; and the introduction of internment in August 1971, which was exclusively directed at the Catholic community. Measures such as these were milestones in the British army's
alienation of Catholics and nationalists. What they also did was generate increased momentum for the ongoing revival of the IRA.

In the 1960s the IRA had become preoccupied with agitation
rather than armed struggle, though by late in the decade the Dublin
government perceived it as a growing threat. But in Belfast the IRA
had always claimed that the protection of the nationalist community
from Protestant attack was a crucial part of its historic purpose; now
it had a chance to step up to the mark. The resurgence of Protestant
paramilitary forces became evident from 1966 onwards, when members of a group that had revived the pre–First World War name of
the Ulster Volunteer Force (UVF) carried out a number of sectarian
killings of Catholics. The IRA were now revitalized, and marshalled
to protect Catholic areas that came under attack. It also split into
rival factions: the more politicised "Official" IRA, widely (and correctly) seen as more left wing, and the more straightforwardly militant and (arguably) conservative "Provisional" IRA. The basic republican perspective was simple enough. Having been obliged to
defend themselves and their community, they argued that what had
placed them in danger in the first place was the continuation of Brit-

ish rule over Northern Ireland. The solution to their predicament was to be a British withdrawal and Irish reunification, an objective that both factions resolved to fight for. Matters came to a head in 1972, when the killing of thirteen unarmed civil rights marchers by British paratroopers in Derry—"Bloody Sunday"—prompted a backlash that generated huge sympathy for the Provisional IRA. The Official IRA carried out a retaliatory bombing in England at the paratroops barracks in Aldershot, where a number of civilian workers were killed.

The early years of the Troubles were by far the most violent. Half of those killed in the conflict up to 1999 were killed prior to 1977: 1,876 out of 3,636 victims. Working-class areas bore the brunt of the destruction. Death and injury were not evenly distributed, and some areas—such as north Belfast—suffered disproportionately. The single worst year was 1972, when 496 people were killed. Alongside those killed by republican paramilitaries and British state forces, the death rate was swollen between 1972 and 1976 by increasingly active loyalist paramilitary groups such as the UVF and the Ulster Defence Association (UDA), who killed 590 people in this period.[1]

In the aftermath of Bloody Sunday, the Northern Ireland parliament was suspended; it was obvious that any replacement would have to follow a different model. The Sunningdale agreement of December 1973 established a new assembly, in which Catholic and Protestant representatives—the Social Democratic and Labour Party (SDLP) and Ulster Unionists, respectively—would share power in a form of consensus government, with stronger links to the Dublin regime being part of the package. This arrangement was denounced as a sellout by Paisley, who in 1971 had founded his own Democratic Unionist Party (DUP) as a rival to the Ulster Unionists, and by loyalist paramilitaries who orchestrated a general strike that resulted in the experiment being abandoned within months. The lesson that the British took from this was bleak. It was obvious that this form of settlement could offer a solution. It was also obvious that it did not command sufficient support to be workable at this juncture; and in that light, the British discreetly abandoned such attempts at peacemaking, opting to settle instead for managing what they viewed as a security problem within Northern Ireland, and making sure it did not spill across the Irish Sea. This did not always succeed: IRA bombings in Britain, most notoriously at Guildford and Birmingham in 1974, in which twenty-seven people were killed, forced Irish matters into public view. They also resulted in appalling miscarriages of justice, as British police forces eagerly convicted innocent Irish emigrants for these bombings, and successive British governments did not seek a settlement of the issues underlying the Troubles.

British hostility to the IRA was magnified by attacks of this kind, and the advent of Margaret Thatcher's Conservative government in 1979 ensured that attempts at compromise were placed further out of reach during a period that featured appalling sectarian attacks. For Thatcher, the IRA were to be treated as criminals, and criminals did not warrant a political response. Of the two wings of the IRA, the Officials had declared a cease-fire in 1972; the Provisionals remained active, and had concluded that British overtures were not to be trusted. After a disastrous cease-fire in 1975, the Provisional IRA began to reorganise in a manner that was intended to sustain a war of attrition that would slowly but surely grind down British resolve and lead to a British withdrawal. Deadlock—and thousands of deaths—resulted from the obduracy of both sides.

The View from the South

Between 1973 and 1977 the republic was governed by a coalition led by Liam Cosgrave, the son of W. T. Cosgrave. This striking example of dynastic politics in Irish life had another parallel: the younger Cosgrave was inclined, just like his father, to take a harsh line against republicans whom he and his government felt were intent on undermining the republic itself. The prospect of the northern conflict spilling across the border was widely feared; the single greatest loss of life in the Troubles was caused by no-warning car bombings in Dublin and Monaghan in 1974 that killed thirty-three people, and the IRA's assassination of the British ambassador, Christopher Ewart-Biggs, outside Dublin in 1976 was seen to foreshadow what might happen if the conflict did escalate across the border. This was a widespread and genuine fear: after all, angry protestors had burnt down the British embassy in Dublin in the aftermath of Bloody Sunday.

As early as 1972, Lynch's government had established the non-jury Special Criminal Court to handle trials of paramilitary forces, and Cosgrave's government built upon this willingness to take such a harsh line. It was beset by accusations of heavy-handedness, including that the police, or Gardaí, were given free rein to deal with republicans via the use of a so-called "heavy gang," whose actions were hardly within the law. Equally, figures such as the former diplomat and academic Conor Cruise O'Brien, who served as minister for posts and telegraphs, extended the existing regime of censorship while also mounting a formidable (and influential) intellectual attack on the nationalistic assumptions that were assumed to motivate the IRA and its sympathisers.

The 1970s was an undeniably dramatic decade, with economic, industrial, and political unrest at home and abroad, social change, and a new level of consumer affluence, along with sharpened debates about religion, equality, and the status of women in Irish life, all while the continuation of the conflict in Northern Ireland had serious implications for civil liberties and cultural life in the republic. Ireland finally succeeded in joining the EEC in 1973, and with regards to agriculture—an export-driven sector largely obliged to take whatever prices it could get—Irish membership of the common market provided a welcome boost for many farmers, albeit mostly the larger ones. There was also political change: Fianna Fáil returned to power under Lynch in 1977, on a platform whose main plank was a generous but populist budget that had major fiscal ramifications over the next decade. Lynch's relationship with Charles Haughey had been poisonous since he had sacked him in 1970, but Haughey had rebuilt his political fortunes and returned to the cabinet. Lynch was replaced by his old nemesis in 1979, and Haughey took a more nationalistic line while in power; what appeared to be a cordial rapport with Thatcher was soured by his condemnation of the Falklands War in 1982. In the same year Haughey's government fell from power after a sustained period of instability, to be replaced by a new coalition of Fine Gael and Labour Party, led by the liberal Garret Fitzgerald. Ironically, his term of office was marked by controversies of the most rigorously conservative kind.

"Wife-Swapping Sodomites"

In 1967 a constitutional review had recommended that the special position of the Roman Catholic Church in the constitution of 1937 be amended; this status was removed by a referendum in 1972. The inexorable weakening of the traditional alliance between church and state, combined with the broader liberalisation of Irish society, created a space in which key issues that were deemed to be of a "moral" nature—the availability of contraception, divorce, and abortion—became battlegrounds. Liam Cosgrave at one point voted against his own government when it introduced legislation to make contraception more widely available in 1974. The visit of Pope John Paul II in September 1979 could be seen to have ushered in a period in which these issues become particular flashpoints. In 1983 the right to life of the unborn was recognised in the constitution following a referendum, and the acrimonious defeat of a 1986 referendum aimed at legalising divorce in limited circumstances suggested that staunch Catholic conservatism, articulated now by vocal groups such as the Society for the Protection of the Unborn Child (SPUC), was now back in the ascendant. This was the context in which a spate of apparitions of the Virgin Mary—statues of whom were allegedly moving of their own volition—were claimed to be taking place at shrines around the country in 1985. A cynic might say that her timing was impeccable.

There was a good deal of hypocrisy at work here, most notably in relation to abortion. Although it was unavailable anywhere in Ireland, north or south, Irish women had availed themselves of it in Britain since it was legalised there in 1967. In many ways, the potency of these issues was interlinked with the ongoing struggle for women's rights that had become more vocal and pronounced since the 1970s. By the end of the 1980s, it did seem that this conservative perspective could no longer command the degree of consensus it once had. In that regard, the election of the liberal lawyer Mary Robinson to the Irish presidency in 1990 was a symbolic milestone. In 1992 the so-called "X" case saw the Irish Supreme Court decide that abortion could be permitted where the life of the mother was in danger (the case in question related to a fourteen-year-old girl who had become pregnant after being raped); the stance of the court in

favour of conditional abortion was supported by 80 percent of voters, according to polls. The introduction of limited provisions for
divorce in 1995 was a further marker of change (prompting one
prominent, albeit disgruntled, conservative activist to dismiss pro-
divorce campaigners as "wife-swapping sodomites").[2] At the same
time, the moral authority of the Catholic Church was fundamen-
tally damaged from the 1990s onwards by revelations about the
scale of physical and sexual abuse against children in church-run
institutions, such as "industrial" schools, and a succession of high-
profile cases of clerical paedophilia—crimes whose impact was magnified in the public eye by the realisation that the church had attempted to cover them up rather than submit its members to the
rigours of secular law.[3]

The Peace Process

In 1981, ten republican prisoners starved themselves to death in
prison in a protest against their official categorisation as criminals.
The hunger strikes prompted an enormous wave of public unease
that made itself felt at the ballot box amidst the turmoil of the early
1980s. In 1981 the Provisional IRA hunger striker Bobby Sands was
actually elected to the British parliament before he died after sixty-
six days without food (two other hunger strikers were elected to the
Dáil). One consequence of the hunger strikes was that some republicans realized there was a political constituency, north and south,
who might vote for a republican party rather than the SDLP, which
under the former civil rights leader John Hume had become established as the voice of nonviolent nationalism in Northern Ireland.
The obvious party to present to such potential voters was Sinn Féin,
which, since the split that created Fianna Fáil in 1926 had been
essentially a mouthpiece for the various incarnations of the IRA. But
it now began to tentatively contest local elections in the north with
a degree of success, and in 1986 split yet again over a decision to
take seats in the Dáil should members be elected. By this time, the
focus of the republican struggle in the north ensured that both Sinn
Féin (led after 1983 by the Belfast republican Gerry Adams, who
had been elected to Westminster on a traditional abstentionist ticket

the same year) and the IRA were northern-based organisations. Yet the option of politics was, at this stage, to go hand in hand with the continuation of the republican "armed struggle": a combination, as Sinn Féin's Danny Morrison famously put it, of the Armalite (semi-automatic rifle) and the ballot box. There were a number of attempts to stymie the rise of Sinn Féin, most obviously the Anglo-Irish Agreement of 1985, which gave the Irish government an unprecedented consultative role (and even a physical presence) in the administration of Northern Ireland, but this met with such a degree of popular outrage from all strands of unionism that its provisions were not fully expanded upon.

By the late 1980s the IRA had reached a military peak when it was rearmed with vast quantities of weapons provided by the Libyan regime of Muammar Gaddafi (who had decided to support another enemy of the British in the aftermath of the Anglo-American bombing of Tripoli in 1986). But republican hopes of political progress were halted in November 1987 when eleven Protestant civilians were killed by an IRA bomb at a Remembrance Sunday service in Enniskillen, County Fermanagh; given the nature of the event that had been attacked, which could in no way be described as being a military target, it prompted widespread revulsion. Gordon Wilson, whose daughter was killed in the bombing, nevertheless publicly forgave those responsible, and his magnanimity touched a chord with many in the republic. It should be said that loyalist paramilitaries were very active killers during the 1970s, 1980s, and into the 1990s, and British state forces carried out some extremely contentious killings as well. But republican paramilitaries were the most prolific killers by far, being responsible for the deaths of just over half of the thirty-six hundred victims of the Troubles, over two thousand of whom were civilians. Loyalists were more likely to target civilians, while the IRA killed more of what it deemed to be "legitimate targets" (though this proved to be a flexible definition). But neither loyalist paramilitaries nor the British army were seeking votes in the republic. Southern hostility to the IRA was made the more pronounced by this fact: voting for Sinn Féin meant voting for a party that supported the "armed struggle" against British rule, and for many, the Enniskillen bombing was the stark reality of what that consisted of.

There were attempts made to end the conflict, most publicly by the SDLP leader John Hume, who met Gerry Adams to discuss a possible IRA cease-fire in late 1988. More meaningful progress came in the early 1990s, with the advent of a new Conservative prime minister, John Major, a new Fianna Fáil taoiseach, Albert Reynolds, and a new U.S. president, the Democrat Bill Clinton, which created a climate that facilitated progress towards an end to the conflict. But the impetus came from republicans. It had been obvious to both the IRA and the British since the early 1980s that they were deadlocked. This raised the prospect that the IRA war of attrition could backfire: that the republican cause would eventually weaken and wither. The prospect of an IRA cease-fire was officially mooted in 1993 when the British and Irish governments committed themselves to discussing the future of Northern Ireland in the event of paramilitary cease-fires. The final years of the troubles saw some notable and vicious killings, especially by the UVF and UDA, but both the IRA and their loyalist counterparts declared cease-fires in 1994. The burgeoning "peace process" was held up by British demands for the decommissioning of paramilitary weapons. This was interpreted as a political necessity for Major's government to retain the support of unionist members of parliament hostile to what were deemed "concessions" to the IRA, who in turn viewed demands for decommissioning as an unacceptable attempt to humiliate them with a symbolic surrender. Bombings in London and Manchester in 1996 put an end to the first cease-fire, but the election in 1997 of new Fianna Fáil and Labour governments in Dublin and London (led by Bertie Ahern and Tony Blair, respectively) opened the door to negotiations, which resulted in the power-sharing arrangement of the Belfast Agreement, also known colloquially as the Good Friday Agreement, in 1998.

Ironically, despite the ending of the paramilitary campaigns, popular sectarianism often came to the fore during the years of the peace process. This was most obvious in the Drumcree standoff of the mid-1990s, when the refusal of the RUC to let an Orange Order parade march through a Catholic area in the Armagh town of Portadown became a symbol for the perceived erosion on the rights and liberties of Protestants, and brought the local MP, David Trimble, to the leadership of the Ulster Unionist Party. The riposte was that such rights were little more than an excuse for aggressive sectarian coat-trailing. While the Drumcree protest faded away over time, the ending of the paramilitary wars seemed to lift the lid off the simmering sectarianism that defined so much of communal life in Northern Ireland, and which had been overlooked by observers whose attention was taken up by the more spectacular activities of the paramilitary organisations. The fragility of the process was shown by the fact that a republican splinter group carried out the deadliest single attack of the Troubles by planting a car bomb in the market town of Omagh, resulting in the deaths of twenty-nine civilians on a Saturday afternoon in August 1998—after the peace agreement was signed.

Following 1998, a process of prisoner release and demilitarisation took place, though wrangling over weapons—seen as an indication of good faith—continued until the final IRA decommissioning of 2005, which was overseen and confirmed by neutral third parties. The Belfast Agreement was modified in 2005 and power sharing was resumed, but with the veteran Ian Paisley—a bitter critic of the original agreement, who had become the de facto leader of unionism as a result—sharing power with the self-confessed former IRA commander Martin McGuinness. Ironically, the parties now obliged to share power—Sinn Féin and the DUP—are those that were once deemed the extremists, while the more moderate parties that were traditionally the focus of attention from Dublin and London—UUP and SDLP—have undoubtedly been marginalised. Communal tensions have endured, but there was no consensus in favour of returning to the violence of a previous era, even though the root causes of conflict remain in place in what remains a deeply divided society. But an imperfect peace was, by virtually unanimous consensus, better than none.

The Celtic Tiger: Boston or Berlin?

The Republic of Ireland in the 1980s was a state gripped by a recession, burdened by a huge national debt, and ravaged yet again by emigration on a huge scale: more than sixty-one thousand people left Ireland in 1988 alone, with two-thirds of them departing for the United Kingdom.[4] Yet in the last decade of the twentieth century the Irish economy became one of the most dynamic in Europe. The roots of this change go back to the implementation of a recovery strategy for the economy under a new Fianna Fáil government led by Haughey in 1987, and aided by its Fine Gael opponents. The strategy had paid off by the early 1990s, as the manifestation of the economic boom later dubbed the "Celtic Tiger" became apparent. The basis for this was major foreign investment, often from the United States (the offshoots of the boom that followed the end of the Cold War) combined with European Union structural funding aimed at overhauling Ireland's infrastructure. The presence of a well-educated Anglophone workforce in a country that was committed to the European Union in general, and to the European single currency (the "euro") in particular, was an attractive prospect.

The spectacular economic growth of the 1990s saw emigration, a traditional litmus test of Irish economic performance, reverse; Ireland instead began to receive immigrants, most especially after the expansion of the European Union into the former Soviet bloc in 2004. Two telling markers of wealth were huge increases in both consumer spending and alcohol consumption on the part of a population with a relatively young demographic. The republic's population, having reached a historic low of 2,818,341 in 1961, by 2011 stood at 4,588,252, and in 2016 had grown to 4,757,976 (the total population of the island of Ireland in 2011, when census returns were taken in both the Republic and Northern Ireland, was approximately 6,403,000). The upsurge in the southern economy had an impact on the emigrant flow: young Irish people were staying at home during the boom, as there were now jobs to be had, and were fond of giving their newly earned cash to retailers and barmen. Physical changes in infrastructure took place, though this level of development had its own drawback: the housing bubble of the early 2000s is what ultimately scuppered the Irish economic "miracle" in spectacular style after 2008.

The growth of the economy was managed to a degree by the process of consensus governance known as "social partnership." The governing system of independent Ireland—government, civil service, media—was established by the 1950s, and from the 1960s the state took a more interventionist role in economic and social planning. The "social partnership" process that emerged in the 1990s was perhaps not as new as it sounded; cooperation among business, unions, and the agricultural sector had been evident since the 1960s in order to permit a negotiated blueprint for economic progress. Strikes and industrial unrest had also been a surprisingly common feature of Irish life from the 1960s to the 1980s, but by the late 1980s unions were wary that, due to the impact of the recession and the resurgence of mass emigration, their position was potentially weakened with regards to any confrontation with the government that might occur. Social partnership was attractive to Irish unions, and the maintenance of industrial peace allowed the state to present the republic to potential investors as free from industrial militancy. This manner of governing was continued in the National Development Plans of the late twentieth century, although there was an expansion in the range of stakeholders involved in such negotiations. Technological advances and late twentieth-century "globalisation" aided its diversification; while the United Kingdom accounted for 90 percent of Irish exports in the 1940s (30 percent of which were cattle), it took in only 30 percent by the 1990s. The long-term strategy of encouraging external investment was seen in the fact that by 1998, computers and chemicals accounted for 40 percent of Irish exports.[5] That said, the manner in which Ireland was promoted as a lightly regulated venue for financial services remains a murky chapter of recent history.

The cultural impact of the boom could be seen throughout Irish society: in infrastructure, housing, artistic output, social life, sport, travel, and, more subjectively, in the ambitions and aspirations of a populace who have experienced a degree of prosperity and opportunity unprecedented in Irish history. Yet the boom also highlighted stark socioeconomic inequalities that have persisted in Irish life, and the 1990s and 2000s saw an ongoing stream of investigations and revelations into corruption and sexual abuse by members of the Catholic Church; recent history has its dark chapters. The ending of the boom in 2008, with the spectacular collapse of a property bubble created by the availability of cheap credit and the reckless willingness to lend it without discretion, will leave its own legacy. The ruinous activities of institutions such as the Anglo-Irish Bank (now liquidated) caused the Fianna Fáil government of Brian Cowen to guarantee the assets of the Irish banking sector, a controversial move that has left a huge financial burden likely to be an issue for years to come. The downturn of 2008 led to a series of austerity budgets, and in 2010 the republic was forced to seek assistance from the International Monetary Fund. Fiánna Fáil, which spent more time in government than any other party since 1922, was devastated at the polls in 2011, to be replaced by a coalition of Fine Gael and the Labour Party. If in 2011 the Irish electorate had punished one ruling party for overseeing the bust, in 2016 they punished two more, as Fine Gael support dropped significantly, the Labour Party were devastated, and Fianna Fáil embarked on a modest recovery. Two phenomena could be discerned between both general elections: a new proliferation of smaller parties and independent, non-party candidates (often campaigning on localised issues), and the fact that Sinn Féin had secured a new position as a significant political force in the Republic as well as Northern Ireland. Between 2011 and 2016 the Irish political system seemed to fragment and shift leftward, though the full implications of this in terms of Ireland's traditional party system remain to be seen.

The 2011 election result in particular was a reflection of social and economic conditions on the cusp of the second decade of the twenty-first century, and it might be worth ending with a brief glance at a political party that can never have a vote cast for them again. The now defunct Progressive Democrats had been founded in the 1980s by dissident Fianna Fáilers, and attracted support for their perceived combination of liberal social policies and especially their commitment to free market economics. As partners in coalition, they became a fixture of Fianna Fáil governments during the boom, and have been blamed for exerting an influence over the larger party, most especially in relation to economic policy. The Progressive Democrats were decimated in 2007 and have ceased to exist, but one of their leaders, Mary Harney, once remarked that the economic policies she and her colleagues advocated were perhaps more in line with the United States than with Ireland's European neighbours. Between that and its significant historical links to North America, Ireland was, Harney suggested, closer to Boston than to Berlin. A cynic might suggest that before 2008 Ireland was too close to Boston and too far from Berlin; after 2008, and especially after the bailout of 2010, another cynic might suggest that Ireland has ended up being far too close to both at different times, with different results. A historian might prove to be a third cynic; but his or her judgement on the recent past might, at this stage, be far too close to call.

Where Historians Disagree

An Epilogue

I N CONTRAST TO ITS predecessor, the history of twentieth-century Ireland is a very lively and contested field indeed. The revolutionary period in particular has thrown up a number of controversies and debates. The first relates to the Irish participation in the First World War, a subject that, until relatively recently, was surprisingly neglected, partly due to the awkward realities of how Ireland achieved its independence. It was difficult to unequivocally commemorate the First World War when Irish military service took place in the British armed forces; those were the same forces, after all, that Irish men and women fought against to achieve independence. This is not to say that the memory of the war was completely neglected, but it was undoubtedly marginalised in Irish public life, and with the outbreak of the Troubles in Northern Ireland it declined even further from public view in the south.[1] Equally, the war was commemorated by members of the Protestant community in the south and by unionists in Northern Ireland. But there is now a rich and growing literature on the Irish involvement in the conflict that saw far more Irish participants and victims than the subsequent struggle for independence.[2]

With regards to the struggle for independence itself, the Easter Rising of 1916 remains contentious: was it a reckless attempt at martyrdom, or a more pragmatic attempt at an uprising that fell at the final hurdle? The most recent assessment by Fearghal McGarry leans towards the latter, though it does not do so uncritically; the fact that large numbers of testimonies from the period have become available in recent years allows one to paint a very different picture of the rebellion based on the experience of those who participated in it.[3] As for the subsequent War of Independence and Civil War, a very controversial issue to have emerged in recent years relates to whether or not the revolution had a sectarian element, and if so, to what degree? The Canadian historian Peter Hart argued that the IRA campaign in Cork had a pronounced sectarian dimension; this has prompted vigorous criticisms of his method, along with wider reassessments of whether or not the argument for republican sectarianism may be true.[4] While it contained sectarian elements—as did Irish society as a whole—sectarian conflict was not the IRA's reason for being. The issue is muddied by the political allegiance of many Protestants as loyalists who would have been hostile to the IRA anyway, and vice versa. A more telling indication of wholesale sectarianism relates to the decline of the Protestant population; but recent research does not support claims that Protestants in the Irish Free State were subject to any campaign of "ethnic cleansing," as the population did not drop any more than might have been expected anyway.[5] That said, the Protestant minority in the south were marginalised and sometimes discriminated against after 1922.[6]

Many of these debates about the revolutionary period are influenced, to some degree, by the experience of the more recent Troubles. With regards to Northern Ireland itself, the question of institutional discrimination against the Catholic minority remains an issue. The existence of such discrimination is not disputed; the extent of it is, however. It should be said that the release and digitisation of the collections of the Bureau of Military History and of extensive pension files for active service in the revolutionary decade, along with the existence of substantial archival collections (such as the papers of Richard Mulcahy and Ernie O'Malley) permit a detailed examination of the Irish revolution that was not possible for earlier generations of historians.[7]

As for the society that existed in the south after the revolution, it has been argued that Ireland underwent a conservative political counterrevolution.[8] Irish neutrality during the Second World War remains a controversial topic, with disagreement between those who suggest that Ireland should have joined the Allied war effort and those who argue that neutrality was the best and most pragmatic choice for a small, relatively poor state.[9] Surprisingly, the social and economic history of Ireland during the war has been overshadowed by an emphasis on diplomatic history and the morality of neutrality, but Clair Wills and Bryce Evans have recently examined the experience of everyday life during the Emergency.[10]

Developments in recent years have had a profound impact on assessments of Ireland since independence, most especially revelations about the manner in which Irish citizens were incarcerated in what has been dubbed an "architecture of containment," largely run by the Catholic Church with the support of the state. Children, often from poorer backgrounds, and single women who were, for whatever reason, deemed to be morally delinquent were incarcerated in a surprisingly extensive network so-called "Magdalene" institutions and "industrial" and "reform" schools. Enforced adoptions and sexual abuse seem to have been rife in these places, and the circumstances and conditions were often horrific. (More recently, revelations of wholesale sexual abuse by members of the Catholic Church have become intertwined with these issues.)[11] The uncovering of the extent of this system of incarceration poses awkward questions about the nature of the state and society that accepted and facilitated their existence, though their history has been explored by official inquiries, journalists, and social scientists rather than by historians.[12] It should be said that the importance of class to discussions of recent Irish history remains underdeveloped in relation to other countries, and women's history can often be seen as a niche interest.

"Revisionism" is the single most potent word in the study of modern Irish history. The inclination to reexamine the Irish past using more "professional" standards of examination and exposition could be seen in the work of Irish historians from the 1930s onwards.[13] This became an imperative with the outbreak of the troubles in Northern Ireland from the late 1960s onwards, which forced many to reexamine long-held beliefs in the context of a new conflict.[14] But, to paraphrase the U.S. historian Perry Curtis, revisionism is like cholesterol; there are good and bad versions. The good version is the basic professional necessity for any historian to reevaluate their subject in the light of new evidence.[15] The bad version is a revisionism that is motivated by ideology—such as hostility towards Irish nationalism—which can end up replacing one type of orthodoxy with another.[16] There is no denying the academic and popular influence of Irish revisionism, though its intellectual history remains to be written. Another influential thesis, as applied to Ireland from literary and cultural studies, was that Ireland was a classic "postcolonial" society, and that many of its social and institutional problems could be traced back to this; that said, it is a thesis that has been much debated and which has not always been accepted by historians. Indeed, it has been seen sometimes as the polar opposite of "revisionism."[17] If these debates can be seen as offshoots of the conflict in Northern Ireland, then mention should be made of an ongoing question that is still being investigated and which has serious implications for recent history: the degree to which members of the British security forces colluded with loyalist paramilitary groups from the 1970s onwards.[18]

As we move closer to the present, recent history has to be explored through its "first drafts": the works of journalists and other commentators. The financial crisis of 2008–10 is too close to have been fully scrutinised by historians, though aspects of it have been explored in some valuable journalistic accounts.[19] One question that might tentatively be asked of historians is: how deep were its roots in Ireland? Even aside from the emergence of the "Celtic Tiger," were the foundations of the Irish manifestation of the global financial crisis laid by deeper structural issues in the Irish economy (such as an unhealthy dependence on construction) and in Irish political culture (such as corruption)? Some recent studies have sought to address this question, or at the very least to point towards an answer.[20]

Finally, by way of conclusion it is worth looking at two excellent and very different major histories of Ireland that had a public impact in the late 1980s (because no comparable history of Ireland has had a similar impact since then!). The first was Roy Foster's *Modern Ireland*, an explicitly revisionist text that synthesised a generation of academic scholarship and presented it to a new audience.[21] His emphasis on the overlooked complexities of Irish history, and his attempt to examine that history on its own terms without constant recourse to the Anglo-Irish relationship, has proven exceptionally influential (though his work has often been critiqued). The second major history of Ireland to make a public splash was Joseph Lee's *Ireland, 1912–1985*.[22] With a much firmer emphasis on modern economic history, Lee also put forth a stark hypothesis that was more challenging in its own way than Foster's deconstruction of "myths": that the Irish state, since its inception, had underperformed relative to the other small European states (such as Denmark and Finland) that were its natural peers, and had fallen short of its full potential. Lee published his book in 1989, before the advent of the "Celtic Tiger." Arguably, his thesis did not fit the prevailing mood of the 1990s and early 2000s, when suggestions that Ireland had underperformed might be dismissed on the grounds that economic expansion and social change at the turn of the millennium proved that it was making up for lost time. Events since 2008 have naturally taken the shine off this rapid progress, and while Lee's much-discussed thesis had slipped from view prior to this, its relevance has surely reemerged, and may be built upon in the future; proof, if it were needed, that the writing of history changes as much as history itself.

Notes

Introduction

1. F. H. A. Aalen, "The Irish Rural Landscape: Synthesis of Habit and History," in *Atlas of the Irish Rural Landscape*, ed. F. H. A. Aalen, Kevin Whelan, and Matthew Stout (Cork: Cork University Press, 2011), 4–31.
2. Ken Nichols, "Gaelic Economy and Society," in *A New History of Ireland*, vol. 2: *Medieval Ireland, 1169–1534*, ed. Art Cosgrove (Oxford: Oxford University Press, 1987), 379–438.
3. Kevin Down, "Colonial Economy and Society," in *A New History of Ireland*, vol. 2, ed. Cosgrove, 439–91.
4. Kevin Whelan, "The Modern Landscape: From Plantation to Present," in *Atlas of the Irish Rural Landscape*, ed. Aalen, Whelan, and Stout, 73–113.

Chapter One. New Faith, New Kingdom

1. Quoted in Brendan Bradshaw, *The Irish Constitutional Revolution of the Sixteenth Century* (Cambridge: Cambridge University Press, 1979), 201.
2. Tony Crowley, *Wars of Words: The Politics of Language in Ireland, 1534–1998* (Oxford: Oxford University Press, 2004), 12–15.
3. Brendan Bradshaw, *The Dissolution of the Monastic Orders in Ireland in the Reign of Henry VIII* (Cambridge: Cambridge University Press, 1976), 229.
4. Christopher Maginn, "Surrender and Regrant in the Historiography of Sixteenth-Century Ireland," *Sixteenth-Century Journal*, 38:4 (2008), 955–74.
5. W. J. Smyth, *Map-Making, Landscapes, and Memory: A Geography of Colonial and Early Modern Ireland, 1530–1750* (Cork: Cork University Press, 2006), 21–53.
6. Quoted in Ciaran Brady, *Shane O'Neill* (Dundalk: Dundalgan Press, 1996), 14.

Chapter Two. Elizabethan Ireland

1. Crowley, *Wars of Words*, 15–18.
2. Quoted in Ciaran Brady, *The Chief Governors: The Rise and Fall of Reform Government in Tudor Ireland*, 1536–1588 (Cambridge: Cambridge University Press, 1994), 138.
3. Rory Rapple, "Taking Up Office in Elizabethan Connacht: The Case of Sir Richard Bingham," *English Historical Review*, 123 (2008), 277–99.
4. David Edwards, "Beyond Reform: Martial Law and the Tudor Reconquest of Ireland," *History Ireland*, 5:2 (1997), 16–21.
5. Patricia Palmer, "'An Headlesse Lady' and 'a Horses Loade of Heads': Writing the Beheading," *Renaissance Quarterly*, 60:1 (2007), 25–57.
6. Anthony McCormack, "The Social and Economic Consequeces of the Desmond Rebellion of 1579–1583," *Irish Historical Studies*, 34:113 (2004), 1–15.
7. Quoted in Rory Rapple, *Martial Power and Elizabethan Political Culture: Military Men in England and Ireland*, 1558–1594 (Cambridge: Cambridge University Press, 2009), 244.
8. James Ware, *Ancient Irish Histories: The Works of Spenser, Campion, Hanmer, and Marlborough*, 2 vols. (Dublin, 1809), i, 166–67.
9. Ciaran Brady, "Conservative Subversives: The Community of the Pale and the Dublin Administration, 1556–86," in *Radicals, Rebels, and Establishments*, ed. P. J. Corish (Belfast: Appletree Press, 1985), 11–32.
10. Christopher Maginn, "The Baltinglass Rebellion, 1580: English Dissent or a Gaelic Uprising?," *Historical Journal*, 47:2 (2004), 205–32.
11. Colm Lennon, "Taking Sides: The Emergence of Irish Catholic Ideology," in *Taking Sides?: Colonial and Confessional Mentalities in Early Modern Ireland*, ed. Vincent P. Carey and Ute Lotz-Heumann (Dublin: Four Courts Press, 2003), 78–93.

Chapter Three. Tyrone's Rebellion

1. Quoted in Hiram Morgan, *Tyrone's Rebellion: The Origins of the Nine Years War in Tudor Ireland* (Woodbridge: Boydell, 1992), 85.
2. Hiram Morgan, "Hugh O'Neill and the Nine Years War in Tudor Ireland," *Historical Journal*, 36:1 (1993), 21–37.
3. Vincent Carey, "'What Pen Can Paint or Tears Atone?': Mountjoy's Scorched Earth Campaign," in *The Battle of Kinsale*, ed. Hiram Morgan (Bray: Wordwell, 2004), 205–16.
4. Quoted in W. P. Kelly, ed., *Docwra's Derry: A Narrative of Events in North-West Ulster, 1600–1604* (Belfast: Ulster Historical Foundation, 2003), 23.
5. Hiram Morgan, "The 'Wild Man of the Woods' and 'the Hunting of the Earl of Rone': Tyrone in English Folk Tradition," *History Ireland*, 15:4 (2007), 9–11.
6. Breandán Ó Buachalla, "'James Our True King': The Ideology of Irish

Royalism in the Seventeenth Century," in *Political Thought in Ireland Since the Seventeenth Century*, ed. D. G. Boyce, Robert Ecclehall, and Vincent Geogheghan (London: Routledge, 1993), 9–14.

Where Historians Disagree

1. Nicholas Canny, "Why the Reformation Failed in Ireland: Une Question Mal Posée," *Journal of Ecclesiastical History*, 30 (1979), 423–50, at 450; Karl Bottigheimer, "The Failure of the Reformation in Ireland: Une Question Bien Posée," *Journal of Ecclesiastical History*, 36 (1985), 196–207. See also Henry A. Jefferies, "Why the Reformation Failed in Ireland," *Irish Historical Studies*, 40 (2016), 151–70.
2. Canny, "Why the Reformation Failed in Ireland," 440.
3. Bottigheimer, "The Failure of the Reformation in Ireland," 197.
4. Lennon, "Taking Sides."
5. James Murray, *Enforcing the English Reformation in Ireland: Clerical Resistance and Political Conflict in the Diocese of Dublin*, 1534–1590 (Cambridge: Cambridge University Press, 2009), 317.
6. Steven G. Ellis, *Tudor Frontiers and Noble Power: The Making of the British State* (Oxford: Oxford University Press, 1995).
7. Bradshaw, *The Irish Constitutional Revolution*; Brendan Bradshaw, "The Tudor Reformation and Revolution in Ireland and Wales: The Origins of the British Problem," in *The British Problem: State Formation in the Atlantic Archipelago*, 1534–1707, ed. Brendan Bradshaw and John Morrill (London: Macmillan, 1996), 39–65.
8. D. B. Quinn, *The Elizabethans and the Irish* (Ithaca: Cornell University Press, 1966); Nicholas Canny, *The Elizabethan Conquest of Ireland: A Pattern Established* (Hassocks: Harvester Press, 1976); Nicholas Canny, *Making Ireland British*, 1580–1650 (Oxford: Oxford University Press, 2001).
9. Brady, *Chief Governors*; Ciaran Brady, "From Policy to Power: The Evolution of Tudor Reform Strategies in Sixteenth-Century Ireland," in *Reshaping Ireland: Colonization and Its Consequences*, ed. Brian Mac Cuarta (Dublin: Four Courts Press, 2011), 21–42.
10. David Edwards, "The Escalation of Violence in Sixteenth-Century Ireland," in *Age of Atrocity: Violence and Political Conflict in Early Modern Ireland*, ed. David Edwards, Padraig Lenihan, and Clodagh Tait (Dublin: Four Courts Press, 2007), 34–78. See also Brendan Kane, "Ordinary Violence?: Ireland as Emergency in the Tudor State," *History*, 99:336 (2014), 444–67.
11. See the relevant essays by Kevin Down and Kenneth Nichols in *A New History of Ireland*, vol. 2, ed. Cosgrove, and by D. B. Quinn and Kenneth Nichols in *A New History of Ireland*, vol. 3: *Early Modern Ireland*, 1534–1691, ed. T. W. Moody, F. X. Martin, and F. J. Byrne (Oxford: Oxford University Press, 1976).

Chapter Four. Plantation

1. Susan Flavin, "Consumption and Material Culture in Sixteenth Century Ireland," *Economic History Review*, 64:4 (2011), 1144–74.
2. Jane Ohlmeyer, *Making Ireland English: The Irish Aristocracy in the Seventeenth Century* (New Haven: Yale University Press, 2012), 42, 48, 136.
3. Raymond Gillespie, *The Transformation of the Irish Economy*, 1550–1700 (Dublin: Economic and Social History Society of Ireland, 1998), 33.
4. Ó Buachalla,"'James Our True King,'" 13–14.
5. Risteard B. Breatnach, "Elegy on Donal O'Sullivan Beare (1618)," *Éigse*, vol. 7, part 2 (1953–55), 174–75. Kindly reproduced by permission of editor Liam Mac Mathúna and publisher National University of Ireland.
6. Joep Leerssen, *Mere Irish and Fíor-Ghael: Studies in the Idea of Irish Nationality, Its Development and Literary Expression Prior to the Nineteenth Century* (Cork: Cork University Press, 1996), 264–77.
7. Quoted in Raymond Gillespie, *Reading Ireland: Print, Reading, and Social Change in Early Modern Ireland* (Manchester: Manchester University Press, 2005), 19.
8. *Historical Manuscripts Commission: Calendar of the Manuscripts of the Marquess of Ormonde*, new series, 8 vols. (London: HMSO, 1902–20), 2:12.

Chapter Five. The Wars of the Three Kingdoms

1. "O'Connolly's relation of the plot to seize Dublin Castle": http://1641.tcd.ie/deposition.php?depID=840001r001a (accessed 7 April 2017).
2. Quoted in Elaine Murphy, *Ireland and the War at Sea*, 1641–53 (Woodbridge: Boydell & Brewer, 2012), 4.
3. Quoted in Thomas Bartlett, *The Academy of Warre: Military Affairs in Ireland* (Dublin: National University of Ireland, 2002), 9.
4. Padraig Lenihan, "War and Population, 1649–52," *Irish Economic and Social History*, 24 (1997), 1–21.

Chapter Six. The Cromwellian Conquest and the Restoration

1. C. H. Firth and R. S. Rait, eds., *Acts and Ordinances of the Interregnum*, 3 vols. (London: HMSO, 1911), 2:598–603.
2. John Cunningham, "Oliver Cromwell and the 'Cromwellian' Settlement of Ireland," *Historical Journal*, 53:4 (2010), 919–37.
3. *The Down Survey of Ireland: Mapping a Century of Change*, Trinity College Dublin, http://downsurvey.tcd.ie/index.html (accessed 9 May 2016).
4. Edmund Ludlow, *Memoirs of Edmund Ludlow, with a Collection of Original Papers* (London, 1751), 146.
5. *The Down Survey of Ireland* (http://downsurvey.tcd.ie; accessed 30 May

2016). See also Kevin McKenny, "The Restoration Land Settlement in Ireland: A Statistical Interpretation," in *Restoration Ireland: Always Settling and Never Settled*, ed. Coleman A. Dennehy (London: Ashgate, 2007), 35–52.

6. Karl Bottigheimer, "The Restoration Land Settlement in Ireland: A Structural View," *Irish Historical Studies*, 18:69 (1972), 19–20.

7. Cecile O'Rahilly, *Five Seventeenth-Century Political Poems* (Dublin: Institute for Advanced Studies, 1952), 76, 79; Vincent Morley, "Views of the Past in Irish Vernacular Literature, 1650–1850," in *Unity and Diversity in European Culture, c. 1800: Proceedings of the British Academy*, vol. 134, ed. Tim Blanning and Hagen Schulze (Oxford: Oxford University Press, 2006), 180–81. Original Irish text reproduced by permission of the Governing Board of the School of Celtic Studies of the Dublin Institute for Advanced Studies.

8. *The Statutes at Large, Passed in the Parliaments Held in Ireland*, 13 vols. (Dublin, 1786), 2:239–45.

9. Leerssen, *Mere Irish and Fíor-Ghael*, 259–64.

10. Quoted in *Verse in English from Tudor and Stuart Ireland*, ed. Andrew Carpenter (Cork: Cork University Press, 2003), 410.

11. Ohlmeyer, *Making Ireland English*, 312.

12. William Petty, "The Political Anatomy of Ireland," in *The Economic Writings of Sir William Petty*, ed. C. H. Hull, 2 vols. (London, 1899), 2:155–57.

Chapter Seven. Two Kings

1. John Miller, "The Earl of Tyrconnell and James II's Irish Policy," *Historical Journal*, 20:4 (1977), 803–23.

2. Quoted in Éamonn O'Ciardha, *Ireland and the Jacobite Cause, 1685–1766: A Fatal Attachment* (Dublin: Four Courts Press, 2002), 83.

Where Historians Disagree

1. Kevin Kenny, ed., *Ireland and the British Empire* (Oxford: Oxford University Press, 2004); Joe Cleary, "Amongst Empires: A Short History of Ireland and Empire Studies in International Context," *Éire-Ireland: A Journal of Irish Studies*, 42:1 & 2 (Spring/Summer 2007), 11–57.

2. Liam Kennedy, "Modern Ireland: Post-Colonial Society or Post-Colonial Pretensions?," *The Irish Review*, 13 (Winter 1992–93), 107–21.

3. Canny, *Making Ireland British*; David Dickson, *Old World Colony: Cork and South Munster, 1630–1830* (Cork: Cork University Press, 2005); W. J. Smyth, *Map-Making, Landscapes, and Memory*.

4. Jim Smyth, "The Communities of Ireland and the British State, 1660–1707," in *The British Problem*, ed. Bradshaw and Morrill, 246–61.

5. Essex to William Harbord, 28 March 1674, in *Essex Papers, Volume I, 1672–79*, ed. Osmond Airy (London, 1890), 200–202.

6. Jane Ohlmeyer, "A Laboratory for Empire?: Early Modern Ireland and English Imperialism," in *Ireland and the British Empire*, ed. Kenny, 29.

7. See the essays in Bradshaw and Morrill, eds., *The British Problem*; Nicholas Canny, "Writing Early Modern Mistory: Ireland, Britain, and the Wider World," *Historical Journal*, 46:3 (2003), 723–47.

8. Jane Ohlmeyer, "The 'Old' British Histories?," *Historical Journal*, 50:2 (2007), 499–512.

9. Eamon Darcy, *The Irish Rebellion of 1641 and the Wars of the Three Kingdoms* (Woodbridge: Boydell & Brewer, 2013); John Gibney, *The Shadow of a Year: The 1641 Rebellion in Irish History and Memory* (Madison: University of Wisconsin Press, 2013).

10. 1641 Depositions, http://1641.tcd.ie (accessed 9 May 2016).

11. Canny, *Making Irish British*, esp. 336–401; Nicholas Canny, "The 1641 Depositions as a Source for the Writing of Social History: County Cork as a Case Study," in *Cork: History and Society*, ed. Patrick O'Flanagan and Cornelius G. Buttimer (Dublin: Geography Publications, 1993), 249–308; Raymond Gillespie, "Migration and Opportunity: A Comment," *Irish Economic and Social History*, 13 (1986), 90–95; Nicholas Canny, "A Reply," *Irish Economic and Social History*, 13 (1986), 96–100; Michael Perceval Maxwell, "Migration and Opportunity: A Further Comment," *Irish Economic and Social History*, 14 (1987), 59–61.

12. David Edwards, "Out of the Blue?: Provincial Unrest in Ireland Before 1641," in *Ireland 1641: Contexts and Reactions*, ed. Jane Ohlmeyer and Micheál Ó Siochrú (Manchester: Manchester University Press, 2013), 99–114.

13. Micheál Ó Siochrú, *God's Executioner: Oliver Cromwell and the Conquest of Ireland* (London: Faber & Faber, 2008).

Chapter Eight. Ascendancy

1. C. I. McGrath, "Securing the Protestant Interest: The Origins and Purpose of the Penal Laws of 1695," *Irish Historical Studies*, 30:117 (1996), 25–46.

2. S. J. Connolly, *Religion, Law, and Power: The Making of Protestant Ireland, 1660–1760* (Oxford: Oxford University Press, 1992), 263–313.

3. Ivar McGrath, *Ireland and Empire, 1692–1770* (London: Pickering & Chatto, 2012), 69–142.

4. Neal Garnham, "Local Elite Creation in Early Hanoverian Ireland: The Case of the County Grand Jury," *Historical Journal*, 42:3 (1999), 623–42; Patrick Walsh, "The Fiscal State in Ireland, 1690–1769," *Historical Journal*, 56:3 (2013), 1–28.

5. James Kelly, "Eighteenth Century Ascendancy: A Commentary," *Eighteenth-Century Ireland*, 5 (1990), 173–88.

6. David Dickson, *New Foundations: Ireland, 1660–1800* (Dublin: Irish Academic Press, 2000), 117.

7. Thomas Bartlett, "Ireland, Empire, and Union, 1690–1801," in *Ireland and the British Empire*, ed. Kenny, 61–89.

Chapter Nine. Hidden Irelands

1. Ciarán Ó Murchadha, "Letter to John Vesey, Bishop of Tuam, July 1711," *Journal of the Galway Archaelogical and Historical Society*, 60 (2008), 117.
2. Kevin Whelan, "An Underground Gentry: Catholic Middlemen in Eighteenth-Century Ireland," in *The Tree of Liberty: Radicalism, Catholicism, and the Construction of Irish Identity*, by Kevin Whelan (Cork: Cork University Press, 1996), 3–56.
3. Breandán Ó Buachalla, "Irish Jacobitism in Official Documents," *Eighteenth-Century Ireland*, 8 (1993), 135.
4. James Kelly, "The Abduction of Women of Fortune in Eighteenth-Century Ireland," *Eighteenth-Century Ireland*, 9 (1994), 7–43.
5. S. J. Connolly, "A Woman's Life in Mid-Eighteenth Century Ireland: The Case of Letitia Bushe," *Historical Journal*, 43:2 (2000), 433–51.
6. W. A. Hart, "Africans in Eighteenth-Century Ireland," *Irish Historical Studies*, 33:129 (May 2002), 19–32.

Chapter Ten. Patriots

1. Jim Livesey, *Civil Society and Empire: Ireland and Scotland* (New Haven: Yale University Press, 2009), 90–127.
2. Máire Kennedy, "Reading the Enlightenment in Eighteenth-Century Ireland, *Eighteenth-Century Studies*, 45:3 (2012), 355–78; Niall Ó Ciosáin, *Print and Popular Culture in Ireland*, 1750–1850 (Dublin: Lilliput Press, 2011), 71.
3. Michael J. Griffin, "The Two Enlightenments of Merriman's Clare," in *Brian Merriman's Midnight Court*, ed. Brian Ó Conchubhair (Syracuse: Syracuse University Press, 2009), 59–69.
4. Quoted in Maurice Bric, "Ireland and the Atlantic World, 1690–1840," in *The Oxford Handbook of Modern Irish History*, ed. Alvin Jackson (Oxford: Oxford University Press, 2014), 466.
5. Vincent Morley, "Irish Political Verse and the American Revolutionary War," *Journal of Irish-Scottish Studies*, 1 (2007) 45–59.
6. Breandán Ó Buachalla, "From Jacobite to Jacobin," in 1798: *A Bicentenary Perspective*, ed. Thomas Bartlett, David Dickson, Daire Keogh, and Kevin Whelan (Dublin: Four Courts Press, 2003), 75–96.
7. Fintan Cullen, *Visual Politics: The Representation of Ireland* (Cork: Cork University Press, 1997), 57–62.
8. J. T. Gilbert, *A History of the City of Dublin*, 3 vols. (1854–59), 3:42–52.
9. David Dickson, Cormac Ó Gráda, S. Daultry, "Hearth Tax, Household Size, and Irish Population Changes, 1672–1821," *Proceedings of the Royal Irish Academy*, 82c (1982), 155.

10. Quoted in Padhraig Higgins, *A Nation of Politicians: Gender, Patriotism, and Political Culture in Late Eighteenth Century Ireland* (Madison: University of Wisconsin Press, 2010), 239.

Chapter Eleven. The French Disease and the Union

1. Quoted in Ian McBride, *Scripture Politics: Ulster Presbyterians and Irish Radicalism in Late-Eighteenth Century Ireland* (Oxford: Oxford University Press, 1998), 168.
2. Ó Buachalla, "From Jacobite to Jacobin."

Where Historians Disagree

1. Jim Smyth, "'Like Amphibious Animals': Irish Protestants, Ancient Britons, 1691–1707," *Historical Journal*, 36:4 (1993), 785–97.
2. Connolly, *Religion, Law, and Power*, 123. It should be said that Connolly subsequently accepted the concept of colonization as valid for sixteenth-century Ireland: S. J. Connolly, *Contested Island: Ireland, 1460–1630* (Oxford: Oxford University Press), 166–68.
3. Vincent Morley, *Irish Opinion and the American Revolution, 1760–1783* (Cambridge: Cambridge University Press, 2002), 12–14.
4. L. M. Cullen, "Catholics Under the Penal Laws," *Eighteenth-Century Ireland*, 1 (1986), 23–36; Thomas Bartlett, *The Fall and Rise of the Irish Nation: The Catholic Question, 1690–1830* (Dublin: Gill and Macmillan, 1992), 17–29; Connolly, *Religion, Law, and Power*, 263–313; John Bergin, Eoin Magennis, Lesa Ní Mhunghaile, Patrick Walsh, eds., *New Perspectives on the Penal Laws* (Dublin: Eighteenth-Century Ireland Society, 2011).
5. Connolly, *Religion, Law, and Power*, 312.
6. McGrath, "Securing the Protestant Interest."
7. Whelan, "An Underground Gentry"; T. C. Barnard, "The Gentrification of Eighteenth-Century Ireland," *Eighteenth-Century Ireland*, 12 (1997), 137–55.
8. Daniel Corkery, *The Hidden Ireland: A Study of Gaelic Munster in the Eighteenth Century* (Dublin, 1925); L. M. Cullen, "The Hidden Ireland: Reassessment of a Concept," *Studia Hibernica*, 9 (1969), 7–47.
9. David Dickson, "Jacobitism in Eighteenth-Century Ireland: A Munster Perspective," *Éire-Ireland*, 39:3 & 4 (2004), 38–99.
10. Toby Barnard, *A New Anatomy of Ireland: The Irish Protestants, 1649–1770* (New Haven: Yale University Press, 2003), vii.
11. S. J. Connolly, "Jacobites, Whiteboys, and Republicans: Varieties of Disaffection in Eighteenth-Century Ireland," *Eighteenth-Century Ireland*, 18 (2003), 63–79; Vincent Morley, "The Continuity of Disaffection in Eighteenth-Century Ireland," *Eighteenth-Century Ireland*, 22 (2007), 189–205.
12. Ó Ciardha, *Ireland and the Jacobite Cause*; Breandán Ó Buachalla, *Aisling Ghéar: Na Stíobhartaigh agus an tAos Léinn, 1603–1788* (Baile Átha Cliath, 1996).

13. Morley, *Irish Opinion and the American Revolution*.

14. Guy Beiner, *Remembering the Year of the French: Irish Folk History and Social Memory* (Madison: University of Wisconsin Press, 2007).

15. Higgins, *A Nation of Politicians*.

16. James Livesey, "Free Trade and Empire in the Anglo-Irish Commercial Propositions of 1785," *Journal of British Studies*, 52:1 (2013), 103–27.

17. Tom Dunne, *Rebellions: Memoir, Memory and 1798* (Dublin: Lilliput Press, 2010).

18. Ó Buachalla, "From Jacobite to Jacobin."

19. McBride, *Scripture Politics*.

20. Kevin Whelan, "The Republic in the Village: The United Irishmen, the Enlightenment, and Popular Culture," in *The Tree of Liberty*, by Kevin Whelan, 59–96.

21. Jim Smyth, "Wolfe Tone's Library: The United Irishmen and 'Enlightenment,'" *Eighteenth-Century Studies*, 45 (2012), 423–35.

22. Breandán Mac Suibhne, "Politicization and Paramilitarism: North-West and South-West Ulster, c. 1772–98," in *1798*, ed. Bartlett et al., 243–78.

23. Ultan Gillen, "The Enlightenment and Irish Political Culture in the Age of Revolutions," in *Peripheries of the Enlightenment*, ed. Richard Butterwick, Simon Davies, Gabriel Sánchez Espinosa (Oxford: Voltaire Foundation, 2008), 181.

Chapter Twelve. The Age of O'Connell

1.   Quoted in James S. Donnelly, "Captain Rock: Ideology and Organization in the Irish Agrarian Rebellion of 1821–24," *Éire-Ireland*, 42:3 & 4 (2007), 66.

2.   Gearóid Ó Tuathaigh, "Gaelic Ireland, Popular Politics, and Daniel O'Connell," *Journal of the Galway Archaeological and Historical Society*, 35 (1974–75), 21–34.

3.   Jacqueline Hill, "National Festivals, the State, and 'Protestant Ascendancy' in Ireland," *Irish Historical Studies*, 24:93 (1984), 37–39.

4.   Cormac Ó Gráda, *Ireland: A New Economic History*, 1780–1939 (Oxford: Oxford University Press, 1994), 10.

5.   Ó Ciosain, *Print and Popular Culture in Ireland*, 177–94.

6.   Thomas Crofton Croker, *Researches in the South of Ireland* (Dublin, 1824), 328–29.

7.   Quoted in Georges Zimmerman, *Songs of Irish Rebellion: Irish Political Street Ballads and Rebel Songs*, 1780–1900 (Dublin: Allen Figgis, 1967), 50, reproduced by kind permission of Four Courts Press.

8.   Gary Owens, "Nationalism Without Words: Symbolism and Ritual Behaviour in the Repeal 'Monster Meetings' of 1843–45," in *Irish Popular Culture*, 1650–1850, ed. James S. Donnelly and Kerby A. Miller (Dublin: Irish Academic Press, 1998), 243–44.

9.   *The Nation*, 15 October 1842.

Chapter Thirteen. Famine and Diaspora

1. Unless otherwise indicated, all statistics are from John Crowley and William J. Smyth, eds., *Atlas of the Great Irish Famine* (Cork: Cork University Press, 2012).
2. Whelan, "The Modern Landscape," 86–91.
3. Don Mullan, ed., *Narrative of the Life of Frederick Douglass, an American Slave* (Dublin: A Little Book Company, 2011), 211–17.
4. Quoted in Thomas Linehan, "History and Development of Irish Population Censuses," *Journal of the Statistical and Social Inquiry Society of Ireland*, 16, part 4 (1991–92), 103.
5. Ó Gráda, *New Economic History*, 17–23.
6. Cormac Ó Gráda, *Black '47 and Beyond: The Great Irish Famine in History, Economy, and Memory* (Princeton: Princeton University Press, 1999), 83.
7. Quoted in Peter Gray, *The Irish Famine* (London: Thames & Hudson, 1995), 140–41.
8. David Fitzpatrick, *Irish Emigration, 1901–1922* (Dundalk: Economic and Social History Society of Ireland, 1984), 21.
9. E. M. Spiers, "Army Organisation and Society in the Nineteenth Century," in *A Military History of Ireland*, ed. Thomas Bartlett and Keith Jeffrey (Cambridge: Cambridge University Press, 1996), 335–57.
10. Virginia Crossman, "The Army and Law and Order in the Nineteenth Century," in *A Military History of Ireland*, ed. Bartlett and Jeffrey, 358–78.
11. Kevin Kenny, "The Irish in the Empire," in *Ireland and the British Empire*, ed. Kenny, 102–3.
12. Kenny, "The Irish in the Empire," 113–21.
13. Alvin Jackson, "Ireland, the Union, and the Empire," in *Ireland and the British Empire*, ed. Kenny, 125.
14. Barry Crosbie, "Ireland, Colonial Science, and the Construction of British Rule in India, c. 1820–c. 1870," *Historical Journal*, 52:4 (2009), 963–87; Matthew Kelly, "Irish Nationalist Opinion and the British Empire in the 1850s and 1860s," *Past & Present*, 204:1 (2009), 127–54.

Chapter Fourteen. New Departures

1. Samuel Clark, *Social Origins of the Irish Land War* (Princeton: Princeton University Press, 1979), 108.
2. David Fitzpatrick, "The Disappearance of the Irish Agricultural Labourer," *Irish Economic and Social History*, 7 (1980), 87–88.
3. Cormac Ó Grada, "Lost in Little Jerusalem: Leopold Bloom and Irish Jewry," *Journal of Modern Literature*, 27:4 (2004), 17–26.
4. S. J. Connolly, *Religion and Society in Nineteenth-Century Ireland* (Dundalk: Dundalgan Press, 1985), 3.
5. Emmet Larkin, *The Historical Dimensions of Irish Catholicism* (Washington, D.C.: Catholic University of America Press, 1976), 77, 84; Emmet

Larkin, *The Pastoral Role of the Roman Catholic Church in Pre-Famine Ireland* (Dublin: Four Courts Press, 2006), 271.

6. Damien Shiels, *The Irish in the American Civil War* (Dublin: History Press, 2013), 30.
7. *The Irish People*, 16 September 1865.
8. W. E. Vaughan, *Landlords and Tenants in Ireland, 1848–1904* (Dublin: Economic and Social History Society of Ireland, 1994), 5–6.
9. Vaughan, *Landlords and Tenants in Ireland*, 17.
10. *Freeman's Journal*, 20 September 1880.
11. Deirdre McMahon, "Ireland, the Empire, and the Commonwealth," in *Ireland and the British Empire*, ed. Kenny, 183.
12. Jackson, "Ireland, the Union, and the Empire," 131.

Chapter Fifteen. Culture Wars

1. Mike Cronin, Mark Duncan, and Paul Rouse, *The GAA: A Peoples History* (Cork: Collins Press, 2009), 99–100.
2. Mary Daly, "Literacy and Language Change in the Late Nineteenth and Early Twentieth Centuries," in *The Origins of Popular Literacy in Ireland*, ed. Mary Daly and David Dickson (Dublin: Trinity College Dublin, 1990), 153–66.
3. Murphy et al., eds., *Atlas of the Great Irish Famine*, 582–83.
4. Catríona Clear, *Social Change and Everyday Life in Ireland, 1850–1922* (Manchester: Manchester University Press, 2007), 70.
5. Quoted in Maureen O'Rourke Murphy and James MacKillop, eds., *An Irish Literature Reader: Poetry, Prose, and Drama* (Syracuse: Syracuse University Press, 2006), 140, 146.
6. P. J. Mathews, *Revival: The Abbey Theatre, Sinn Féin, the Gaelic League, and the Co-operative Movement* (Cork: Cork University Press, 2003), 35–45.
7. Mathews, *Revival*, 66.
8. McMahon, "Ireland, the Empire, and the Commonwealth," 192–94.
9. Senia Paseta, *Before the Revolution: Nationalism, Social Change, and Ireland's Catholic Elite, 1879–1922* (Cork: Cork University Press, 1999), 29. See also Ciaran O'Neill, *Catholics of Consequence: Transnational Education, Social Mobility, and the Irish Catholic Elite, 1850–1900* (Oxford: Oxford University Press, 2014).

Where Historians Disagree

1. Niall Ó Ciosáin, *Ireland and Official Print Culture, 1800–1850: A New Study of the Poor Inquiry* (Oxford: Oxford University Press, 2014).
2. Richard McMahon, "'A Violent Society?': Homicide Rates in Ireland, 1831–1850," *Irish Economic and Social History*, 36 (2009), 1–20.
3. Ó Gráda, *Ireland: A New Economic History*.
4. David Dickson, *Dublin: The Making of a Capital City* (London: Profile Books, 2014).

5. Ó Gráda, *Black '47 and Beyond.*

6. Crowley, Murphy, and Smyth, eds., *Atlas of the Great Irish Famine.*

7. Timothy G. McMahon, "Religion and Popular Culture in Nineteenth-Century Ireland," *History Compass*, 5 (2007), 845–64.

8. Tom Inglis, "Origins and Legacies of Irish Prudery: Sexuality and Social Control in Modern Ireland," *Éire-Ireland*, 40:3 & 4 (2005), 9–37.

9. Elaine Farrell, "'Infanticide of the Ordinary Character': An Overview of the Crime in Ireland, 1850–1900," *Irish Economic and Social History*, 39 (2012), 56–72; Cliona Rattigan, "'Done to Death by Fathers or Relatives': Irish Families and Infanticide Cases, 1922–1950," *History of the Family*, 13 (2008), 370–83.

10. Niall Ó Ciosáin, "Gaelic Culture and Language Shift," in *Nineteenth-Century Ireland: A Guide to Recent Research*, ed. Laurence Geary and Margaret Kelleher (Dublin: UCD Press, 2005), 136–52.

11. Nicholas Wolf, "'Scéal Grinn?': Jokes, Puns, and the Shaping of Bilingualism in Nineteenth-Century Ireland," *Journal of British Studies*, 48:1 (2009), 51–75.

12. Michael de Nie, "British Conceptions of Ireland and Irishness in the Nineteenth Century," *History Compass*, 3 (2005), 1–6.

13. Philip O'Leary, *The Prose Literature of the Gaelic Revival, 1881–1921: Ideology and Innovation* (University Park: Penn State University Press, 1994).

14. Mathews, *Revival.*

Chapter Sixteen. Revolution

1. David Fitzpatrick, "The Logic of Collective Sacrifice: Ireland and the British Army, 1914–1918," *Historical Journal*, 38:4 (1995), 1017–30.

2. *Freeman's Journal*, 21 September 1914.

3. Quoted in Alice Curtayne, *Francis Ledwidge* (London: Martin, Brian & O'Keeffe, 1972), 83.

4. Quoted in F. S. L. Lyons, *John Dillon: A Biography* (London: Routledge & Kegan Paul, 1968), 373.

5. Quoted in *Dictionary of Irish Biography*, 9 vols. (Cambridge: Cambridge University Press, 2009): "O'Keeffe, Patrick."

6. Eunan O'Halpin, "Counting Terror: Bloody Sunday and 'The Dead of the Irish Revolution,'" in *Terror in Ireland, 1916–1923*, ed. David Fitzpatrick (Dublin: Lilliput Press, 2012), 141–57.

7. Quoted in D. M. Leeson, *The Black and Tans: British Police and Auxiliaries in the Irish War of Independence, 1920–21* (Oxford: Oxford University Press, 2011), 14.

8. National Archives of Ireland Treaty Exhibition: http://treaty.nationalarchives.ie/wp-content/uploads/2011/12/Anglo-Irish-Treaty.pdf (accessed 10 May 2016).

9. *Dáil Éireann Official Debates*, 21 January 1922, col. 32.

10. Quoted in Oonagh Walsh, *Ireland's Independence, 1880–1923* (London: Routledge, 2002), p. 102.

Chapter Seventeen. Two Irelands

1. Quoted in Ó Gráda, *New Economic History*, 441.
2. Terence Dooley, "Land and Politics in Independent Ireland, 1923–48: The Case for Reappraisal," *Irish Historical Studies*, 34:175 (2004), 175–97.
3. Quoted in John Coolahan, *Irish Education: History and Structure* (Dublin: Institute of Public Administration, 1981), 55.
4. Lindsay Earner-Byrne, "Reinforcing the Family: The Role of Gender, Morality, and Sexuality in Irish Welfare Policy, 1922–1944," *History of the Family*, 13 (2008), 360–69.
5. Moira Maguire, "The Carrigan Committee and Child Sexual Abuse in Twentieth-Century Ireland," *New Hibernia Review*, 11:2 (2007), 79–100.
6. Gertrude Gaffney, "The Death Knell of the Working Woman," in *Great Irish Reportage*, ed. John Horgan (Dublin: Penguin Ireland, 2012), 25–30.
7. Quoted in John Gibney, "GUBU, Gregory and Cosmic Cover-Ups: 1982 State Papers," *History Ireland*, 21:1 (2013) 49.
8. Gearóid Ó Crualaoich, "De Valera's Other Ireland," in *De Valera's Ireland*, ed. Gabriel Doherty and Dermot Keogh (Cork: Mercier Press, 2003), 155–65.

Chapter Eighteen. The Second Republic

1. James Kelly, "The Operation of the Censorship of Publications Board: The Notebooks of C. J. O'Reilly, 1951–1956," *Analecta Hibernica*, 38 (2004), 223–369.
2. John Healy, *No One Shouted Stop!* (Achill: House of Healy, 1988), 43.
3. Robert J. Savage, "Film and Broadcast Media," in *Oxford Handbook*, ed. Jackson, 268–86.
4. Roisin Higgins, *Transforming 1916: Meaning, Memory, and the Fiftieth Anniversary of the Easter Rising* (Cork: Cork University Press, 2012).
5. Carole Holohan, "Challenges to Social Order and Irish Identity?: Youth Culture in the 1960s," *Irish Historical Studies*, 38:151 (2013), 389–405.

Chapter Nineteen. Between Boston and Berlin

1. David McKitterick, Seamus Kelters, Brian Feeney, and Chris Thornton, *Lost Lives: The Stories of the Men, Women, and Children Who Died as a Result of the Northern Ireland Troubles* (Edinburgh: Mainstream, 2000), 1473–76.
2. *The Irish Times*, 6 July 1995.
3. Brian Girvin, "Church, State, and Society in Ireland Since 1960," *Éire-Ireland*, 43:1 & 2 (2008), 74–98.

4. Enda Delaney, *Irish Emigration Since 1921* (Dublin: Economic and Social History Society of Ireland, 2012), 5.

5. Adrian Redmond, ed., *That Was Then, This Is Now: Change in Ireland, 1949–1999* (Dublin: Central Statistics Office, 2000), 91–93.

Where Historians Disagree

1. Jane Leonard, "The Twinge of Memory: Armistice Day and Remembrance in Dublin Since 1919," in *Unionism in Modern Ireland*, ed. Richard English and Graham Walker (Basingstoke: Macmillan, 1996), 99–114.

2. Philip Orr, *The Road to the Somme: Men of the Ulster Division Tell Their Story* (Belfast: Blackstaff Press, 1986); Philip Orr, *Field of Bones: An Irish Division at Gallipoli* (Dublin: Lilliput Press, 2005); Keith Jeffrey, *Ireland and the Great War* (Cambridge: Cambridge University Press, 2000); John Horne, ed., *Our War: Ireland and the Great War* (Dublin: Royal Irish Academy, 2008); Myles Dungan, *Irish Voices from the Great War* (Dublin: Merrion Press, 2014); David Fitzpatrick, "Irish Consequences of the Great War," *Irish Historical Studies*, 39:165 (2015), 643–58.

3. Fearghal McGarry, *The Rising: Ireland: Easter 1916* (Oxford: Oxford University Press, 2010).

4. Peter Hart, *The IRA and Its Enemies: Violence and Community in Cork, 1916–1923* (Oxford: Oxford University Press, 1998); Niall Meehan, "Uncovering Peter Hart," *Field Day Review*, 10 (2014), 102–47; Andy Bielenberg, John Borgonovo, and James S. Donnelly Jnr, "'Something of the Nature of a Massacre': The Bandon Valley Killings Revisited," *Éire-Ireland*, 49:3 & 4 (2014), 7–59; John Regan, *Myth and the Irish State* (Dublin: Irish Academic Press, 2014).

5. Andy Bielenberg, "Exodus: The Emigration of Southern Irish Protestants During the War of Independence and Civil War," *Past and Present*, 218 (2013), 199–233; David Fitzpatrick, *Descendancy: Irish Protestant Histories Since 1795* (Cambridge: Cambridge University Press, 2014).

6. Ian d'Alton, "'A Vestigial Population': Perspectives on Southern Irish Protestants in the Twentieth Century," *Éire-Ireland*, 44:3 & 4 (2009), 9–42; Catherine O'Connor, "Mixed Marriage, 'a Grave Injury to our Church': An Account of the 1957 Fetherd-on-sea boycott," *History of the Family*, 13 (2008), 395–401.

7. Bureau of Military History: http://www.militaryarchives.ie/collections/online-collections/bureau-of-military-history-1913-1921 (accessed 13 May 2016); Military Service Pensions Collection: http://www.military archives.ie/collections/online-collections/military-service-pensions-collection (accessed 13 May 2016).

8. John M. Regan, *The Irish Counter-Revolution, 1921–1936* (Dublin: Gill and Macmillan, 1999).

9. Geoffrey Roberts, "Three Narratives of Neutrality: Historians and Ire-

land's War," in *Ireland and the Second World War: Politics, Society, and Remembrance*, ed. Brian Girvin and Geoffrey Roberts (Dublin: Four Courts Press, 2000), 165–79; Eunan O'Halpin, "The Second World War and Ireland," in *Oxford Handbook*, ed. Jackson, 711–25.

10. Clair Wills, *That Neutral Island: A Cultural History of Ireland During the Second World War* (London: Faber, 2007); Bryce Evans, *Ireland During the Second World War: Farewell to Plato's Cave* (Manchester: Manchester University Press, 2014).

11. Catriona Crowe, "The Ferns Report," *Éire-Ireland*, 43:1 & 2 (2008), 50–73.

12. Eoin O'Sullivan and Mary Raftery, *Suffer the Little Children: The Inside Story of Ireland's Industrial Schools* (Dublin: New Island, 1999); James M. Smith, *Ireland's Magdalene Laundries and the Nations Architecture of Containment* (South Bend: University of Notre Dame Press, 2007); Eoin O'Sullivan and Ian O'Donnell, eds., *Coercive Confinement in Post-Independence Ireland: Patients, Prisoners, and Penitents* (Manchester: Manchester University Press, 2012); Sarah-Anne Buckley, *The Cruelty Man: Child Welfare, the NSPCC, and the State in Ireland*, 1889–1956 (Manchester: Manchester University Press, 2013); *Final Report of the Commission to Inquire into Child Abuse*, 2009, http://www.childabusecommission.com/rpt/pdfs/ (accessed 30 Nov. 2014).

13. Ciarán Brady, ed., *Interpreting Irish History: The Debate on Historical Revisionism*, 1938–1994 (Dublin: Irish Academic Press, 1994).

14. A seminal text is Conor Cruise O'Brien, *States of Ireland* (London: Hutchinson, 1972).

15. R. F. Foster, "We Are All Revisionists Now," *The Irish Review*, 1 (1985), 1–5.

16. Kerby Miller, "Re-Imagining Irish Revisionism, in *Reimagining Ireland*, ed. Andrew Higgins Wyndham (Charlottesville: University of Virginia Press, 2006), 223–43.

17. Clair Connolly, ed., *Ireland and Postcolonial Theory* (Cork: Cork University Press, 2003); Stephen Howe, *Ireland and Empire: Colonial Legacies in Irish History and Culture* (Oxford: Oxford University Press, 2000).

18. A recent account is Anne Cadwallader, *Lethal Allies: British Collusion in Ireland* (Cork: Mercier Press, 2013).

19. Frank McDonald and Kathy Sheridan, *The Builders* (Dublin: Penguin Ireland, 2008); Fintan O'Toole, *Ship of Fools: How Stupidity and Corruption Sank the Celtic Tiger* (London: Faber, 2009); Shane Ross, *The Bankers: How the Banks Brought Ireland to Its Knees* (Dublin: Penguin Ireland, 2009); Pat Leahy, *Showtime: The Inside Story of Fianna Fáil in Power* (Dublin: Penguin Ireland, 2009); Simon Carswell, *Anglo Republic: Inside the Bank that Broke Ireland* (Dublin: Penguin Ireland, 2011).

20. Richard B. Finnegan, "Forums, Courts, Cabinets, and Tribunals: The Governing of Ireland Since the 1960s," *Éire-Ireland*, 43:1 & 2 (2008), 126–53; Conor McCabe, *Sins of the Father: Tracing the Decisions that Shaped*

the *Irish Economy* (Dublin: History Press, 2011); Mary Daly, Frank Barry, Brian Girvin, and Eoin O'Leary, "Booms and Busts: Cycles in Irish Economic History and the Current Downturn," *Irish Economic and Social History*, 38 (2011), 18–88; Elaine Byrne, *Political Corruption in Ireland, 1922–2010: A Crooked Harp?* (Manchester, 2012); Frank Barry, "Diversifying External Linkages: The Exercise of Irish Economic Sovereignty in Long-Term Perspective," *Oxford Review of Economic Policy*, 30:2 (2014), 208–22.

21. J. J. Lee, *Ireland, 1912–1985: Politics and Society* (Cambridge: Cambridge University Press, 1989).

22. R. F. Foster, *Modern Ireland, 1600–1972* (London: Allen Lane, 1988).

Further Reading and Online Sources

MANY OF THE SOURCES used in the writing of this book are indicated in the notes, and the essays titled "Where Historians Disagree" at the end of each part are intended to serve as guides to further reading. So is this section, which provides a brief selection of additional major works in English (some of which have been cited already) and key online sources that should whet the appetite of anyone who wants to know more.

Thomas Bartlett, *Ireland: A History* (Cambridge: Cambridge University Press, 2010) is a major and up-to-date survey history of Ireland that begins in 431 AD, though J. C. Beckett, *The Making of Modern Ireland, 1603–1923* (London, 1966) is still worth reading. R. F. Foster's *Modern Ireland, 1600–1972* (London: Allen Lane, 1988) is an important, if contentious, revisionist account. It might not be ideal for the beginner, but it remains essential reading whether one agrees with Foster or not (and it is very readable). For a series of more detailed studies on a huge range of topics from the earliest settlers to the 1980s, the various—and massive—volumes of T. W. Moody et al. (eds.), *A New History of Ireland* (9 volumes, Oxford: Oxford University Press, 1976–2010) are well worth exploring. They are a bit like the proverbial curate's egg; in some cases the studies they contain have been overtaken by more recent scholarship (especially with regards to the sixteenth, seventeenth, and eighteenth centuries), but they still contain a huge amount of first-class material. More recent and up-to-date perspectives are provided in Richard Bourke and Ian McBride (eds.), *The Princeton History of Modern Ireland* (Princeton: Princeton University Press, 2016). The physical environment is examined in F. H. A. Aalen, Kevin Whelan, and Matthew Stout (eds.) *Atlas of the Irish Rural Landscape* (Cork, 2011), and the various instalments of the Royal Irish Academy's *Irish Historic Towns Atlas* project.

There are also some very important works of reference that can be dipped into as required: Alvin Jackson (ed.), *The Oxford Handbook of Modern Irish History* (Oxford: Oxford University Press, 2014), S. J. Connolly (ed.), *The Oxford*

Companion to Irish History (Oxford: Oxford University Press, 2011), Robert Welch (ed.), *The Oxford Companion to Irish Literature* (Oxford: Oxford University Press, 1996), Joe Cleary and Clair Connolly (eds.), *The Cambridge Companion to Modern Irish Culture* (Cambridge: Cambridge University Press, 2005), Philip O'Leary and Margaret Kelleher (eds.), *The Cambridge History of Irish Literature* (2 volumes, Cambridge: Cambridge University Press, 2006), Dáithí Ó hÓgáin, *The Lore of Ireland: An Encyclopedia of Myth, Legend, and Romance* (Cork: Collins Press, 2006) and the *Dictionary of Irish Biography* (9 volumes, Cambridge: Cambridge University Press, 2009). Musical traditions can be explored in Barra Boydell and Harry White (eds.), *The Encyclopedia of Music in Ireland* (2 volumes, Dublin, 2013), art and architecture in Andrew Carpenter et al. (eds.), *Art and Architecture of Ireland* (5 volumes, New Haven: Yale University Press, 2014), and virtually all types of Irish writing in Seamus Deane et al. (eds.), *The Field Day Anthology of Irish Writing* (5 volumes, Cork and Derry: Cork University Press/Field Day, 1991–2002).

Useful general studies of important topics are Leslie Clarkson and Margaret Crawford, *Feast and Famine: Food and Nutrition in Ireland, 1500–1920* (Oxford: Oxford University Press, 2001), Thomas Bartlett and Keith Jeffrey (eds.), *A Military History of Ireland* (Cambridge: Cambridge University Press, 1996), Marianne Elliott, *When God Took Sides: Religion and Identity in Ireland* (Oxford: Oxford University Press, 2009), Kevin Kenny (ed.) *Ireland and the British Empire* (Oxford: Oxford University Press, 2004), Christopher Morash, *A History of the Media in Ireland* (Cambridge: Cambridge University Press, 2010), and Diarmaid Ó Giolláin, *Locating Irish Folklore: Tradition, Modernity, Identity* (Cork: Cork University Press, 1999). Finally, an anthology that introduces many of the debates that have animated Irish historians in the twentieth century is Ciaran Brady (ed.), *Interpreting Irish History: The Debate on Historical Revisionism, 1938–1994* (Dublin: Irish Academic Press, 1994).

Major, though contrasting, interpretations of the sixteenth century are provided in Steven G. Ellis, *Tudor Frontiers and Noble Power: The Making of the British State* (Oxford: Oxford University Press, 1995), Brendan Bradshaw, *The Irish Constitutional Revolution of the Sixteenth Century* (Cambridge: Cambridge University Press, 1979), and Ciaran Brady, *The Chief Governors: The Rise and Fall of Reform Government in Tudor Ireland, 1536–1588* (Cambridge: Cambridge University Press, 1994). A very useful series of essays is Ciaran Brady and Raymond Gillespie (eds.), *Natives and Newcomers: Essays on the Making of Irish Colonial Society, 1534–1641* (Dublin, 1986), while two newer collections are worth exploring: David Edwards, Padraig Lenihan, and Clodagh Tait (eds.), *Age of Atrocity: Violence and Political Conflict in Early Modern Ireland* (Dublin: Four Courts Press, 2007) deals with the violence of the early modern period, while Patrick J. Duffy, David Edwards, and Liz Fitzpatrick (eds.), *Gaelic Ireland, c. 1250–c. 1650: Land, Lordship, and Settlement* (Dublin: Four Courts Press, 2001) goes some way towards balancing a traditional concentration on the British colonial communities and government. With regards to colonisation,

Nicholas Canny, *Making Ireland British, 1580–1650* (Oxford: Oxford University Press, 2001) and W. J. Smyth, *Map-Making, Landscapes, and Memory: A Geography of Colonial and Early Modern Ireland, c. 1530–1750* (Cork: Cork University Press, 2006) are essential works; the latter is a novel work of historical geography that ranges into the eighteenth century. Finally, identity politics and literature in a variety of genres and languages are explored in Joep Leerssen, *Mere Irish and Fíor-Ghael: Studies in the Idea of Irish Nationality, Its Development and Literary Expression Prior to the Nineteenth Century* (Cork: Cork University Press, 1996).

Many of these works are also relevant for the seventeenth century, in which the 1640s and 1650s loom large. Important recent studies are Jane Ohlmeyer and Micheál Ó Siochrú (eds.), *Ireland 1641: Contexts and Reactions* (Manchester: Manchester University Press, 2013), Micheál Ó Siochrú, *God's Executioner: Oliver Cromwell and the Conquest of Ireland* (London: Faber, 2008), and Aidan Clarke, *Prelude to Restoration in Ireland: The End of the Commonwealth, 1659–60* (Cambridge: Cambridge University Press, 1999). The restoration and the reign of James II can be explored in Coleman A. Dennehy (ed.), *Restoration Ireland: Always Settling and Never Settled* (London: Ashgate, 2007), and J. G. Simms, *Jacobite Ireland, 1685–91* (London: Routledge & Kegan Paul, 1969) remains a useful account. Another useful collection of essays on Ireland's relations with its immediate neighbours is Brendan Bradshaw and John Morrill (eds.), *The British Problem: State Formation in the Atlantic Archipelago, 1534–1707* (Basingstoke: Macmillan, 1996). Mary Ann Lyons and Thomas O'Connor, *Strangers to Citizens: The Irish in Europe, 1600–1800* (Dublin: National Library of Ireland, 2008) is an attractive introduction to the subject.

There are very good accounts of eighteenth-century Ireland in David Dickson, *New Foundations: Ireland, 1660–1800* (Dublin: Irish Academic Press, 2000) and S. J. Connolly, *Religion, Law, and Power: The Making of Protestant Ireland, 1660–1760* (Oxford: Oxford University Press, 1992), and Toby Barnard examines the Protestant community and "ascendancy" in *A New Anatomy of Ireland: The Irish Protestants, 1649–1770* (New Haven: Yale University Press, 2003). This can be balanced by Éamonn O'Ciardha, *Ireland and the Jacobite Cause, 1685–1766: A Fatal Attachment* (Dublin: Four Courts Press, 2002) and Vincent Morley, *Irish Opinion and the American Revolution, 1760–1783* (Cambridge: Cambridge University Press, 2002). L. M. Cullen, *The Emergence of Modern Ireland, 1600–1900* (London: Batsford Academic, 1981), offers insights into social, cultural, and economic life and is still worth reading. The popular politics of the 1770s and 1780s is the subject of Padhraig Higgins, *A Nation of Politicians: Gender, Patriotism, and Political Culture in Late Eighteenth Century Ireland* (Madison: University of Wisconsin Press, 2010), while Thomas Bartlett, David Dickson, Daire Keogh, and Kevin Whelan (eds.), *1798: A Bicentenary Perspective* (Dublin: Four Courts Press, 2003), provides a series of studies of the origins, progress, and legacy of the 1798 rebellion. An important study of folklore and "social memory" relating to 1798 is Guy Beiner, *Remembering the Year of the French: Irish Folk History and Social Memory* (Madison: University of Wisconsin Press, 2007).

The popular culture of pre-famine Ireland is explored in James S. Donnelly and Kerby A. Miller (eds.), *Irish Popular Culture, 1650–1850* (Dublin: Irish Academic Press, 1998). Cormac Ó Gráda, *Ireland: A New Economic History, 1780–1939* (Oxford: Oxford University Press, 1994), is another important study. Probably the single most significant work on nineteenth-century Ireland in recent years is John Crowley and William J. Smyth (eds.), *Atlas of the Great Irish Famine* (Cork: Cork University Press, 2012), an enormous compendium that covers much more than just the famine. Two older works on the nineteenth century that are still worth reading are Gearoid Ó Tuathaigh, *Ireland Before the Famine, 1798–1848* (Dublin: Gill and Macmillan, 1972) and Joseph Lee, *The Modernisation of Irish Society, 1848–1918* (Dublin: Gill and Macmillan, 1973). Very often Irish historians concentrate on political history, but the social history of the post-famine era can be explored in Catriona Clear, *Social Change and Everyday Life in Ireland, 1850–1922* (Manchester: Manchester University Press, 2007). For the twentieth century, J. J. Lee's *Ireland, 1912–1985: Politics and Society* (Cambridge: Cambridge University Press, 1989) remains an essential text; it makes for a lively and stimulating read. Another very readable work with much to say on Irish cultural life is Declan Kiberd's *Inventing Ireland: The Literature of the Modern Nation* (London: Cape, 1995), which offers a panoramic view of Irish literary history since the famine in both languages, influenced by post-colonial theory. David Fitzpatrick, *The Two Irelands, 1912–1939* (Oxford: Oxford University Press, 1998), offers a slightly acerbic overview of the Irish revolution and its consequences, while Diarmaid Ferriter, *The Transformation of Ireland, 1900–2000* (London: Profile Books, 2004), tackles the twentieth century at great length with a focus on social and cultural history. A useful compendium of statistics is Adrian Redmond (ed.), *That Was Then, This Is Now: Change in Ireland, 1949–1999* (Dublin: Central Statistics Office, 1999). This can be downloaded from the website of the Irish Central Statistics Office (CSO), which also contains a great deal of material on social and economic life in Ireland from the nineteenth century to the present (http://www.cso.ie), though information on Northern Ireland after 1920 does not form part of its remit. Statistical information relating to Northern Ireland can be found on the website of the Northern Ireland Statistics and Research Agency (NISRA, http://www.nisra.gov.uk). The Conflict Archive on the Internet project (CAIN, http://cain.ulst.ac.uk) contains a huge quantity of material relating to the Northern Ireland conflict from 1968 onwards.

This brings us to online sources. An important bibliographical resource is the Royal Irish Academy's Irish History Online project (https://www.ria.ie/re search-projects/irish-history-online). It should be noted that databases of printed material for the early modern period, such as Early English Books Online (EEBO, http://eebo.chadwyck.com/home) and Eighteenth Century Collections Online (ECCO, http://quod.lib.umich.edu/e/ecco), will contain a great deal of primary source material relating to Ireland, though these may only be accessible through subscribing institutions. Projects such as Google Books are also worth exploring for Irish material.

An invaluable online archive containing material from British official sources, from the eighteenth to the twentieth centuries, is *Documenting Ireland: Parliament, People, and Migration* (http://www.dippam.ac.uk). Large quantities of Irish newspapers, both historical and contemporary, have online archives; many of these are collated online in the *Irish Newspaper Archive* (https://www.irishnewsarchive.com). Maps can be accessed via the website of the Irish Ordnance Survey (http://www.osi.ie), while a useful adjunct for place names in Irish and English is the Placenames Database of Ireland (http://www.logainm.ie). Folkloric material in both Irish and English is being made available on the website of the National Folklore Collection (http://www.duchas.ie/en).

Visual material (including material referred to in the text) can be accessed on the websites of both the National Library of Ireland (http://www.nli.ie) and the National Gallery of Ireland (http://www.nationalgallery.ie). A large quantity of news footage relating to twentieth-century Ireland is available on the British Pathé website (http://www.britishpathe.com), while the online archive of RTÉ, the Irish state broadcaster (http://www.rte.ie/archives/about), hosts significant quantities of audio-visual and photographic material relating to modern Ireland from the 1960s onwards.

Finally, the main journals in the field of Irish history are *Irish Historical Studies, Irish Economic and Social History, History Ireland, Eighteenth-Century Ireland, Analecta Hibernica,* and the *Proceedings of the Royal Irish Academy,* most of which are available on databases such as JSTOR (http://www.jstor.org), though major English and American journals such as *English Historical Review, Historical Journal,* and *Journal of British Studies* will often include articles on Ireland. All of the works listed above will have extensive bibliographies and guides to further reading. This is just a very small—and subjective—selection from a huge range of material. If you've come this far, you've only just begun.

Index